Sketches of Brighton – 1827

Sketches of Brighton – 1827

By a French nobleman

Translated by Suzanne Hinton

First published in 2016 by Belle Vue Books
www.SuzanneHinton.uk

ISBN 978-0-9956032-0-2

Designed and typeset by Carnegie Book Production

Printed and bound in the UK by Gomer Press

Acknowledgements

I am most grateful for the generosity of the following who have permitted me to use their images: the Alexander Baring Archive, Cuckfield Museum, Peter Groves, Steve Myall, John Wells-Thorpe and Shirley Veater.

Graham Jaunay, Alexandra Loske, Geoff Mead, and Jennifer Drury (editor of the *My Brighton and Hove* website) have all been most helpful with advice, contacts and information.

The Society of Authors has given invaluable advice on contracts.

Above all, thanks to staff at The Keep at Brighton (Kate Elms, Jenny Geering, Shona Milton, amongst many others) for their immense patience in explaining the fine new microfilm readers in the Reference Room at The Keep, and in sourcing missing editions of 1827 newspapers.

And finally, many thanks to Kevin Bacon, Digital Development Officer at Royal Pavilion and Museums (Brighton and Hove City Council), for providing the bulk of the images in this text.

Gravé à Vienne par Dav: Weiss 1815.

Le Comte de Lagarde

Translator's introduction

On Saturday 11 October 1827, the *Brighton Gazette* announced the arrival in Brighton of Auguste Louis Charles de la Garde-Chambonas, Comte de Messence. The Count was forty-four years old and a seasoned traveller, but this was the first time he had set foot on English soil. He was in England to enjoy himself, to make new acquaintances and to renew old friendships. Above all, he was in England to attempt to correct the rather negative impression that the French held of their near neighbours.

The English had all but forgotten the Napoleonic wars which had lasted throughout the first fifteen years of the nineteenth century. They were busy expanding industry at home, increasing trade overseas, and imposing political, economic and intellectual control wherever possible across the surface of the globe. The French were stinging beneath the defeat of Napoleon and struggling to come to terms with the fall of the First Empire. A Bourbon monarchy had been restored in 1815, but this did not mean that by 1827 the French population of intellectuals, travellers and nobility was ready to become bosom friends with the subjects of His Majesty George IV, the Hanoverian.

The Count de la Garde was born in 1783. His mother died in childbirth, his father shortly after. The young orphan was taken under the wing of his uncle, who enjoyed the splendid name and title of Scipion Charles Victor Auguste de la Garde, Marquis de Chambonas. As with the English nobility, a marquis trumps a mere count or earl. Scipion was therefore the senior member of the La Garde clan. However, in France, the final years of the eighteenth century were not an ideal time to flaunt your titles of nobility. Scipion supported the Revolution in France in its early days, and held, briefly, the office of Minister of Foreign Affairs within the Legislative Assembly in 1792. By the end of that year, he had been denounced and he found it prudent to disappear into internal exile until 1795. It was within France that he rode out the storm of 'The Terror' which followed the execution of Louis XVI in 1893. With the emergence of Napoleon Bonaparte at the head of the three-man Directoire in 1795, Scipion felt able to emerge from hiding, but not to live openly in his own home land.

Scipion therefore set out for Hamburg, taking with him his young son and his twelve-year-old nephew. This was the first of Auguste's wanderings. Travel was to become a way of life with him. The map below reveals the extent of the young man's movements before he reached the age of thirty-one. At the Restoration of the French monarchy in 1815, Auguste, aged 31, was ready to return to France. He lived there for the rest of his life. He lived there, but was unsettled; he spent a large part of each year travelling to foreign parts.[1] By the time he reached England in 1827, he had added the labels of Germany, Holland, Italy, Sicily and Russia to his valises.

What sort of education had Auguste received amidst all the chaos of the revolutionary period? His mind had, naturally, been broadened by travel itself. But there was also a solid basis of schooling. He had spent his internal exile in the town of Sens where his uncle had been Governor in 1789 and Mayor in 1791. There he had attended the grammar school. The school had been snatched from the Jesuits, but it was still run by the clergy. The education provided did not have such a religious focus as that of the Jesuits, but nevertheless attracted the disapprobation of the revolutionary authorities as it was later closed at some point during 'Year II' of the new regime (1793/1794). So already at the age of ten, the boy's education had been disrupted.

As a very young child, Auguste had often been entrusted to his godmother and to his godmother's close friend, Madame de Bernard whose daughter, Jeanne, was just six years older than Auguste. Jeanne had been a childhood friend and, on Auguste's return to France in 1801 aged 18, she became his mentor. Why did a young lady of just 24 years old become mentor to such a well-travelled youth? Jeanne Bernard was an astounding woman. In 1792, aged fifteen, she had married, or been married to, a banker thirty years her senior, Jacques Récamier.[2] Madame

1 As recounted by the Count de Fleury in his 1901 introduction to Auguste's *Souvenirs of the Congress of Vienna 1814–1815*, published by the Librairie historique et militaire.

2 See Chapter 5

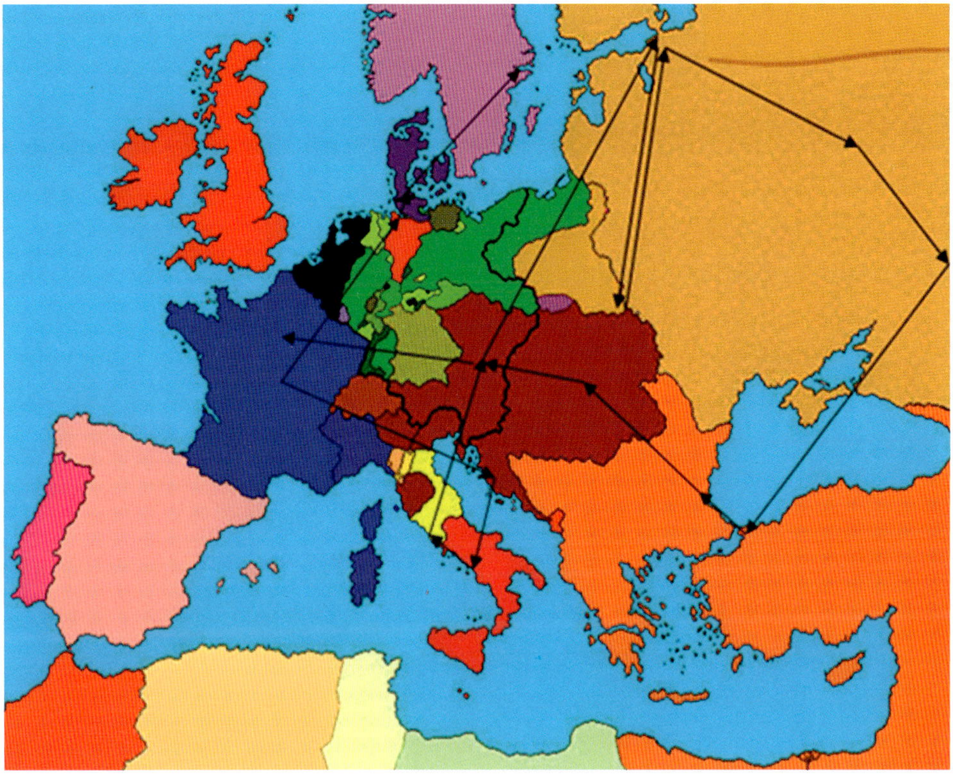

The travels of Auguste, Comte de la Garde, between 1793 and 1815

Récamier had had wealth, intelligence and contacts. These rapidly enabled her to create one of the most successful literary *salons* in Paris.

It was in this highly respected *salon* that Auguste came into contact with men and women who were to have a lasting influence on him. It was there he met Frédéric-César de la Harpe. La Harpe was an influential educator with a powerful background. As a Swiss politician, he had fought for an equitable co-federal organisation of cantons in his own country in the 1790s. He had had to flee several times. On one occasion he had become tutor to the future Tsar of Russia, Alexander I; on another he had taken dictatorial power in Switzerland, been deposed and fled to Paris. La Harpe became tutor to Auguste. A formidable influence.

Auguste's education was therefore built upon practical knowledge of the lands he had visited, a sound school-based education and contact with some of the finest minds of his age. It is little wonder that he could feel at ease among the upper echelons of English society when he reached Brighton in 1827.

By all accounts, Auguste de la Garde was not only a well-educated man; he was a charmer. He easily found sponsors and protectors, the first being his uncle, but even more importantly, in 1806, he had caught the eye of the influential Belgian Prince de Ligne, an extremely wealthy man of letters and former soldier. For two years, Auguste lived in the prince's household at his palatial residence in Vienna. The Prince de Ligne had had four sons, all of whom had died[3] by the time of the Congress of Vienna (1815) at which their father played such an important role, at least socially. There can be little doubt that the prince must have seen in the 30-year-old Auguste a substitute for the sons he had lost. In his future writings, Auguste would always take every opportunity to show, perhaps rather extravagantly, his appreciation of the treatment he received from the prince.

The map of Auguste's travels prior to the Congress of Vienna shows him in Marmont (Dalmatia – or modern day Croatia), Naples and Rome. These were all missions to the courts ruled by various members of the Napoleonic dynasty. Auguste had acquired these prestigious missions through the influence of Prince Eugène de Beauharnais,[4] the step-son of Napoleon Bonaparte. Auguste had obviously worked his magic on Prince Eugène in the early years of the century, thus acquiring employment, and contacts in very high Imperial places as he made his way around Dalmatia and Italy.

A third and rather unexpected influence came to work on Auguste when he visited the estate of Count Felix Potocki in Poland. While he was there, Auguste seems to have taken a delight in both agriculture and science, but more importantly it would seem that, during his stay, he had the leisure and the enthusiasm to make some first steps in his literary career. Count Potocki had a beautiful wife, Sophia. Sophia had bewitched and seduced her first husband, her second husband (Potocki himself), her second husband's son, and many, many others. These men lavished gifts on the wayward Sophie. Potocki's gift had been to create for her a

3 The eldest son of the Prince de Ligne had died in battle aged 33; his third, in 1813 on the eve of the Congress, aged 47; the two others had died in 1771, aged 3 and 6 respectively.

4 Eugène was the son of Josephine de Beauharnais, Napoleon Bonaparte's first wife. Napoleon had crowned himself Emperor in 1804 and was then in a position to bestow honours on his step-son. He created Eugène Viceroy of Italy in 1805 and officially adopted Eugène in1806, when Eugène was already 27 years old. Prince Eugène had proved himself to be an efficient, although possibly not brilliant, military leader.

magnificent park on land he owned at Uman in the Ukraine: the Park Sofiyivka.[5] A friend of Potocki, the Polish lyrical poet Stanislav Trembecki, had written a lengthy poem, the *Sophiowka* extolling the beauties of the park, albeit in a rather didactic fashion. Auguste was fired to translate this poem from the Polish into French and to develop the instructive aspect of the work by adding informative details about Poland and her people. On the strength of this, it is claimed that Auguste was elected to the 'academies of Warsaw, Cracow, Munich, London and Naples'.[6]

Auguste did not need to earn a living. He was wined and dined around Europe. Despite his uncle having been relieved of much of his lands and his income as a noble and an exile, it would seem that Auguste had managed to find some sort of private income. It is clear that he was never without a bed to sleep in – and probably a most comfortable one at that. However, he was now in a position to present himself as a writer. By the time he reached England he had already published, in 1815, the *Sophiowka* mentioned above: a tour de force consisting of ten pages of general introduction, thirty-five pages of translated verse and some sixty pages of notes on the poem and on Poland. His love affair with Poland continued when he composed, just four years later, a sixty-five-page poem on the death of the great liberator of Poland, Thaddeus Kosciusko. This work earned him Polish citizenship, an honour of which he was most proud.

The following extract, which might well be highly apocryphal, is taken from 'Napoleon and His Times' by Charlotte de Sor. The book was published in 1837 and purports to be the reminiscences of the Duke of Vicenza as told to de Sor.[7] From 1802 until 1812, the duke had been Emperor Napoleon's Ambassador to the court at St. Petersburg. What he is reported to have said, translated below, better explains, perhaps, why the honour of Polish citizenship had been bestowed on Auguste:

> 'Alongside the most weighty diplomatic missions given to me by the Emperor, there were occasionally duties which had minimal importance. Napoleon demanded an account of everything that was happening [*in St. Petersburg*], and his retentive mind caught at every

5 The park is still as beautiful today and is also home to the Ukrainian National Arboretum and the National Academy of Sciences: www.sofiyivka.org.ua

6 This seems unlikely, certainly in the case of England where there is no Royal Academy to represent writers. It is significant that the Académie Française, a most literary of French institutions, is not listed.

7 *Souvenirs du duc de Vicence*, Volume 1, by Charlotte de Sor (1837).

tiny detail. He forgot nothing. In 1809 or possibly 1810, I received a very specific order to have watched a Frenchman who had sought refuge in Russia. This is more or less what occurred.

'Count Charles de la Garde had been living in Poland, whether because he was an exile or whether for other reasons is not clear. Being on intimate terms with all the best aristocratic families in the land, he took it into his head to put onto the Polish throne a king of his own making, and his eye was taken by Lucien Bonaparte as being one who might grant him the crown. It was a most curious idea! He organised a little plot, believing he had won over a few Poles to his pipedream, and, full of his project, set off for Italy. Whether he had seen Lucien or not is of little importance, for the whole thing was preposterous. But the Emperor, who disliked confusion, took the prank very badly and the order came to arrest the king-maker and to send him to Paris, where he would most likely have spent a few months in the Temple [*prison*] or Vincennes where he could contemplate the dangers of playing with fire. The unfortunate conspirator, having been warned in time, found sympathetic friends in Naples. [...] He changed his name, calling himself the Chevalier de Messence, and as the Emperor had no real desire to extradite him, he did nothing to pursue the matter. He merely ensured that the man be watched, constantly. The Chevalier was living in St. Petersburg, but you will not be surprised to learn that he did not present himself at the [*French*] Embassy and that he avoided all contact with myself. Notes concerning him arrived for me and I forwarded them to my office. I gave my orders and that was that. There had been talk of him as an émigré, as a conspirator, so in my mind I had the image of this Chevalier de Messence as being a man of at least 40 or 50 years old.

'As it happened, there were more and more rumours about the deeds and activities of the Chevalier [...] People were talking of the talent, the elegance, the kindness of the Chevalier; he composed songs and he sang, delightfully, the ballades for which Boïeldieu wrote the music, he could improvise and this had, so it was said, great success with women. Now, I found it difficult to reconcile such fine accomplishments with the advanced years with which I had been endowing the man. It was not my place either to talk of him, nor to seek him out, and yet I would not have been averse to catching a glimpse of this nimble-footed Lovelace.

'One evening I was at the theatre, and during the interval, I visited some of the boxes of my acquaintances. Princess Dol*** caught sight of me and beckoned to me, so I entered her box. A few moments later, a friend arrived in the company of an extremely young man who looked both high-spirited and most elegant in his dress. 'Mr. Ambassador,' said the Princess playfully, 'allow me to present one of your compatriots, the Chevalier de Messence.' Both the Chevalier and I were astounded by this turn of events, but he, being a man of the world, bowed low and within five minutes, he had disappeared from view.

'If truth be told, I found this secretly most amusing. This bold leader of the conspiracy which was to free Poland and endow it with a king of his choosing was, quite simply, a very pleasant young man whose curly blond hair and boyish face made him look 20 or 22 at the most. I wrote to the Emperor, telling him that the police had taken this prank too seriously, and that this Chevalier de Messence could plot to his heart's content in the back lanes of the city, but that I was not of the opinion that he could fire up revolt in any other place. There the story ended; the Emperor never mentioned the subject again.'

Auguste's full name was Auguste Louis Charles de la Garde-Chambonas, Chevalier de Messence. There were several of the de la Garde family who had the name Charles. However, the dates given, the itinerary followed by 'Charles' and the description of the man all lead to the supposition that the text refers to the Auguste who visited Brighton in 1827.

Auguste's other works before he came to Brighton were *A Glimpse of Alexandersbad and Louiseberg in Bavaria*, also published in 1819: at a mere 53 pages long it was one of his shortest works, but one of the first books ever to be illustrated with lithographs. The fact that the publisher was willing to use a new and expensive technology on such a short work shows that the author himself must have already stood in high esteem. In 1824, Auguste published *A Journey from Moscow to Vienna; through Kiev, Odessa, Constantinople, Bucharest and Hermannstadt*[8] (1824, 440 pages), based on a series of letters he had sent to a friend, Jules Griffith between May 1811 and June 1812. Throughout the years 1803 to 1827 he was producing song lyrics with such evocative titles as *C'est une larme* (Just a Teardrop); *Les Époux fugitifs* (The Runaway Newlyweds); *Pourtant je t'aime encore* (And I still love you yet); *Le Soupir* (The Sigh).[9]

8 Present day Sibiu in Romania.
9 Many of these scores are kept in the Municipal Library in Lyon, France.

By 1827, Auguste must already have been considering writing, or perhaps had already written, his *Anecdotal recollections of the Congress of Vienna: 1814–1815*[10] but this work was not published until 1843. It is his major piece of writing and has been translated into both English and German. Already Auguste was well versed in the art of recounting what he saw and heard around him. It is clear, however, that his interest in Society verged on the frivolous, even in such august company as the signatories to the 'Final Act of the Congress of Vienna'.

One admirer of Auguste's song lyrics was Queen Hortense of Holland. In many ways, it is surprising that he did not meet Hortense until 1819, for she was the sister of his benefactor, Prince Eugène. Indeed, not only was she Napoleon's step-daughter, but by marrying Napoleon's brother, Louis, she had become both Napoleon's sister-in-law and Queen of Holland. Hortense had been born in the same year as Auguste, 1783. In 1802, at the request of Napoleon himself, she had married Louis[11] and, on becoming Queen in 1806, had moved to The Hague where she lived until Louis was deposed in 1810. From then on, Hortense, now styled the Duchess of Saint-Leu, spent much of her time in Switzerland, but it was at her home at Augsburg, in Bavaria, that Auguste first met the former queen. Hortense is said to have been a great admirer of Auguste's songs and there seems little doubt that they were friends. According to Hortense, in a note she wrote to Auguste, it was she herself who had set these songs to music.

In the 1833 English translation of Hortense's 'Mémoires', the following note from Hortense to the Count de la Garde appears:

> I owe you a thousand thanks, my dear sir, for the charming romances you have sent me. I had already set to music some of them which had fallen accidentally in my way before I knew their author. I am gratified by the pleasure of your acquaintance, and the opportunity of telling you how much I am flattered by your politeness in preparing such a delightful collection. Your two other productions I read with deep interest: they display abilities, which, although a woman, I can justly appreciate, for whatever is deeply felt is always within our comprehension.

---

10 Auguste's own title: *Fêtes et souvenirs du Congrès de Vienne: Tableaux des salons, scènes anecdotiques et portraits 1814–1815* was mercifully shortened to *Anecdotal recollections of the Congress of Vienna: 1814–1815* by Albert Vandam in his 1902 translation.

11 Napoleon III, Emperor of France from 1852 until 1870, was one of the three legitimate children borne by Hortense. She also had an illegitimate son who was later given the title of Duke de Morny.

> With this note, you will receive a book of my own romances, which I beg you to accept as a remembrance. Let it express the pleasure I have derived from your poems, and my sentiments of sincere esteem and respect.[12]

The 'Memories of Hortense de Beauharnais' have been generally ascribed to Auguste, as were some notes on a visit to her home in Augsburg. Towards the end of his life, several of Auguste's songs and Hortense's settings of them were published, along with the Mémoires, in 'Le Livre d'art de la Reine Hortense'. This was a luxury edition illustrated with lithographs, chromolithographs and gold edging. A truly fitting end to Auguste's career as a writer, as this seems to be the last major work to come from his pen.

Very little is known of Auguste's life after his visit to England. The London Literary Gazette lists him as being present at a meeting of the Medico-Botanical Society in London on 14 March 1828 at which he was admitted as a member of the Society. Apart from his publications, there is little firm evidence of how long he remained in England or of when he returned to France. The only indisputable fact is that he died in 1853 at the age of seventy.

How had Auguste arrived in Brighton? Coming from France, he had no option other than by boat. This was the means of transport used by the fleeing aristocrats in the 1790s. It was good enough for Auguste. He chose to make the crossing from Dieppe on the steamship Eclipse. Steam, however, did not make the crossing any more pleasant, as Auguste does not fail to tell us in his account.

Auguste must have arrived in Brighton with a sheaf of introductions to the great and the good. He must also have arrived in Brighton with letters of credit, or at least a fair amount of gold carefully concealed about his person. He had reserved a room, not in one of the two or three very best hotels, but in a hotel which nevertheless accepted only the most refined clients. This was a man who was intent on meeting a very specific aspect of Brighton society: the Nobility and the Gentry.

Before reading what Auguste has to say, it may be interesting to look at Brighton as it appeared to the majority of its visitors and its inhabitants. The town – not yet a city – was no longer just the preserve of nobility, their servants and the local tradesmen who served them. By 1827, any Mr. and Mrs. Baker might well

12 Taken from the English text of *The memoirs of Hortense de Beauharnais*, published in 1833 by Key and Biddle of Philadelphia (translator unknown). It is suggested by Key and Biddle that these memoirs were written by La Garde himself.

have been affluent enough to leave the London shop in the hands of their overseer and apprentices and to indulge in a week or two by the seaside. How did ordinary mortals arrive in Sussex on their way to Brighton?

There were no trains. There were no railway tracks into the town. There were no buses. No motor vehicles. Even the bicycle had not yet been invented. A steam coach, not in public use, would splutter its way intermittently on trial runs along the rutted roads, but it would not be until 1833 that either Walter Hancock or Sir Charles Dance[13] managed to offer their short-lived regular services. So how would Mr. and Mrs. Baker have travelled from London to Brighton in early October 1827?

The answer was simple. Mr. and Mrs. Baker would have taken the stagecoach. This was not a comfortable experience according to twenty-first-century standards. However, by 1827 John McAdam's process for creating cambered, closely-packed road surfaces was already in general use on the main roads of the land: coaches were well supplied with padding (at least inside) and springs; the horses were well chosen and well matched; the coachmen had become serious professionals. Coaching was big business with punctuality and safety as major concerns, both for the travelling public and the coach proprietors. The traveller from London to Brighton could find a coach leaving Piccadilly, Holborn, the Borough or Elephant and Castle at any time during daylight hours. The journey would take a mere six hours.

In the October 1828, a coaching enthusiast and journalist, 'Viator Junior', was moved to write for his editor at the 'Sporting Magazine':

> Within my recollection the Brighton Road is always a good one; but from the innumerable improvements made on it during the last ten or twelve years it is now as close to perfection, and very nearly as much shortened, as it ever can be. On neither of the new lines of road is there occasion more than twice or thrice for the drag-chain, even with the most stiff-necked team; and the old road, with the exception of Reigate and Clayton Hills [...] is equally free from difficulty or danger. [...]
>
> As I hold all safety patents about coaches exceedingly cheap, I have not given myself the trouble of examining 'Cook's Patent Life Preserver,' which is fitted to Mr. Gray's 'Bolt-in-tun' coach, the 'Patriot'; but I will tell a rather good anecdote of an incident of which I was witness just a few days ago. Just as Pickett was starting with his 'Union' coach out of Holborn, up comes a fussy old citizen, puffing and blowing like a grumpus: 'Pray, coachman, is this here the Patriotic

13 Quoted by Charles G. Harper in *The Brighton Road*, published by Chapman and Hall in 1906.

> Life Preserver Safety-coach?' 'Yes, sir,' says Pickett, not hearing above one-half of his passenger's question; 'room behind, sir; jump up, if you please; very late this morning.' 'Why, where's the machinery?' cries the old one. 'There, sir,' replied a passenger (a young Cantab, I suspect[14]), pointing to a heavy trunk of mine that was swung beneath; 'in that box, sir, that's where the machinery works.' 'Ah!' quoth the old man, climbing up quite satisfied, 'wonderful inventions nowadays, sir; we shall all get safe to Brighton; no chance of an accident in this coach.'[15]

As ever, the impression of comfort and safely have more to do with the impression of progress than with actual comfort and safety.

Coaching could be a cutthroat business: in early 1827

> [...] the Comet safety coach [...] reduced its fares to 16*s.* inside and 8*s.* outside. [...] When the Comet and the New Times were both running to and from Brighton, the fare by the former was 10*s.*[16] and the latter 15*s.*; but from the very beginning fares have varied: I think 25*s.* was the most ever asked; while in the heat of the opposition, 5*s.* was often accepted and sometimes passengers were carried for nothing, to keep them off the other vehicles.[17]

Although Viator does counter with:

> [...] having an unhappy prejudice against cheap articles in general, of all cheap things in this world (except cheap wine), I hold cheap coaches in the greatest and most particular abomination; and whenever I see the words 'Cheap Travelling' posted up at the door of an office, I always feel disposed involuntarily to add 'and nasty' to the advertisement.

So Mr. and Mrs. Baker are obliged to travel by coach. Whether they have chosen a coach taking the Holborn–Croydon–Redhill route (51½ miles) or the Borough–Mitcham–Reigate route (51⅝ miles), after a long and perilous ride, they will get

14 There was a fashion in the Regency period and beyond for young lords to take up coach driving as a sport. Occasionally better-educated men, such as this 'Cantab' or 'Cambridge graduate' took to the roads professionally. The proprietor of their coach would not hesitate to advertise widely the qualifications of their highly educated drivers.

15 George C. Harper *The Brighton Road* (1906 edition).

16 In 1825 a well paid footman would earn about £26/0/0 a year. An 8/- trip to Brighton would cost him the whole of his wages for one week. In the first years of the twenty-first century, a train journey from London to Brighton return would cost between £3.00 (special promotional offer) and £35.00: this would represent the labour of between 15 minutes and two hours for a person earning the average wage.

17 Quoted by William C. Blew in *Brighton and its Coaches: A History of the London to Brighton Road* (1894), published by J. C. Nimmo.

their first glimpse of the farmland which feeds Brighton as they breast the ridge of the South Downs at Pyecombe. They are tired. They are mired. They are leaving behind them the mineral-rich clay of the Weald; leaving behind them trees, quaint thatched cottages, all the delightful scenes that Auguste describes at the end of his narrative, as he finally makes this journey in the reverse direction. Auguste will be leaving the area. Mr. and Mrs. Baker are arriving; into the barren, chalky landscape of the hinterland of Brighton. Sheep dominate agriculture. Sheep nibble; they nibble at the grass, at the scrub and at the heath. Over the centuries, they have denuded the Downs, leaving the outline of the hills stark and smooth. Trees will be a rarity as the stagecoach moves nearer to Brighton. It is indeed a barren landscape. Why have our two travellers come? On this October afternoon, it is windy with the odd shower; the road is exposed but there are glimpses of the sun. It is well known that the area south of the Downs benefits from a sunny climate. Clean bracing air with a modicum of sunlight will do them good.

It is true there was one shingle beach *near the sea,*
But elsewhere he hunted in vain for a tree,
For round about Brighton wherever you walk,
The country, so call'd, is a desert of chalk.[18]

The coachman has a slightly easier time of it once past Pyecombe. The road slopes slowly down leaving behind the tiny Norman church of the village perched on its hill whilst on the crest of Clayton Hill, Mrs. Baker spots a pretty white post windmill. The mill is known locally as 'Jill'. She had been built there just six years previously and was going to have to wait until 1872 before she is joined by her mate, the dark 'Jack' windmill.

As with many practicable roads, the way to Brighton follows its way along a valley. Between Pyecombe and Patcham, the Downs rise steeply on both sides. Where the plough has turned the thin soil, white gashes of chalk have appeared. The need to satisfy the hunger of Brighton's increasing population, as well as that of her seasonal guests, has lead to a move from sheep grazing to arable farming. It is this disturbance of the fragile layer of topsoil which is hastening the flow of loam from the hills to the valley. Whenever it rains, even the metalled road risks being covered in a layer of mud.

---

18 Extract from the poem ascribed to Horace Smith: 'Clio Grub at Brighton' published in the *New Monthly Magazine* in 1830 and reprinted as a book *The Midsummer Medley* and 1832.

Pyecombe – Junction of the two roads

The four and one quarter miles from Pycombe to the ancient village of Patcham are covered in just under an hour. Mr. Baker is no doubt relieved to know that there will be no more hills. He will not now be required to leave the coach, and he certainly will not be required to lend a hand to push. Mrs. Baker has not been too concerned about having to walk a little, although she is going to have to find a servant to clean the mud-splattered hem of her dress as soon as she arrives at their lodgings. For her, it has been the many tales she has heard of accidents which have been worrying her: a heavily laden coach might overturn, a horse might bolt or fall, the coachman might drive his team too fast, a rut in the road might break an axel or a wheel. Indeed, she knows that she will not be safe until she had stepped out of the coach, onto firm ground, for even within the town itself, spills could and would happen. Blew gives an account of the following accident which occured in 1833:

> Mr. Snow had undertaken, on Thursday last, to drive one of the new coaches, the Quicksilver, which leaves Brighton at 5 o'clock. The horses became unmanageable soon after starting. When they reached the sharp projecting corner in Marlborough Place, beyond the King and Queen, a cart was standing at a lampost near that spot, and, in making a sweep to avoid it, the coach was overturned; unfortunately

> the injury which such an accident must, under any circumstances, have occasioned, was increased by the passengers being thrown against the iron rails of the North Steine, several of which were absolutely broken. From this spot the coach was dragged, after being upset, by the unmanageable horses a considerable distance before they could be stopped. The passengers were conveyed to the King and Queen, the Gloucester Hotel, &c., where surgical assistance was immediately obtained.

Mrs. Baker has hoped that, by travelling as an inside passenger, she might meet a member of the nobility, or at least a minor notable, on his or her way to spend the season in Brighton. She has been doomed to disappointment. The more wealthy class of persons travelling to the town are able to afford their own transport. The list of passengers involved in the accident described above, reveals the class of people who used the stage coach: there was 'Mr. Sugon, who is well known here as an annual visitor [...] Mr. Pearson, the Common Councilman; Captain Hunter, Mr. Beale, a butcher at Clapham, whose wife and child were inside, as well as many others.'

And so the coach has reached Patcham. The coachman has paid his toll at the turnpike gate at the juction of Mill Road and the London Road. Little could he have imagined that nearly two hundred years later, the site of that gate would be dwarfed by the massive concrete structure of the A27 Brighton by-pass and that his ghost would be deafened by the constant rumble of a myraid of internal combustion engines thundering their way from Lewes to Shoreham.

Approaching the village of Patcham, to their right the coach passengers will catch their first glimpse of a building clad in black mathematical tiles. This is Patcham Place, a fine, square mansion, remodelled at the end of the eighteenth century to adapt the sixteenth-century building to the modern age and the modern style. Its façade gleams gently in the fading light; the travellers begin to feel that they are, at last, nearing the fashionable metropolis. This impression maybe a little diminished for them by the sight of the rather

Preston Manor, the house and Church 1818

ramshackle Black Lion Inn and, further on, the tiny cottages of the village lining their road, but a glimpse of the familiar outline of a squat thirteenth-century church tower, almost identical to that at Pyecombe, has reassured Mrs. Baker that she is in a good Christian part of her country. This impression is reinforced when she sees a third square tower as the coach approaches the next village, Preston. Here, at Preston, Mrs. Baker is much comforted to see an elegant Palladian manor house. Two such substantial homes so close together. Ah! civilisation. Ah! Brighton – or Brighthelmstone as she has heard it called – is, indeed, near. Now Preston has been passed, the horses find the going a little heavier once again, for the road closely follows the course of the Wellsbourne stream. The September rains have, as usual, caused the stream to overflow, as it has not yet been severely culverted and curtailed by latter-day road builders. Clay, sands, chalk rubble and flints have all been washed off the hillsides to right and left of the road, so the valley floor presents no smooth surface to the traveller.

About a half mile nearer the town, Mrs. Baker spots a group of cottages set on the hillside,[19] but then no more signs of civilisation until the coach reaches the junction of New England Road, London Road and two unnamed roads leading up the hillside to her left. Modern day readers will recognise this as the busy Preston Circus. To left and right, elegant detached villas line the London Road. What a thrill to see these grand, newly built houses, although disappointment briefly takes a hold when she sees, a little further on, the meaner, artisans' homes glimpsed in Queens-place. As far as Mrs. Baker can judge, these cottages have been built of common pebbles from the beach. Let's hurry past.

87 London-road, built shortly after 1822
Image © John Wells-Thorpe

19 The old cottages at Nos. 5 and 6 Lovers' Walk are possibly all that remain of Preston Dairy Farm. (Carder)

Queens-place, built around 1815

At last! the sparkling new Church of St. Peter's. Not yet officially opened, but complete in all its external details. A magical vision is before her. This is Brighton.

Unlike Auguste, Mr. and Mrs. Baker are not going to be staying in the Gloucester Hotel. Instead, they carry on south, past the Royal Pavilion, barely visible in early evening twilight: there will be plenty of time to admire it in the following days, and so they alight, weary but excited, at the Clarence Inn in North Street.

A boy carries their boxes to their hotel, the King's Head in West-street, which they have chosen for its exciting connection with King Charles' escape to France. There we leave them to the privacy of the rest of their stay.

To ***Brighton*** *he went, and secured a retreat*
In the pebble-built house of a narrow back street,
With a staring bow-window, to let him explore
What was passing in either bow-window next door.[20]

What sort of town was Brighton in 1827? Auguste's account is of grand assemblies, nobility and Society gossip. All that did, of course, exist and Auguste recounts the facts and his impressions in detail. But there was more to the town than that.

King George IV, the former Prince Regent, had made his last visit to the town earlier in the year of 1827; the Prime Minister, George Canning owned a home in the town but had recently died after a mere 119 days in the highest office in the land. It would seem that the town, once the seat of the royal court-by-the-sea, had

20 From 'Clio Grub at Brighton' by Horace Smith, *c.* 1830.

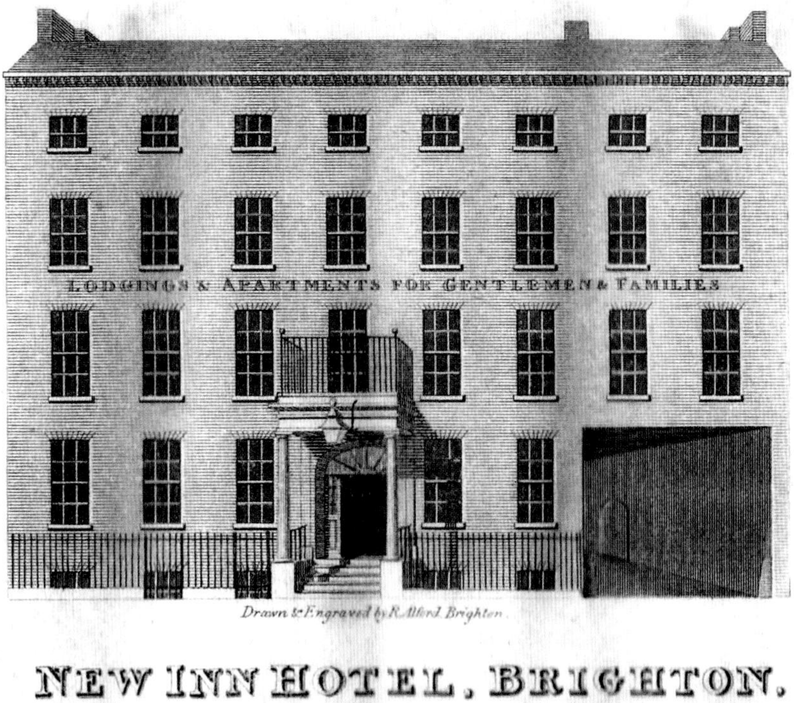

The Clarence Inn, North Street, 1818
Image reproduced by kind permission of Peter Groves

passed its zenith. It could well have been on the decline with the disappearance of so much royal and powerful patronage. The truth was very different.

In 1821, the permanent population of Brighton had been some 24 500 souls. By 1831, just four years after Auguste's visit, the town had over 40 000 inhabitants. Even before the arrival of the railway in 1841, the population of the town continued to rise rapidly throughout the 1830s. The town was in the midst of a building frenzy. Regency Square had been laid out and was not yet complete. Brunswick Town, with Brunswick Square at its heart, had been laid out but remained unfinished. Kemp Town had been planned and many, but not all, of the carcases of the houses built but yet not inhabited. Auguste will visit acquaintances in each of these parts of the town, but he does not mention the fact that they are still more or less still building sites. When Auguste goes to dinner with Thomas Read Kemp at N°. 22 Sussex Square, he does not mention that the area must have been virtually deserted: only eleven of the properties on the whole of the Kemp Town estate were occupied at the time.[21]

The process of enclosing the land on the Downs was increasing. Rich landowners were consolidating their holding. Instead of owning scattered strips, they were now able to let out large tracts of land to prosperous tenants. Flocks of 1 000 or more sheep were not uncommon, and in late September 1827, for example, at Findon Fair, some 12 miles to the west of Brighton, 12 000 sheep were entered into the sale, although few were bought, Sussex being in the second half of a double dip recession. The move from pastoral to tillage was in full swing. There was little room for the smallholder on his narrow strips of land. New agricultural practices were also pushing labourers away from the countryside: larger ploughs and larger fields encouraged farmers to employ casual labour rather than housing their own work force.

> Machine for Digging Potatoes. – Mr. Michael Bury of Swords, Eng.,[22] has invented a machine, simple in its construction and principle, by which with 2 horses and 1 attendant, an acre of potatoes may be dug up in 1 hour. Also, an acre of ground, previously ploughed for oats or other grain, can be harrowed by it in an hour, with 2 horses and 1 attendant, thereby effecting, in the branch of harrowing, a saving of upward of 93 per cent, or in other words, doing the work of 82 horses and 16 attendants, with 2 horses and 1 attendant. – *American Paper*
>
> Brighton Herald, 1 September 1827

21 Carder, Timothy, *The Encyclopaedia of Brighton*, 1990.

22 At the time, the whole of Ireland was united with Britain. This American journalist was evidently unable to grasp the administrative difference between Britain and England.

Families displaced from the land moved, naturally enough, to Brighton where there was work. But at much the same time as this influx from local areas, two other factors, the end of the Napoleonic Wars and the unlikely event of any other imminent war, brought many former soldiers back to their home area: the majority fit to work, but many crippled and capable only of the lightest household duties. In Brighton, there was work for all the family from labourer, to dairymaid to ornamental flunky.

A form of enclosure was also taking place within Brighton. Here a distinction must be made between the Lanes of Brighton and the Laines of Brighton. The Lanes, nowadays beloved of tourists in the search for jewellery and quaintness, represent the footprint or street pattern of what was left of the old fishing village of the early 1700s before Dr Richard Russell made sea-bathing fashionable. The North Laine, today the haunt of university students on the hunt for a trendy cafe or that outlandish vintage dress, is what remains of the strip-farming system within the town. Streets such as Church Street (formerly Spring Walks) and Gloucester Street running from west to east down the slope to the valley mark the pathways between the strips of farming land. The streets of small terraced houses running north to south (Bond Street, late eighteenth century; Gardner Street, early nineteenth century; Kensington Place, 1820s) were all built on these strips of land. It is no coincidence that, in the centre of Brighton, streets and twittens[23] still bear the name of Gardens: Kensington Gardens, Frederick Gardens and Queens Gardens being the most obvious.

Local entrepreneurs had realised the advantage of large plots of land. One of the first of these was the wealthy Thomas Read Kemp, MP for Lewes. Kemp (or possibly his father, Thomas) had bought small parcels of land from town folk such as Thomas Friend, Farmer Western, Mr. Vinall and Mrs. Soper. Kemp was aware of the advantages of consolidating his holding. He amassed a portfolio of former agricultural property in the east of the town. He sold land in the west to Joshua Flesher Hanson. Hanson consolidated a large area of land by buying up not only Kemp's holdings, but also those of the Duke of Dorset and others. Hanson was a speculator and Hanson speculated. On his newly acquired land he laid out a lawn covering some one and a half acres of wind-blown cliff top; he decreed that sixty-nine houses should be built on his land around that lawn; he issued covenants as to the appearance of the

23 Twitten: a Sussex dialect word for a path or passage between two walls or hedges. OED.

houses. Whether it was Hanson who thought up the name 'Regency Square' is unknown, but the houses of Regency Square started to rise in 1818. The development was a success, inspiring others, amongst them Thomas Read Kemp, to emulate such a moneymaking idea.

By 1827, the 45-year-old Thomas Read Kemp was well on the way to constructing his monument, Kemp Town. It was a gamble. The estate was over a mile from the Assembly Rooms, the Libraries, the Royal Pavilion and the 'life' of the town. The one advantage might have been the distance from the dirt and smoke that this 'life' created. A sad sequel to this adventure is that Kemp finally had to pass much of his land to his builder, Thomas Cubitt, as the houses sold far less quickly than expected. Auguste's account of his meeting with T. R. Kemp gives no clue to the underlying anxieties that Kemp must have been facing at the time.

The cityscape of Brighton was in turmoil. One of the only references which Auguste makes to the fact that so much building and improvement work is going on is in the early pages of his account. He strolls on the promenade, meets some agreeable company and then proceeds to inspect the improvements being made along the shoreline. Noisy work is underway on the promenade in two main areas. The first is the building of a road between the extreme southern end of the Steine to join it to the King's Road to the west. This will be Grand Junction Road. Its creation necessitated the destruction of the very derelict Battery built in 1760 but unused since 1783.

> 'Great inconvenience is felt by our fashionable visitors from the alteration making on the King's-road; all carriages are forced to go through Ship-street or Middle-street, till it is completed.'
>
> Brighton Gazette 8 September 1827

Any Brighton visitor or resident who experienced the massive cable laying activities for cable television in the 1990s or the wholesale replacement of the Victorian drains in the first years of the twenty-first century, will feel great sympathy with those who suffered nearly 200 years ago.

The second improvement was the creation of a Brighton to Shoreham road, namely an extension to the Kings Road going west past Regency Square and Brunswick Square. It is the latter which Auguste inspected. Auguste's claim that his friend Sir Robert Wilson was responsible for these improvements is a little fanciful. It is true that the Commissioners who oversaw the good running of the town were indeed ensuring its improvement, but it was Mr. Robinson, Clerk of Works to the Commissioners, who had been put in charge of the work.

> Workmen are constantly and actively employed in completing the Regency-square Esplanade, under the immediate inspection of Mr. Robinson, to whom the public are greatly indebted for the active part he has taken in promoting this work. On Tuesday, we are sorry to say, a sewer and a cess-pool, which were forming on the beach under the esplanade, were destroyed by the sea.
>
> BRIGHTON GAZETTE, 11 October 1827

Even at the heart of the fashionable part of town, the 'workmen of the New Gas Company are employed in laying down a new main across the Old Steine'.[24] No inhabitant, no resident, no visitor could walk without hindrance or inconvenience. Auguste is so intent on 'puffing' Brighton that he did not dream of mentioning any of this upheaval.

The ten fine houses of Brunswick Terrace West had not yet been built for, according to the *Brighton Gazette*, on 11 October 1827, Charles Busby had only very recently bought the land on which he and Amon Wilds were going to build their magnificent terrace. A month later, Thomas Cubitt is reported as making 'arrangements for obtaining the field between Portland-place and Kemptown with a view to erecting a square'.[25] Marine Square, just to the east of Portland Place, had been completed only three years earlier. Even to the north of the town, building was in full swing. When Auguste was taken to Ireland's Pleasure Gardens, an area of Brighton now completely buried under the houses and gardens of Park Crescent, he seemed to have been oblivious of the fact that, on the other side of the road, Hanover Crescent was growing, brick by brick under a forest of wooden scaffolding. Later during his visit, Auguste was invited to dine with Major Philip Stewart and his family at 28 Oriental Place. Does Auguste deign to mention that, although Oriental Place itself was more or less complete,

24 *Brighton Gazette* 8 September 1827.

25 Most probably the reference is to Eastern Terrace which dates from 1827–28. (Carder)

Early bow windows at N°s. 5 and 6 Little East Street. Listed by English Heritage as being built in the late eighteenth or early nineteenth century. Architect unknown.

less than 200 yards away, the builders employed by local magistrate, magnate and director of the East India Company, Sir David Scott, were working on the foundations of the magnificent Sillwood Hall? No, he does not.[26]

Although today it is considered that Brighton is a town full of the bow windows of 'Regency[27] architecture', it should be remembered that the four main architects in the town were capable of producing building in very different styles.

Ammonite capitals

Whilst in partnership together, Amon Wilds senior, Amon Henry Wilds junior and Charles Busby were at the peak of their careers. Amon, father and son, left their mark in the ammonite capitals adorning vast numbers of 'Regency' properties, but it must not be forgotten that in 1827 the following were being built or were recently completed:

26 Sillwood Hall later had a chequered history as a hotel in the late nineteenth century, part of Debenhams department store in the late twentieth century and elegant flats in the twenty-first.

27 George IV was Regent from 1811 until 1820. Architecture is no respecter of reigns. Many genuinely Regency building were built some years after 1820.

By 1823, Wilds Senior and Busby had completed the Western Pavilion (Western Road), an Indian-inspired homage to the Royal Pavilion.

Amon Henry Wilds had built the Unitarian Chapel (New Road) in the Greek Revival style in 1820.

Meanwhile, Busby had recently designing the neo-Classical St. George's Church in Kemp Town in 1824–25 (see engraving page 46).

Charles Barry, for his part, was quite comfortable in supplying the town with a severely classical hospital building as well as contributing to the town's stock of splendid Gothic structures, such as St. Peter's Church, which opened on 1 January 1828.

Edmund Gilbert[28] sums up this builders' bonanza in the following way:

> In 1823 alone the estimated number of bricks consumed in the town was 5 millions; 12,000 loads of sand were taken from the beach, and 3,000 loads of timber were used. As there was no local stone, bricks and plaster were the material for building and gave unity to the stuccoed squares and terraces. At the beginning of 1826 over 500 new houses were being built.

The following accounts from local newspapers give a hint of the fact that building, gardening and even pastoral activities were taking place side by side in the town.

> A very fine wether[29] sheep, belonging to Mr. Acton, Brighton-place, was stolen on Tuesday evening or early on Wednesday morning, from a field on Church Hill, and taken to an unfinished house in Montpelier-road, where it was slaughtered. Some carpenters, who were at work on the spot, discovered the skin and entrails, and from the manner in which the skin had been stripped, there is reason to believe it was done by an experienced butcher.
>
> Brighton Gazette, 11 October 1827

Alas, Auguste seems not to have noticed the sad reports of accidents in the local newspapers. In just one edition of the *Brighton Gazette*, on 29 November 1827, two serious accidents were reported:

28 Edmund M. Gilbert *Brighton: Old Ocean's Bauble*, 1954.
29 Wether sheep: A male sheep, a ram; esp. a castrated ram. OED.

> On Thursday last, as a number of men employed in building a house at Kemptown, were busily at work, the scaffolding suddenly gave way, and four of them were precipitated to the ground from nearly the top of the house. The sufferers were immediately taken up, and conveyed as expeditiously as possible, to the Infirmary in Middle Street, where, under the skilful surgical care of Messrs. Taylor and Bugey, we are happy to learn that they are going on well. The names of the poor men are, John Harris, whose thigh was broken, Humphrey Bean, badly bruised, James Wilson ribs broken, James Cook, head much hurt and otherwise injured; but he is so far recovered as to render his residence in the Infirmary unnecessary. The other men on the building saved themselves by clinging to the scaffold poles. It is said that the accident happened through some negligence in fitting the put-logs; if so, it deserves the most severe animadversion. It is dreadful that men's lives should, through negligence, be placed in jeopardy.

Negligence was imputable not only to the overseers of building sites. Local residents may also be guilty of not taking proper care of their surroundings. A week prior to the two accidents described above, the *Brighton Gazette* takes the 'parish officers' to task in the following diatribe:

> We wish to call the attention of the parish officers of Hove to the condition of several places near Brunswick-square which are left in a dangerous state. There is a well near the top of Waterloo-street, left entirely open day and night. As buildings are daily increasing in this neighbourhood, it behoves the officers to see that the public safety is not endangered by excavations. We hope that this hint will not be lost on them, as we hear that loud complaints are made of the evil.

Several letters to the newspapers complain of the filthy condition of the town. The *Brighton Gazette* describes Pool Lane as 'a horrid place.' Rainy weather seemed to have had the one advantage of washing the streets clean. For the pedestrian, pavements, where they existed, were of brick and presumably quite acceptable, even to ladies in their long skirts. The carriageways between the pavements were less acceptable, being either hard and cobbled, deep in gravel, or muddy:

> …so much gravel has been laid down that it became on Monday impossible for the coaches to pass over it, and they were actually compelled (a thing never perhaps done before) to turn off near the New Church, and go by the circuitous route of the Ditchling-road, afterwards passing down one of the narrow streets again into the London-road, Surely the menders of our ways might contrive to regulate these things better.
>
> Brighton Gazette, 9 November 1827

All carriageway surfaces would have been liberally scattered with horse manure, which Auguste does not condescend to mention, despite the fact the most of his acquaintances move about the town on horseback or in horse-drawn carriages.

In the late autumn of 1827, large parts of Brighton must have been smelly and dirty. Although Auguste bemoans the fact that his hotel room was unheated, many of the more wealthy houses must have been issuing large amounts of coal smoke from the chimneys in an attempt to keep their inhabitants warm. The rate books show that the collection of ashes from houses was big business, and a dirty one. In east Brighton, a mere quarter mile from the new Kemp Town estate, the gas works had been importing vast quantities of gritty coal by hauling it over the beach from dirty coastal tramp ships and then burning the coal to obtain gas. The beach must have been black with coal dust.

The town was a hive of activity and boasted:

- four iron foundries (one being situated, ironically, in the delightfully named Spring Gardens)
- nine braziers and tinplate workers along with six whitesmiths[30] and bell hangers and two wire drawers
- thirteen brewers and two maltsters (think of the smell!)
- sixty-five butchers, many of whom would have been slaughters as there is no separate listing in the directory for slaughterers
- twenty-six coal merchants and four coal dealers

30 Whitesmith: One who polishes or finishes metal goods, as distinguished from one who forges them; also, more widely, a worker in metals. OED

- fifteen cow keepers and dairymen (in streets which the twenty-first century considers as 'select': Church Street, Western Road and Ship Street
- four curriers[31] and leather curers (pure urine was still being used in the curing process)
- thirteen dyers and scourers[32]
- two lime burners (essential to the building trade in Brighton)
- twenty-five blacksmiths

These industries employed large numbers of people, not all of whom were keen to go to their labours of a morning, as the *Herald* explains:

> A novel scene took place on Friday morning in Church-street. It seems one of the apprentices at Messrs. Palmer and Towner's foundry, had over-slept himself for several mornings; and the men, to cure him, went to his lodgings about eight o'clock, with flags flying, &c. Having brought him forth, maugre[33] all his efforts to escape from their grasp, they bound him fast to a truck, and then in triumph dragged him on his chariot down Church-street and back to the foundry in Trafalgar-street. At the foundry gates he was received by a promiscuous mob of persons, who seemed much pleased with the sport, although the poor apprentice appeared to have a sorry time of it, and would no doubt rather have gone to bed some night and for ever forgot to awake, than go a second time through such a purgatorial initiation.

Although the lad might have been living in his parents' house, it is more likely that he is in lodgings as he had been indentured from outside the town and, like many servants, could rarely go home to see his parents.

There were, however, also pleasant noises in the streets. Auguste comments on the night watchmen who sing out the hour and the weather. On 4 October, the 'fine band of the 7th Hussars, which had not played for more than a week, drew

31 Currier: One whose trade is the dressing and colouring of leather after it is tanned. OED.

32 Scourer: One who cleans wool, cloth, clothes, etc. OED.

33 Maugre: Notwithstanding; in spite of everything. Obs. OED.

a large assemblage of spectators to the Steine on Sunday.' Later in the month, Auguste saw a similar performance and was most impressed with the large and varied crowd it drew. Brighton residents are not slow in complaining, however, and there seemed to be one noise which drove them to distraction. On that same October day, as the inhabitants were delighting in listening to the band, the *Brighton Gazette* was reporting discontent:

> We hear that several highly respectable inhabitants have preferred a complaint before one of our Magistrates relative to a practice which has long since been felt as a serious evil, by a very populous and opulent circle of the inhabitants of this town. The nuisance referred to is firing off cannon at all hours of the day and night, on board the packets, and on the Chain Pier. The startling afright of which this is productive, especially to ladies confined to bed by illness, is too generally felt and lamented to require any explanation... and hope that the Powers that be will abate the 'mischievous nuisance'.

It is entertaining to think that the firing of cannon might be mainly to alert the hotel owners that their clients would soon be arriving.

Hyde Park Corner in London epitomises the English love of free speech. In 1827, Brighton was not to be outdone. The *Brighton Herald* reported on 8 September:

> A person belonging to the Society of Ranters, has for the last few Sabbaths past, been holding forth, in the afternoon, to a small but attentive audience, from a capstan on the beach, at the bottom of Cannon Place.

There was plenty of outdoor entertainment for the idlers who took the air in the town or along the esplanade. There was even the 'tuneful vendor of matches now about our streets [who] warbles in fine style "Hurrah for the bonnets of Blue" and totally eclipses the once famous minstrel who sold his wares to the tune of "Rosemary Lane"'. But what was there in the way of entertainment indoors? On this subject Auguste is an expert. His account covers the theatre, the libraries, the balls, musical soirees and the baths. He describes them all in detail. He belongs to the upper ranks of society who have an *entrée* to such amusements. How did the middle classes find entertainment? What did the servants do for fun in their limited free hours? The newspapers of the day give us relatively little indication.

As England moved away from the excesses of the Regency to the more straight-laced middle-class attitudes of a later period, it is possible that respectable Mr. and Mrs. Baker would have been satisfied with a stroll on the promenade, a chat to friends and acquaintances on the Steine, listening to the band on Sunday afternoon after church and cheaper seats in the theatre if the play were not too serious.

The aristocracy could gather for balls and concerts in the Assembly Rooms or in the better class of inn. As ever, lower down the social scale, there were attempts to ape the next social class up, and thus on 12 November 1827, the following advertisement for a 'tradesman's ball' in Hastings appeared in the *Brighton Gazette*. It is unlikely that tradesmen from Brighton would have ventured so far, but it would not be unreasonable to deduce that similar ball or balls might have been held in Brighton:

PELHAM ARCADE

Messrs. J. Hart and Finch most respectfully inform the Inhabitants of Hastings and its Vicinity, that Mr. Jones' Engagement for the Evening Amusements having terminated, they have made arrangements with the proprietors for continuing them occasionally throughout the winter, and in pursuance thereof, there will be a Tradesman's ball, on Tuesday Nov. 13, 1827. – Admission for Gentlemen, 4*s*. 6*d*. Ladies, 4*s*. Tea and Coffee included [...]

Four Gentlemen of great respectability will act as Stewards.

If Mr. and Mrs. Baker wished to put on their most elegant Sunday best and if they had a penny to squander, they may well have been allowed to promenade on the Chain Pier as Auguste so often did. Reading the newspaper for Mr. Baker or an uplifting novel or religious tract for Mrs. Baker might have completed their entertainment, although while the gentleman was watching a cricket match at Ireland's grounds in the north of the town the lady may have enjoyed a little light shopping in daylight hours. Auguste must have visited the shops, but seems to have been more impressed by the way they were gas lit rather than their contents. However, there was something for every purse and something from every continent. There were traders ranging from booksellers (16) to glass, china and earthenware dealers (11) to chemists (11) to jewellers and silversmiths (9) to milliners (27).[34]

Image reproduced by kind permission of Brighton Royal Pavilion, Museums and Libraries

Many of these trades were being carried on in premises which in the twentieth century would not be recognised as shops. It was not uncommon for men and women to carry on their trade at home and to rely on the publication of their address in the local directory. This would lead their clients to them.

If a client wished merely to browse, he or she would do better to attend one of the regular sales of goods in the Fancy Repositories. There were 8 of these listed in 1828, and nearly all were situated on the East Cliff, clearly a more select part of town. Closest to the heart of town was the Royal Bazaar described in *The Watering Places of Great Britain.*[35]

34 *Pigot's Directory* 1828.
35 *The Watering Places of Great Britain and Fashionable Directory*, published 1833.

> THE ROYAL BAZAAR, on the Grand-parade, is a building originally designed for a picture gallery, for the exhibition of the works of foreign artists. The room, which is spacious and very neatly fitted up, is lighted from above; the counters are ranged round the walls and in the centre, leaving a walk round the room.

Apparently the Bazaar[36] was let out to various dealers, one of whom, Catherine Richardson, placed the following advertisement in the *Brighton Herald* on 3 November:

> ROYAL BAZAAR,
> GRAND PARADE, BRIGHTON
>
> *Selling at the upper end of the Bazaar, under the large Painting*
>
> Catherine Richardson begs to announce to the Nobility, Gentry and Inhabitants of Brighton, that she has just returned from London, with a large assortment of fashionable Jewellery, all town-made, with Splendid Cut and Plain Coral, with Rock Coral Negligies,[37] Bracelets and Ear rings to match, Gold Ear rings plain, and set with Turquoise, fine Amethyst, Garnet and Topaz Ear-rings and Brouches, Coral and Garnet rings, fine Coral Crosses, Gold Chains; Sheffield plate Candlesticks, Snuffers and Stands. The above are selling for small profits, at the upper end, under the large painting. – Old Jewellery bought or taken in exchange.
>
> C.R. gratefully returns her thanks to the Nobility and Gentry, and Inhabitants of Brighton, for their liberal support to her during the 20 years she has been in business; and trusts with strict attention to their demands, and offering the best Goods upon the most reasonable terms, to insure a continuance of their patronage.
>
> Ladies' Fashionable Gilt Neck Chains and Bracelets just arrived.
> ☞ A large quantity of Agate Beads from India, selling *remarkably cheap.*
> Take Notice – At the upper end of the Bazaar, under the Large Painting.

36 The building which housed the Bazaar was demolished in about 1959 with the widening of Morley Street. The numbers in Grand Parade now go directly from No. 27 to No. 29, the intervening property having disappeared.

37 Negligie: A necklace or girdle of (usually irregularly set) beads, pearls, etc. (early nineteenth century) OED

Catherine's grammar and spelling may have been a little suspect to a modern reader, but she knew how to advertise. On 24 November, the *Brighton Herald* was able to report that 'The Bazaar on the Grand Parade has been fashionably visited during the week.' If Catherine's wares were a little too prosaic for popular taste, the following month, J. Good was advertising rather more exotic wares, proving that the English were prepared to forgive the French their recent warlike stance and that they, the English, were more than ready to purchase French wares:

> FANCY REPOSITORY
>
> 18, EAST STREET, BRIGHTON
>
> **J. GOOD**
>
> Most respectfully informs the Nobility, Gentry and Inhabitants of Brighton, that he is recently returned from Paris with a splendid and extensive assortment of Jewellery, consisting of Russian, Greek, Roman, and other bracelets, bracelet snaps, ear-rings, brouches, rings, lockets, necklaces, chains, buckles, and ornamental combs of the most fashionable descriptions; likewise a large collection of ornamental china from Sevre, and other celebrated manufacturies, comprising vases, cups and saucers, inkstands, toilette bottles, match cups, and bower stands of the newest and most elegant designs. Dresden, Saxon, and other figures, a great variety of Opal ornaments, in vases, eau-de-cologne and toilette bottles, cups and saucers, smelling bottles, and bronze, Or-molu and alabaster articles, of the most novel patterns; a quantity of the best plain white china for breakfast set, nursery lamps, inkstands, &c. &c. Eau-de-Cologne, from the *Manufactory at Cologne*, imported through Rotterdam direct by J. Good; perfumery from Lubin, of every kind; and an assortment of crayons of various colours.
>
> The whole of the above elegant assortment of French articles were selected by J. Good himself, and he can therefore recommend them with confidence to the public.
>
> N.B. – Just received direct from Paris, a very superior assortment of Parisian curls and ornamental hair.

If the middle-classes could shop to amuse themselves, what could the servants, shop men and skilled or unskilled workmen do to fill their leisure hours? The newspapers give virtually no indication. However, given the fact that both men and women found themselves hauled before Sir David Scott and his fellow magistrates for drunkenness, it might not be an unfair stereotype to suggest that the main form of entertainment for servants and labouring classes was in the public house. *Pigot's Directory* lists sixty-four taverns and public houses. Many of these would be no more than the front room of a small house in one of the poorer streets of the town, but this was where working class people could relax, or just get very drunk. Thompson and Fearon of Holborn Mill, London put as the strap line to their small advertisement in the *Brighton Gazette* in November: 'GREAT FALL IN GIN' and go on to list the price of an Imperial gallon of English gin at 5*s.* 4*d.* and the same product 'of higher strength' at 6*s.* 8*d.* Even the most impoverished 'mother' could have bought a considerable amount of 'ruin'[38] at that price. In the public house, there would probably be singing. When Auguste and his like were listening to Madame This or Signore That singing the latest popular airs in the theatre or in one of the libraries, plain Mrs. This and Joe That might hear the same songs in very different circumstances.

38 A middle-aged cook would have been earning (full board and lodging found) about £9 or 180 shillings a year.

Brighton prices in November and December 1827

The luxuriant produce of our provincial fruit trees has reduced the price of common cider and perry to fourpence a gallon.

per bottle	*s.*	*d.*
Old Port Wines 1821	2	2
Fine Sherry	2	2
Cape Madeira	1	6
Champagne	6	0
Claret	4	6
Moselle	4	0

Boots		
1st quality	Waterproof Town Made Wellington Boots	21*s.*
2nd ditto	Very prime	18*s.*
3rd ditto	Good	16*s.*
4th ditto	Unequalled at the price	15*s.*
Shoes		
1st quality	Waterproof Shooting Shoes	11*s.*
2nd ditto	Walking and Dress	8*s.*
3rd ditto	Ditto very good	6*s.*
4th ditto	Unequalled at the price	5*s.*

☛ The lady patronesses of the Almack's Balls are perhaps not aware that such is the spirit of opposition among most of the resident gentry in the metropolis, (arising from the want of employment among the working classes) that in the ball room not a lady is to be seen with shoes of French manufacture, which has induced the principal boot and shoe makers in London to manufacture goods of superior quality, and sell at such reduced prices as will defy the competition of foreigners.

Satin Shoes ...... 5*s*. 6*d*. to 6*s*. 6*d*.
T. Dutton,
27, East-street, Brighton; and 53, Blackman-street, Southwark.

per lb		
	s	d
Black tea	4	0
Double refined	1	0
New Figs	0	8
French Plums	0	8
West Indian Raw Sugar	0	7
Lumps	0	10

In March 1800, the price of the quartern loaf was seventeen-pence, when new bread was forbidden to be eaten, and the baker was liable to a penalty of five shillings per loaf if he sold it before it was 24 hours old. In October, 1827, the price of the quartern loaf is seven-pence (and in some shops it may be purchased for sixpence-halfpenny), making a difference between the two periods referred to.

Hunting was a pursuit which brought together both rich and poor, but for very different reasons. The rich were there to show off their thoroughbred horses and their hunting pink, as Auguste so quickly notes when a hunting party took breakfast at his hotel. The poor were there to look after the horses, supervise the hounds and, in the countryside, act as beaters. There was no real meeting of classes.

Cricket and horse racing had both been established in the town in the eighteenth century. These were the pursuits of the rich from which the poor could benefit and which the poor could enjoy from the sidelines. However, as Auguste's visit took place in winter, he was unable to enjoy the pleasures of cricket, for the last match of the season, due to have been played on 8 October, had had to be cancelled 'the weather being so unfavourable' (*Brighton Gazette*) and there was no race meet at Brighton during his stay. At the time, however, Hastings had a racecourse. Those who could afford it (prices not revealed in the newspaper advertisement) could take a day trip on the 'ECLIPSE STEAM PACKET (weather permitting)' leaving the Chain Pier, Brighton at eight o'clock on the morning of Wednesday 26 September or at the same time on Sunday 29 September. The return trip left Hastings at 3 o'clock on the same afternoons, but the advertisement hastened to point out that there was a possibility of a four-night stay in Hastings, if the traveller took the boat out on the Wednesday and back on the Sunday. No offer of a cheaper fare!

Falconry was an entertainment much enjoyed by Auguste. The crowd he describes at the event he attended must have contained many an excited working man or woman, despite the fact that they were merely distant spectators, either as 'loungers' or servants.

On another occasion, the walking endurance test that Auguste witnessed was merely one of many such feats of stamina. These were occasions on which vast sums of money changed hands between members of the aristocracy and on which small, but to them significant, sums of money changed hands from workman to workman. In the eighteenth century, there had been cock fighting and bear baiting. If this was going on in 1827, the local newspapers were silent on the matter. The bear encountered by Auguste in the gypsy camp suffered the indignity of having to perform for its supper, but did not seem to undergo any further ill-treatment. This may well have been in part due to the recent establishment of the Society for the Prevention of Cruelty to Animals in 1824.

Gambling was rife, or had been until very recently, in all classes. At the races, at the cricket match, at sailing or yacht races, during card games, be it in grand mansions and humble beer houses, bets were taken on almost anything by anybody.

A very fine tandem[39] match took place yesterday morning (Monday), between Capt. Swain and Mr. George Wilson, for fifty guineas aside, to drive, in tandem, twelve miles. It was done on a four miles piece of ground, on the great Brighton road. The Captain won the match by near two minutes. A great deal of betting took place, and the odds, when Captain Swain had done his first six miles, were seven to one in his favour.

Brighton Gazette, 12 November 1827

This is an aspect of Brighton life which has changed very little over the years. The city now boasts 39 bookmakers' shops, a greyhound racecourse and a horse race course, not forgetting the Internet access to betting 'rooms'. The reader of Auguste's account is therefore as surprised as Auguste is to find, apparently, that there was 'so little liking for cards'. Is this already the beginning of a slightly puritanical 'Victorian' backlash against such sinful pursuits within the home?

Throughout at least the early part of the nineteenth century, young girl servants would have a couple of hours a week to 'cavort' with their friends. A 'long holiday' was perhaps two days at Mothering Sunday when, if she was lucky, the girl could go home to see her parents, often a journey of many miles. The better class of servant, the butler, the housekeeper and the footman, most likely kept themselves to themselves and in large households might have made their own, discrete entertainment. The music hall did not come to Brighton until the 1850s.

There was one other place where rich and poor would assemble in the same building. It was the Theatre Royal in New Road. Admittedly the rich and poor had separate booking windows and entrances, but they went to see the same performances. Auguste enjoys the charity performance of 'The Merchant of Venice'. There would not have been many of the 'lower classes' to see that particular play, possibly as the subject matter and author may not have appealed, but more likely because the prices had been increased for the one-night performance. Normally, however, prices were not exorbitant: the maximum price for a box was 5 shillings; you could have a comfortable seat in the pit for 2*s*. 6*d*.; or go up into the Gods for 1/-. Most respectable people would be happy to attended an early evening

39 Tandem: A two-wheeled vehicle drawn by two horses (or other beasts of draught) harnessed one before the other. OED.

performance and pay the prices listed above. However, there were nights when there were performances starting at 9.15pm. Then you could have your seat in the gallery for a mere 6*d*. In July, which at that time was the beginning of the Season, theatregoers could have seen 'The Hundred Pound Note'[40] followed by the comic play 'Wives as they were and Maids as they are'; or, later in the month, a real crowd-pleaser, 'The Belle's Stratagem' with 'The Maid of Milan' which introduced that delightful new song 'Home Sweet Home'.

November brought both serious Shakespeare and a reprise of the 1819 burletta 'Rochester, or King Charles the Second's Merry Days'. It is not clear whether Auguste was in Brighton in the days before Christmas, but already pantomime was a firm favourite with Brighton audiences since the first production of 'Christmas Gambols' in 1823.[41]

Apart from the common passion for gambling, the rift between classes was wide. The middle and upper classes were suspicious of any class lower than their own. In Manchester, eleven 'working class' protestors demanding more representation in parliament had been mown down by the military at 'Peterloo' (the massacre in St. Peter's Field) in 1819. In 1830, agricultural workers would initiate the Swing riots in Kent and Sussex in an attempt to halt falling wages and impede the increasing use of mechanical farming methods. This fear is reflected by both the *Brighton Gazette* and the *Brighton Herald* in late 1827. The *Gazette* was relatively sanguine when it found that the Commissioners had been receiving complaints:

> ... low people of both sexes are congregating in the Royal Colonnade especially in wet weather ... had they [the Commissioners] intended to do anything about it, they would have done it before now. Besides, they have got things of more importance to attend to, than to waste their time on such petty matters. One of the beadles, if he had directions, would be enough to put a stop to the nuisance.
>
> Brighton Gazette, 11 October 1827

40 A farce by Richard Brinsley Peake. No to be confused with *The Million Pound Note* published by Mark Twain in 1893.
41 Henry C. Porter *The History of Theatre in Brighton*, 1886.

A reader of the *Herald* reacted to the lower classes a little more hysterically:

To the Editor of the *Brighton Herald*

Sir – Having always understood that Mrs. Fitzherbert was a great friend of Brighton, I was really astonished and shocked when on passing the Steyne Lane a few evenings since, I observed nearly opposite to the carriage entrance of the mansion of the above named lady, a low, dirty-looking GIN SHOP thronged with unfortunate females, and men of the lower class. The doors being open, I could distinctly hear their conversation, which was such as decency forbids me to repeat. By what means, Mr. Editor, does this nuisance, in the face of every thing that is respectable, arise? Or why is it suffered to exist. Surely, the inhabitants of Brighton ought better to consult their own interests, and study to please those by whom they live.

I am, Mr. Editor

Your obed. Servant

A Visitor

Marine Parade Oct 4 1827

The lower classes seemed to have held little interest for Auguste other than his amazement at 'the phalanx of servants in sumptuous liveries' who handed him out of his carriage as he arrived at the home of Thomas Read Kemp.

Of course, one way the employed or the unemployed might have passed their time was in the smuggling industry. Smuggling had reached its peak in Brighton during the Napoleonic wars when high import duties had been placed on so many of the luxury goods from the Continent and which the English craved. The following report shows us that the alcohol consumed at the Assembly Rooms or even in private houses might well have had illegal origins:

A smuggling-boat succeeded in running 500 tubs [*of gin*] on Thursday night, opposite Brunswick Terrace. The Blockage men, who resisted the smugglers, were overpowered and disarmed, after receiving several severe wounds. It is supposed that two or three of the smugglers were either killed or severely wounded.

BRIGHTON HERALD, 20 October 1827

Smugglers were generally a hard working lot. Not honest according to the law, but not reprehensible in the eyes of many a good 'bourgeois' who reaped the benefits. These benefits might be come by legally: locals, residents and visitors flocked to 64 Cavendish Street and also to 26 St. James's Street. These two establishments were: 'the magazines for condemned seizures' made by excise men belonging to the civil Board of Customs or men of the Coast Blockade Service under the command of the Admiralty. There, so the *Brighton Herald* reports, somewhat poetically, the premises are 'crowed to excess daily, to obtain a view of those matchless Oriental treasures, which have caused to the unfortunate adventurers many a weeping eye and aching heart.' But there romance ends and commerce takes over as the *Herald* continues: 'The sale commences this day, under the superintendence of the renowned Captain Johnson, who is commanded to proffer the same duty free.' On the other hand, many a citizen did not bother to keep within the law:

> ... The ugly stories of encounters between coastguards and smugglers, some of them stories of inhumanity rare, as I like to believe, in our dear England, had died into history in my childhood. Smuggling had become so barefaced and was so persistently supported by the townsfolk in Brighton and otherwhere, that there was nothing for it but for the excisemen to wink at it as often as possible, very occasionally to make a show of resistance, and at the worst, clap a culprit into gaol for a few weeks by way of a reminder that the law of Protection did yet exist, if only to be broken! There was not, I believe, a housewife in all the town but knew where to get her tea and brandy without paying duty, nor a lady that had not learned the trick of considerably reducing the outlay of her pin-money over 'real French' fineries, without curtailing her stock of silks and laces at all; not an innkeeper that would not wink as he assured you, you could not get such cognac as his at *that* price elsewhere! [...] It was an open secret that every extra fine consignment from the Continent found its way first to the Pavilion, that the King might skim the cream off it; while in more than one instance the poor fellow that brought it over was fuming his heart out in Lewes gaol...[42]

Vagrancy, on the other hand, was anathema, particularly to the Directors and Guardians of the Poor who would have to cover the expense of sending vagrants to the workhouse on Church Hill (approximately on a site between the northern burial ground of St. Nicholas Church and Buckingham Road). The magistrates

42 Maude Egerton Hine King: *Round About a Brighton Coach Office*, 1896.

did their best to rid the town of this plague but, like so many plagues, it was a difficult one to eradicate:

> Our worthy Magistrate, Sir D. Scott, took occasion to observe from the Bench, on Monday, that the efforts of the Magistrates and Officers in clearing the town of vagrants, were rendered abortive by the prevalence of street charity; for so long as this false system of benevolence prevailed, so long would vagrants infest the place in defiance of beadles and commitments.
>
> BRIGHTON HERALD, 27 October 1827

It is worth comparing the *Herald*'s attitude to that of the Evening Argus in 2000:

> The 'Don't Give to Beggars' campaign has won overwhelming support from our readers.
>
> Yesterday people were asked: 'Should we give to beggars?' The result was a resounding: 'No.'
>
> Of those taking part in our current website poll, 86.5 per cent said no and 13.5 per cent said yes.
>
> An Argus telephone poll was evenly split, with 50 per cent saying the public should not give to beggars and 50 per cent saying they should.
>
> The 'Don't Give to Beggars Campaign' was launched following reports that Brighton and Hove people were inadvertently lining the pockets of drug-dealers when they gave cash to beggars.
>
> THE EVENING ARGUS (Brighton), 6 October 2000

Mr. Chasseraud was the Overseer in the town's Workhouse in 1827. The Workhouse did not have a bad reputation. Indeed, it had some 270 inhabitants at the time Auguste was in the town, although when he admires the delights of St. Nicholas' Churchyard, he does not seem to have noticed that less than 200 yards away was an altogether more forbidding boundary wall and building. Despite this fine new building, and perhaps more importantly, despite the seemingly copious if simple diet, attitudes were still harsh:

> Mr. Chasseraud v. White. Mr. Chasseraud stated the prisoner came to his house and demanded relief; he sent him to the black hole, where his conduct was of the most violent description, and he nearly broke out of the place. Sentence: discharged on a promise to remove to London.
>
> BRIGHTON GAZETTE, 22 November 1827

As long as the vagrants were not a burden on the parish, all was well.

As still happens in the twenty-first century, there was a migration of the needy towards Brighton. There are two rather distressing clauses in the Brighton Town Act which allow 'the Directors and Guardians of the Poor to grant Certificates and take Bonds for the maintenance of Bastard Children' (Clause 236). A Certificate accompanied any illegitimate child which had been born outside the Parish. It ensured that the parish in which the child had been born paid for the upkeep of the child whilst it was in Brighton. And matters could be worse for the unfortunate child. Clause 237 of the Bond is bleak: 'Children may be discharged or hired out'.

Auguste does not speak of these matters. Instead, he tells the jolly tale of a little rich boy who gets lost and becomes a chimney sweep but who is then rescued. Fortunately the days of such child labour were drawing to a close:

> We hear that a machine to sweep chimneys with a view to supersede the use of climbing boys, has been had from London, and that one of our Town chimney sweeps has agreed to use the same.
>
> BRIGHTON HERALD, 6 October 1827

Alas, the early nineteenth century must still be considered as the harsh, bad old days of hanging or deporting criminals at the drop of a judge's black cap. One single column of the *Sussex Advertiser*, on October 1827, reveals the following punishments:

William Hatcher, for Assaulting Charles Sherwin, – One month's Imprisonment

James Thorne, for an Assault on Charles Knight; and George Divian for a like offense on Sarah Cobden, were each fined 20*s*. and discharged

William Mills, charged with Assaulting Wm. Rawlings and William Peele; and George Hatcher, charged with a like offense on Charles Sherwin, were tried and *acquitted.*

Joseph Hobden, convicted on two indictments of stealing at Brighton, one tub, one horse-cloth, a hammer, and sundry other articles, the property of J. Lashmar, was sentences for the first offence to *One week's Imprisonment,* and for the second to *One year's Imprisonment to Hard Labour, and during the latter period to be once publicly Whipped.*

James H. Platt, for stealing at Brighton, five printed books and a handkerchief, the property of S. T. Russell, Esq. – *Six month's Hard Labour, and once publicly Whipped.*

William Newnham, for stealing at Brighton, two handkerchiefs, one collar, and one pair of stockings, the property of James Surman – *Six month's hard Labour, and once publicly Whipped.*

David Williams, for stealing at Brighton, one pair of boots, a pair of breeches, and one pair of trowsers, the property of John Batterbury – *Three calendar months to Hard Labour.*

It would seem that the body was of far less importance than material possessions. The apparently rather fearsome Hatcher brothers could beat up both men and women and get away with a short term of imprisonment or even just a fine. The theft of a possession would lead, not only to severe imprisonment, but the indignity and pain of a flogging. Twenty-first-century values are, on the whole, the opposite and the above is inclined to shock latter-day sensibilities. And yet the magistrates were capable of great humanity as shown in the following:

> A young woman, named Smith, whose husband, we believe, is a pilot at Newhaven, addressed Mr. Milford, complaining of ill treatment from her husband; her information was about to be taken, but Mr. Milford, considering that probably it might be more pleasant to the complainant if her information were taken privately, adjourned the sitting, and we are consequently unable to state how Parsons was disposed of.
>
> Brighton Herald, 8 September 1827

Visitors came to Brighton mainly for their health. Even the inhabitants needed health care. The injured workmen referred to above were taken to the Infirmary in Middle Street. Looking at the buildings in Middle Street in the early twenty-first century, it can be seen that the early nineteenth-century buildings in the street are small. The Infirmary must have been cramped. It was therefore decided in the early 1820s that a new hospital was needed. Land was acquired to the east of central Brighton and Charles Barry, who had also been commissioned to build St. Peter's Church in the centre of Brighton at much the same time, was appointed as architect. Although it was the town Commissioners who were responsible for building the hospital, charitable contributions were also called for. In his account of Brighton, Auguste mentions a sale of work for the 'French and Spanish refugees'. However, the Fancy Fair for the benefit of the new hospital was an even vaster affair. Its organisers reported that it produced 'a sum far surpassing what we, or any other sanguine friend of the Charity had anticipated. Our most venturous hope did not extend beyond a thousand pounds; while the actual amount realized is Thirteen Hundred and Sixteen Pounds, Twelve Shillings, and Six pence'.[43] As is still the case with many major charities, it was the ladies who did the bulk of the organising. The foundation stone of the Sussex County Hospital and Sea Bathing Infirmary had been laid eighteen months before Auguste arrived, but work was still in full swing late in 1827 and the building was not opened until June of the following year.

43 The equivalent of 200 years' pay for the footman mentioned above.

If Auguste had been in need of major bodily repairs, he would have had to rely either on the Infirmary, on one of the thirty-three surgeons or on one of the eight physicians in the town.

As there were only three dentists listed in Pigot's 1828 *Directory*, it is possible that many of the surgeons would have dealt with dental problems. In the early twenty-first century, a good income might tempt someone who has lost a tooth to opt for the exorbitantly expensive dental implant. In 1827, anyone with problem teeth would go for the latest treatment to 'MR. FISHER, SURGEON DENTIST' of 59, Old Steyne, Brighton. Mr. Fisher thought it well worthwhile to take a prominent front page advertisement in the *Brighton Gazette* on 11 October 1827 to advertise his '*mode and terms* of supplying the various losses or deficiencies of the **TEETH**, where mechanical contrivance is required from a single tooth, to a complete set.' Messsrs. Levander and Jones of London advertised:

Under the Patronage of the Faculty

NATURAL AND ARTIFICIAL TEETH

Fixed on an entirely New and Superior Principle:

So adapted to the mouth and gums as to elude the eye of discovery. Those Ladies and Gentlemen whom the rapid progress of Caries may have deprived of those essential instruments of mastication, may have any defect or loss of Teeth remedied, from one to a complete set, without pain or inconvenience to the wearer, at a little more than half the usual charges, by Messrs. Jones and Lavender, Surgical and Mechanical Dentists, 127 St. James's-street, Brighton.

BRIGHTON HERALD, 3 November 1827

How many clients queued up to purchase Butler's Vegetable Tooth Powder or Butler's Silver-wired Tooth Brushes must remain a matter of conjecture.

To complete the set of those who tinkered with the ailing body, we must not forget those who dealt with the lame and the hard of hearing:

The building on the left is the Sussex County Hospital which opened on 11 June 1828; that on the right is St. George's Church. Although this image dates from 1841, the vacant spaces around both buildings must have been much as Auguste would have seen them.
Image reproduced by kind permission of Brighton Royal Pavilion, Museums and Libraries

> Mr. and Mrs. Potter, Chiropodists, removed from East-street to N°. 10, Bond-street (near the Royal Colonnade), North-street, Brighton. Corns, bunions, defective nails, &c. (however obstinate or long standing) cured with perfect safety, and without the least pain [...] Attendance from eleven till four,– The Poor (gratis) from four till five.
>
> Brighton Gazette, 11 October 1827

Mr. Wright, Surgeon-Aurist to her late Majesty Queen Charlotte, Lecturer in Anatomy and Physiology on the Organ of hearing intends [...] to be at Brighton on Wednesday next, the 12th inst., and three following days, during which he will receive patients, before 10 in the morning, or from one till four.

BRIGHTON HERALD, 8 September 1827

In the early nineteenth century, there is no doubt that personal hygiene was much improved when compared to that of the powdered and elaborately swathed eighteenth century. However, few and far were the houses provided with bathrooms, let alone water closets. Although the S-trap had been invented in 1775 and a siphon system patented in 1819, the water closet was still only for the wealthy.

When Thomas Attree leased No. 69 Regency Square to Mr. James Dumbrell in December 1828, the inventory, for the second floor of the house, lists 'Water Closett; mahogany seats [*sic*] with white basin stained glass window' (the punctuation of the original document makes the exact position of the stained glass window ambiguous, but it would be nice to think that the water closet was embellished with such a grand window); on the first floor was a 'Water Closett [with]mahogany fittings complete with blue and white pan'. In all of the houses of Regency Square the main reception room, or Drawing room as it was then called, was situated on the first floor, at the front of the house. It is noticeable that this water closet, on the *pian nobile,* had a patterned pan, whereas the next floor up had only a plain white pan. The servants in the attic and the children of the house, in the nursery or in their bedrooms on the third floor, were not indulged with a water closet on their floor. The chamber pot was the order of the day.

In the basement of No. 69 was a 'pipe from Force Pump to Water Closett and Force Pump and Iron handle fixed in wood frame with nuts and screws'. It is not clear if the further reference to 'Closett' in the basement refers to a water closet or merely a cupboard, but it is not unusual for Regency houses to have an outside water closet for the servants' use during the day. Water was provided for the water closet by means of 'one stout Tub shelf at foot, lead pipe from pump to Water Closet and for conveyance of water from roof containing four upright pipes and Slant ditto and one wood ditto Shute from ditto Reservoir Stout Iron bound Reservoir Brass tap'. Much of this inventory lacks clarity, but the evidence seems to point to a sophisticated system of plumbing within an upper middle class home. There is, in the inventory, however, not a word about anything resembling a bathroom. Hot water would still have been brought up in ewers by a long-suffering under-maid for her mistress or her master.

As the century moved closer towards the Victorian age, cleanliness moved nearer to godliness. More and more nineteenth-century visitors came to appreciate a dip in the sea from the shelter of a horse-drawn bathing machine. Auguste graphically describes how their parents and grand-parents had entrusted their health to the drinking of sea water mixed with milk as prescribed by the early promoters of the benefits of the Briney. What so surprises today is that a sea bath in the 1820s, during the late-autumn Season, was taken generally at six o'clock in the morning. The custom of bathing at dawn has not generally survived to the present day. The explanation for such early dips lies more in the 1825 'Brighton Town Act' than in visitors' personal preferences. Clause 198 of the Act stipulates: 'No person or persons to Bathe any where in front of the Town, between the hours of Eight o'clock in the morning and Nine in the evening. Fine 20/- for every offence against this clause.'

There was no magic about seawater. The salt content would help sterilise the skin, thus alleviating many chronic skin conditions.

The other, more comfortable, way of taking water externally was to visit one of the seven bathhouses in the town. The most well known being the one which Auguste visited and which he compared favourably to bath- and massage-houses in other parts of the world. By 1827, Sake Dean Mahomet's[44] establishment was on a prominent site on the esplanade, at 39 East Cliff, the site being that of the Queens Hotel in the early years of the twenty-first century. Today, this hotel boasts a luxurious leisure centre and spa, thus continuing a long tradition associated with the site. Indeed, the site was so prominent on the 'old' esplanade that, as Fisher[45] points out:

44 Both Mahomet and Mahomed are used to refer to Sake Dean. The former is more common.

45 *The Travels of Dean Mahomet: An Eighteenth-Century Journey Through India* edited with an introduction and biographical essay by Michael H. Fisher, University of California Press.

> From the 1820s, the town built broad seawalls in front of the cliff and filled in the intervening space eventually to create a wide 'Grand Junction Road' and esplanade. Beyond any financial losses incurred by this disruption in his usual custom, Sake Dean Mahomet had to pay for part of the construction. While the ultimate result was a more secure foundation for his bathhouse, during the construction, anyone seeking to visit his baths would have encountered noise and debris. Complaints by Dean Mahomet to the Town Commissioners about inadequate lighting and disruption met with little satisfaction.

A minor advertising skirmish occurred in the pages of Pigot's 1828 *Directory*. The first shot was fired by Mahomet who described himself as 'shampooing surgeon and inventor of the Indian medicated vapour baths.' Just along the road, a certain J. Molineux was not to be outdone. He had recently set up business at N$^{o.}$ 36 East Cliff[46] and vaunted his 'Indian and Turkish Medicated Sea Waters, Vapour and Shampooing[47] Baths.' However, Mahomet held the trump card. He had placed a large advertisement in the same publication in which he assert that he was the one and only 'Shampooing Surgeon to His Majesty, King George IV' and it is true that he had valuable royal patronage, for in 1825 George IV had had installed an Indian vapour bath within the royal bathroom at the Royal Pavilion. The Royal tub had cost the grand total of £25/0/0. Conceding a certain defeat in the domain of 'Baths', Molineux was not to be bested when it came to 'Cupping'[48] in the list of trades. Whereas Dean Mahomet Junior is merely 'late pupil to Mr. Mapleson, cupper to his Majesty' (Oh, the indignity of being so far removed from the royal flesh), John Molineux was proud to announce that he was cupper 'by appointment to his Majesty's household.' The big advantage that both men had seized was the craze for the Oriental, fostered by the Prince Regent with his fantastical palace less than half a mile away.

---

46 It is unfortunate for historians that the name East Cliff is, nowadays, applied by the Brighton and Hove City Council to designate a conservation area east of the Old Steine. The East Cliff of 1827 referred to the cliff top which stretched from roughly the position of the Palace Pier to the Grand Hotel. The East Cliff lay to the west of the lower end of the Steine.

47 To subject (a person, his limbs) to massage. Now rare, except as designating a part of the process of a Turkish bath. OED.

48 Cupping: *Surgery*. The operation of drawing blood by scarifying the skin and applying a 'cup' or cupping-glass the air in which is rarefied by heat or otherwise. (Also called distinctively *wet cupping*. *Dry cupping*: the application of a cupping-glass without scarification, as a counter-irritant) OED.

Mahomet's Baths prior to the construction of Grand Junction Road (c. 1822). The road to the left is a continuation of King's Road. It leads to East Street. By the time La Garde reached Brighton, the troublesome capstan had been removed or at least disabled.
Image reproduced by kind permission of Brighton Royal Pavilion, Museums and Libraries

> Why are the Commissioners like Molineux's bathing brushes? D'ye give it up? Because they're always in hot water.
>
> BRIGHTON GAZETTE, September 1827

The clearest description of the baths in the town is given by Timothy Carder.[49] Carder clarifies the locations of the other baths listed in *Pigot's Directory*. Auguste would have had a choice of having his massage, steam-bath or baths at numerous establishments: at Mr. Williams' Royal Baths 'at the bottom of the Old Steine'; at George Wood's Original Royal Baths advertised as being in the Old Steine;

49 Timothy Carder: *The Encyclopaedia of Brighton* 1990 Entry 7.

he could have patronised Mr. Lamprell's Baths at the furthest seaward end of East Street if he had wished to participate in communal indoor swimming; Awsiter's Baths were just next door; he could have gone to the establishment of F. Fernehough[50] at the Artillery Baths (now buried beneath the ballroom of the Grand Hotel) Finally, Auguste could have bathed at the New Steine Baths in Devonshire Place. He chose not to, preferring Sake Dean's more prestigious establishment.

According to Carder, Lamprell's Baths were housed in a 'circular domed building 53 feet across nicknamed "The Bunion"'; 'it projected into Grand Junction Road somewhat when the road opened in 1829'. This is certainly borne out by the *Brighton Herald* on 1 September 1827:

> SEA WALL.– The contractor for building this wall, has had a remarkably fine time for carrying up the western extremity, level with the beach. Much of the old Blockhouse [*Battery*] has been brought to light, and large fragments of it are embedded in the foundations of the new wall. The tide being on the neap, and the weather still fine, the contractor, on Wednesday last, put on a gang of excavators in front of Lamprell's baths, in the hope that he should be able to carry the wall round this *critical point*, ere the tide should again put in, and the weather become too rough for prosecuting this work. The men the other night, we observed, were busily employed in excavating the beach by fire-light, taking every advantage, when the tide is out, to expedite the undertaking.

Clearly there were no trades unions in Brighton, as yet!

It is fascinating to consider that those huge chunks of eighteenth-century fortifications lie under the area between southern ends of present-day East Street and Brills Lane. Why Brills Lane? For the simple reason that Charles Brill, Mr. Lamprell's nephew, inherited the baths in 1840. The fortifications do

50 Fernehough had established the Artillery Baths in 1813, but it would seem that they had been bought and developed by Robert Hobden in 1824.

not lie immediately under the pedestrian pavement of the twenty-first century promenade as the road widening improvements of the late nineteenth century have pushed both roadway and pavement seawards.

Water was still taken internally for health, but it was of the 'mineral' variety, both natural and artificial. Auguste visited first the natural Chalybeate spring (now a marshy corner of St. Ann's Well Park in Hove);

> When tasted, it is soft, not unpleasingly martial, and temperate in point of heat. It has the smell that is always perceptible in ferruginous waters, but heavy when compared with the brisker odour of Pyrmont or Spa.[51]

Next he went to the German Spa in Queen's Park (Chapter 6). At the German Spa he clearly took a great deal of interest in the manufacture of artificial spa waters which was being carried on there by Frederick Struve. Struve was an entrepreneurial analytical chemist. He had been born in Saxony in 1781 and had already perfected his method of producing 'artificial natural spa water' in the early years of the century. He had set up 'manufactories', well disguised as pump rooms, across Europe in the early nineteenth century. By the time he had arrived in Brighton in 1825, he knew exactly what he wanted.

Struve's elegant spa, with its classical colonnade, sat perfectly in the southern part of the new park-cum-residential development being planned in that part of the town.[52]

If you had spent too long in seawater, your skin may have dried out somewhat. If the spa waters had not relieved your internal problems, you might still be suffering discomfort. There was plenty of help at hand. Any one of the eleven chemists (not to mention the two apothecaries) in the town would be only too ready to sell you the following which was advertised each week in the *Brighton Gazette*:

---

51 Sicklemore (Snr) R.: *History of Brighton and its Environs, 5th edition with elegant engravings*, 1827.

52 Various authors, *The Story of Queen's Park, Brighton*, Brighton Town Press, 2009.

The German Spa in the mid-1820s. In the distance is St. George's Chapel and some very unhealthy looking smoke.
Image reproduced by permission of the Wellcome Library, London

To Families Bathing, enjoying Aquatic Excursions, Travelling in Sun and Dust, or visiting Close Assemblies, are recommended the following:–

Genuine Articles are indispensible for personal comfort and attraction,

Rowland's Kalydor, for the Complexion

An inestimable, mild, and innocent production, powerfully efficacious in thoroughly exterminating

Eruptions, Tan, Pimples, Freckles, Redness, and all cutaneous imperfections ...

To Preserve and Beautify the Human hair, after Sea Bathing, during Travelling and Violent Exercise, or Violent Perspiration, and to retain in it vigour to the latest period of life,

Rowland's Macassar Oil

If you were in need of a remedy for the colic, you could purchase Hallam's Antibilious Pills – 'strongly recommended for "Bilious Complaints, Headache, Heartburn, and habitual Costiveness".'[53] At N°. 5 St. James-street, T. G. Sarel was regularly announcing himself as the 'ONLY Chemist to His Majesty' (within Brighton, presumably) and that he was agent for:

> Snook's Genuine Aperient Pills
>
> A Most excellent Medicine for Bile, Indigestion, Pains, Giddiness of the Head, Piles, Dropsical Complaints ... their composition is excellent as they do not contain Antimonial or Mercurial preparation whatever, and therefore when taken, do not require the least confinement or alteration of diet ... they destroy worms, purify the humours, and evacuate all foul corruption to which the Intestines are so liable, whereby so many diseases are produced – never gripes unless the inside be very foul, and then but little.

A very clever piece of advertising: if you take these pills, you will not have to spend hours in the water closet and if you get any griping pains, it is your fault, not that of the Pill, as your insides must be particularly 'foul'. If you are 'afflicted with Nervous disorders' you will, of course, require 'Dr Fothergill's Nervous Drops'. According to the advertiser of these Drops they are 'sold in Bottles, at 4*s*. 6*d*.; 11*s*. and 22*s*.[54] by the Principal Medicine Vendors of the Kingdom'.

Another way to deal with the foulness of the body was to perfume it. The usual place to buy your perfume would be at the hairdressers. Pigot's 1828 Sussex *Directory* lists seventeen 'Perfumers and Haircutters' but no separate 'Perfumers'. This was fine for any gentlemen who, like Auguste himself, did not have his own manservant to cut his hair. He would choose his products on the haircutter's premises. However, most gentlemen and the vast majority of ladies would have had their hair cut and dressed at home. Perish the thought of undergoing such personal attentions in a semi-public place. These ladies and gentlemen would send

53 Costiveness: The state or condition of being costive; confinement of the bowels, constipation. OED.

54 In 1827 a butler was paid £35 per annum and tea and sugar (700 shillings in pre-decimal money), a housemaid earned about £8/0/0 (160 shillings). From the Diary of John Longe, Vicar of Coddenham.

their servants out to purchase perfumes, oils and pomades, or would have ordered them from a local supplier to be delivered to the house.

It is here, in the advertisements for perfumes, that the influence of France and the French language upon the town starts to become obvious. On the front page of the *Sussex Advertiser* for 15 December 1827, in a broad and prominent column of text, the first item which catches the eye is the name of a very French sounding personage:

> **J. Delcroix Of No. 125 New Bond Street**
> Removed from 33, Old Bond Street, London
>
> Begs leave to inform the Nobility and Public of Brighton and its vicinity, that he is constantly supplying Mr. Good, Perfumer to His Majesty and Her Royal Highness the Duchess of Gloucester, East Street;
>
> Mr. Bonner Perfumer, St. James's-street; and
>
> Mr. Hunter, Perfumer, Bazaar;
>
> With his genuine and unequalled Foreign Perfumery, mostly imported from his Manufactory at Grasse, in the South of France, which enables him to assure the Public of its superior quality, and to maintain its universal pre-eminence.
>
> Delcroix's Esprit de Lavande aux Mille-fleurs, so delightful in its fragrance, that many are basely deceiving the Public, by selling a spurious article, with his name and address; he therefore cautions the public not to purchase at houses unconnected with his authority.
>
> Bouquet du Roi, Bouquet Militaire, Bouquet Britannique, Bouquet Despang, Esprit de Rose, and every sort of the choicest Perfumes for the Handkerchief, &c,
>
> Delcroix's Inexhaustible Salts, and Esprit Volatil de Vinaigre à la Rose, for reviving depressed spirits, and preventing the ill effects of infected air.
>
> Delcroix's efficacious Pomade Divine

Ruge of the Finest Colours and Quality

Blanc de Perle, Crème des Sultanes, and Milk of Roses, for softening and whitening the skin,

Delcroix's fragrant Vegetable Extract for cleaning and beautifying the hair.

His Pomade Régénératrice for the growth and preservation of the hair, and invariably causing it to appear soft and beautiful.

Delcroix's never-failing Poudre Unique, for dyeing the hair without injuring the skin in the slightest manner, if applied agreeably to the easy direction. Delcroix's Poudre Subtil for removing superfluous hair, most effectually, and without the least inconvenience or pain.

Delcroix's Anti-scorbutic Elixir, and Anti-scorbutic Tooth Powder, for preserving the teeth and gums from decay, relieving the tooth-ache, and cleansing and preserving the beauty of the enamel from scorbutic infection.

Vegetable Polish Paste, Pasta del Castagna, and his genuine Naples Soap, he can with confidence recommend to Gentlemen for ease and comfort in shaving.

Delcroix's Mecca, Aromatic, and Valencia Almond Oil Soaps, of the greatest purity. Also his Brown and White Windsor Soaps, and all other articles of Perfumery of the very best description. Genuine Swiss Arquebusade, and Eau de Cologne, imported from the two best makers.

It would not be surprising if, at the end of his advertisement, Mr. Delcroix had pre-empted the famous words of the L'Oreal company by stating: 'Because you're worth it'. In this advertisement are found all the same twenty-first-century concerns which modern beauty products address: a desire for beautiful hair, sparkling teeth, fear of hair loss, painful depilation. Fortunately, we do not have the same problems of scurvy and our 'infected air' has different origins from than of the early nineteenth century. Auguste is quick to comment on the overcrowded rooms to which he is invited. Many a lady would have to have recourse to her *sal volatile*[55] in its elegant little glass bottle, to revive her in the heat and the crush.

The modern day visitor to Brighton is more than happy to spend her time in the town tanning her skin rather than attempting to keep it delicately white. In the 1820s, no respectable lady would wish to look like an outdoor servant by letting the faintest hint of naturally sun-kissed colour tinge her person. A real lady would apply her *ruge*, but very little else in the way of colour, for the highly coloured *maquillage* of her grandmother's time was now well past and the dangers of brilliant white, lead-based powders and paints were already known. Only the more vulgar class of woman would think of applying kohl to the eyes and eyebrows. Thanks to the efforts, throughout the twentieth century and into the twenty-first, of the Trading Standards Department of town and city councils across England, we have relatively little to fear from counterfeit beauty products – the counterfeiters are attracted more by watches and music than by unguents. However, in 1827, the high cost of these imported goods meant that there was a steady trade in fake and probably dangerous substances to be applied to the body.

Delcroix is careful to name products from all the major European countries of good repute. It is significant, however, that he does not fear to use French names for the vast majority of his products. As a Frenchman, not only does he spell the names correctly, he is even bold enough to place accents on some of the words.

Delcroix is assuming that he is addressing a class of people to whom French is a familiar language. He is not wrong. Auguste goes into company where a roomful of Englishmen will use his language rather than their own native English. He is much impressed by the linguistic skills of those he meets. So is French used merely by the aristocracy?

It would seem not. The two main Brighton weekly newspapers were the *Brighton Gazette*[56] and the *Brighton Herald,*[57] both selling at 7*d*. Who would read these newspapers? A house maid would not have bought, and might not even have been able to read, a newspaper. The butler, however, might well have done so. As seen above, his annual salary of £35 0*s*. 0*d*. would represent some 23 old pence (23*d*.) per day. As his food and lodging were found for him, he could indulge 7*d*. once a week on some reading matter. The more likely readership would be the

55 Ammonia, used to restore a lady suffering from the 'vapours'.

56 The *Brighton Gazette and Lewes Observer; or Chichester, Worthing, Eastbourne, Hastings and Tunbridge Wells Fashionable Chronicle and General Advertiser.*

57 The *Brighton Herald; or Sussex, Surrey, Hampshire and Kent Advertiser.*

middle and upper classes. The advertisements placed in these newspapers show that traders are banking on the popularity of French fashion:

> **Mrs. Shepherd**, Parisian corset maker and Dressmaker, 118, St. James Street, Brighton gratefully acknowledges the distinguished patronage of the Nobility, Gentry, &c. and begs to inform Ladies that she continues to make the most approved pattern Corsets in French and English Materials.

At 32 East Cliff, 'opposite Molineux's baths', S. Barnett is advertising:

> ...Indian and French Silks ... French plain and figured Gros-de-Naples [...] fine French Cambrics, 100 Black Satin and other full-sized fashionable cloaks, lined with Ermine, Black Velvet Capes, handsomely trimmed, &c Chantilly Veils and Pelerines of the most exquisite patterns, Valenciennes, Meckling and Lisle Lace, White and Black French Blonds of superior quality, real French shoes [...]

'Mr. Octave, Coiffeur, de Haute classe, from Paris' is paying to advertise, in an attempt not to be outdone by 'Mr. Creuseton, Coiffeur de la Rue de Paix' who invites clients to visit his establishment at 18 Camelford Street. 'Madame Gosse, of the Académie Royale de Musique à Paris' begged to inform the 'Nobility and Gentry' that she had removed to 10 Western Cottages (renamed Sillwood Road in 1871). 'York House' at 20 St. James's Street was advertised as a 'French and British Silk Depot', selling, amongst much else, 'Mantil Zephire Sutoir,[58] à la Giraffe[59] a beautiful variety of gauze Ribbons de Chez le roi'. On an inside page of the *Brighton Herald* is a large advertisement for:

58 Although November seems to be an inappropriate time to be selling such wares, the 'mantil zephire' would seem to be a mantel or cloak made of a light-weight fabric know as 'zephyr' It is possible that the 'sutoir' is 'sautoir' or light chain with which to attach to cloak across the front of the wearer.

59 The art historian Dr Alexandra Loske of the Royal Pavilion has pointed out that the first giraffe ever to be imported into Britain arrived in 1827 as a gift for the king, George IV. The poor beast died in 1829.

Education in France.– An English and French Boarding School, within a few minutes' walk of Dieppe, Young Gentlemen are liberally boarded and instructed in the usual branches of polite Education, or prepared for the Universities. The situation selected for this establishment is particularly eligible; and every attention is paid by the proprietors to the health, comfort, and improvement of their pupils.

A prospectus and references from Clergymen of the greatest respectability in the counties of Kent and Sussex, may be obtained at the office of this paper [...].

Brighton Herald, 6 October 1827

One is tempted to wonder how the French say 'Dotheboys Hall'! But it may well be that such a school, or ones like it, gave the boys a sound foundation in French, English and Latin and any other knowledge they required in their future life.

Most surprising are the announcement-cum-advertisements entirely in French such as the two in the *Brighton Herald* on 10 November 1827. They are quoted here in full so that any modern reader may practise his or her French:

Beaux Arts.– Madame de Comoléra, membre de l'Académie de Peinture de France, et Peintre de la Manufacture Royale de Sèvres, a l'honneur de prévenir les dames et les amateurs des beaux arts, qu'elle est nouvellement arrivée à Brighton, et qu'elle a chez elle une collection d'ouvrages d'un très grand fini et d'un genre dont elle seule est l'inventeur ; que l'on peut voir tous les jours de deux heures à cinq heures en son domicile, No. 4, East Cliff. Madame Comoléra donne des leçons chez elle et chez les dames, et est l'auteur de la superbe table peinte à l'huile, la seule qui existe dans son genre qui a tout excité l'admiration des amateurs et qui est maintenant dans la possession de S.A.R., la Duchesse de Clarence.

This day is published, by Henry Colburn New Burlington Street, London,

The O'Briens and The O'Flahertys; a

National Tale. By Lady Morgan. 4 Vols.

"A plague upon both your houses!" – *Shakespeare*

II

Private Anecdotes of Foreign Courts. By

the Author of the "Memoirs of the Princesse de Lamballe."

2 vols. 8vo 28*s*.

III

Blue Stocking Hall; a Novel. 3 vols. post 8vo 27*s*.

IV

The traveller's Oracle; or Maxims for Loco-

motion. By William Kichiner, M.D. Author of the

"Cook's oracle," "The Art of Invigorating and Prolonging

Life", &c. &c. Second Edition. In 2 pocket vols 15*s*.

V

The Mummy; A Tale of the Twenty-Second Century.

3 vols. post 8vo. 28*s*. 6*d*.

VI

Reuben Apsley. By the Author of "Brambletye

House," "The Tor Hill," &c. Second Edition.

in 3 vols post 8va. 31*s*. 6*d*.

VII

Two Years in New South Wales. By P. Cun-

ningham, Esq. R.N. Second Edition, Revised, with Map

In 2 vols. post 8vo 18*s*.

VIII

Vicissitudes in the Life of a Scottish Soldier.

Written by Himself. 1Vol 12 mo. 7*s*. 6*d*.

We cannot fail to be impressed, as Auguste intends us to be, by the fact that he has met both the delightful Lady Hotham (née Susan-Maria O'Brien), and Lady Morgan's influential publisher, Henry Colburn. The many governesses working in private houses throughout the town would have relied on their mistress to buy novels for the home bookshelves and to make them available to the more impoverished but literate members of the household. The schoolmaster was, perhaps worse off. He would have been paid in the region of £40 per annum, out of which he might well have to find his own board and lodging. Mr. Cunningham's book in the advertisement above, costing nearly £1/0/0, would have been way beyond the young schoolmaster's pocket.

Taylor and Son at 134 North Street were advertising all 45 volumes of Rees' 'Cyclopædia' for the staggering sum of £50 and, for a mere £30, they were offering, in 75 volumes, the complete works of Sir Walter Scott, a writer for whom Auguste declares himself to be 'full of admiration'. Rees and Scott were very much at the high end of the market. The fact that Taylor was selling 12 volumes of Fielding's works for 5 shillings seems to indicate two things: first, that Scott, being still alive and at the height of his popularity, could command far higher prices for his books than the long-dead[61] and unfashionable Fielding; second, the extremely low price of the Fielding could also indicate that Taylor and Son were acting as second-hand book sellers. Auguste describes the auction at which the vast library of the late Prime Minister, George Canning, was disposed. Although many of the books were bought by individuals, as Auguste explains, it must have been true that the bulk was sold off to dealers. It is also likely that books no longer fashionable enough for the Libraries in the town would have been disposed of in much the same way. Our impoverished school-master may well have been able to purchase the books he needed, so long as he was able to find a second-hand copy, courtesy of Mr. Taylor and his son.

The tradition of the Circulating Library is a long one in Brighton, the first having been opened in the town in 1760. By 1827 there were eight libraries, all respectable, but some more respectable than others: *The Watering Places of Great Britain* stresses this aspect of social life:

61 Sir Walter Scott 1771–1832. Henry Fielding 1707–52.

In these establishments amusement and instruction are admirably combined; and from the variety of them which exist, every taste may be gratified, except it be a vicious one,

[*the compiler goes on to list*]

> TUPPEN AND WALKER'S ROYAL MARINE LIBRARY, on the Marine-parade, is well supplied with every popular work, especially such as are calculated for the fair sex [...];
>
> ST. JAMES'S PUBLIC CIRCULATING LIBRARY is of a somewhat different character, being devoted to works of standard merit rather than to those of a lighter class. The reading-room of this establishment is naturally frequented by a highly respectable circle of visitors [...];
>
> LODER'S LIBRARY, in North-street is an extensive concern, embracing above twenty thousand volumes in every branch of science. Hither may the student resort, secure from the interruptions of the giddy and the gay [...];
>
> WRIGHT'S ROYAL COLONNADE LIBRARY is conveniently situated at the corner of North-street and the New-road. It is very respectably and numerously attended; and the proprietor has rendered it worthy of the patronage of his numerous subscribers. The periodical publications, and the French and English newspapers, are taken in [...]Terms 21*l.* per annum;[62] six months 15*l.*; three months 9*l.*; one month 6*l.*;
>
> WHITTEMORE'S RELIGIOUS, MORAL AND ENTERTAINING LIBRARY, 76, West-street.[63] This Library is furnished with the most popular works in theology, moral essays, interesting biography, voyages, and travels, and light reading, purely of a moral cast, so that parents may, with safety allow their children to select any book from the catalogue. The Reading-room is supplied with morning and evening papers, the provincial papers, the most popular monthly periodicals, the Edinburgh, Quarterly, and Theological Quarterly Reviews, and every new work of merit as soon as published.

Apart from books and newspapers, what else was there to entertain the 'Nobility and the Gentry' in a Library? Auguste himself tells us much about the activities and these are confirmed by the entry in '*Watering Places*':

---

62 £21 0*s*. 0*d*.

63 *Pigot's Directory* 1828 gives J. Whittemore at 7 Great East Street. The *Watering Places ... Directory* of 1831 lists several additional libraries which either opened in the intervening years, or which simply did not appear in *Pigot's Directory*.

> … these Libraries are distinguished by the crowds which resort to them every evening; here may be seen the beauty and fashion of the town, gratifying themselves with the pleasures and amusements which surround them, among which the game of loo[64] and the vocal and instrumental music, are not the least.

As can be seen from his writings, Auguste interested himself greatly in grand, international politics (see in particular Chapter 5). Many of the debates he reports have a contemporary ring to them. He would have found adequate information about all aspects of current affairs from local newspapers, from the London newspapers available in the libraries, and from the people he met. He is the first to admit that he barely understood the workings of British politics – and he breathes hardly a breath about local Brighton politics.

Politically, the town was relatively quiet. Brighton was not a parliamentary constituency. The nearest MP was Thomas Read Kemp, member for Lewes, as his father had been before him. Auguste boasts of meeting several parliamentarians (both from the House of Lords and the House of Commons) but does not point out the inequalities in representation across England. It is generally assumed that Auguste was living in London in 1832 when many of these iniquities were addressed by the passing of the Representation of the People Act, more commonly known as the 'Reform Act'.

In Brighton one hundred and sixteen Commissioners, who were – almost – democratically elected (male ratepayers being the only electors), were bound by the 1825 'Brighton Town Act'. The Commissioners were managing to keep the town clean, although there were occasional complaints in the newspapers about the dirty state of the streets. Robert Jackson, the contractor charged with cleansing the town, felt, on one occasion, his work to have been disparaged and sent to the *Herald* an account of his efforts:

64 A round card-game played by a varying number of players. The cards in three-card loo have the same value as in whist; in five-card loo the Jack of Clubs ('Pam') is the highest card. A player who fails to take a trick or breaks any of the laws of the game is 'looed', i.e. required to pay a certain sum, or 'loo', to the pool. OED.

Copy of the Return to the Inspector above alluded to

King's Road was swept to the bare flints on the evening of the 18th, and the morning of the 19th instant: the dirty part of it was scraped on the 22nd, and part of it was scraped on the evening of the 25th, the whole finished this morning, being three times in eight days.

Oct. 26 1827 Signed R. JACKSON

The Commissioners were charged with:

- lighting the town (Clause 41);
- ensuring that the populace emptied its privies responsibly (Clause 54);[65]
- providing fire engines (Clause 61);
- ensuring that no new houses had a thatched roof (Clause 94);
- regulating the provision, sale and distribution of coal (Clauses 163–185). This was clearly a major preoccupation and source of income in the town as the Commissioners were able to impose a rate of 3 shillings per cauldron of coal imported 'across the beach'. The correct disposal of ashes also came under this clause;
- regulating Hackney carriages, pleasure boats and bathing machines (Clauses 187–192)
- caring for the poor (Clauses 219–237). The care of the poor, maintenance of the Poor House and levying a rate for both indoor and outdoor 'Relief', devolved to the Directors and Guardians.

In their meetings, the Commissioners discussed such matters as whether to pay the police force (a band of just 16 men and two Superintendents) or not. This seems to have been agreed to by the Directors and Guardians at a meeting on the evening of Monday 22 November 1827. The decision relating to the possibility of a new organist for the new church, St. Peter's, descended into the farcical. The meeting had been called:

65 A necessary duty as the *Monthly Gazette of Health* for 1825 shows: 'The practice of sinking the reservoirs [*of water closets*] into the shingles we also find to be common in some parts of Brighton. The water is therefore not only rendered unfit for articles of diet, but even for washing the floors of a house, the effluvium being so strong as to contaminate the air of the rooms.'

> ... for the purpose of fixing a salary, and appointing a person to officiate as Organist at the New Church; but neither the Town Hall, nor the Commissioners' room, being large enough to accommodate the great number of the inhabitants assembled, it was resolved to adjourn to a large room in the Workhouse, where, the Rev. Vicar[66] having taken the chair, after a great deal of desultory and uninteresting discussion, the following resolutions and amendments were moved:
>
> – 1st. That the salary of the Organist be fixed at £40 per annum.
>
> – 2nd. That the salary of the Organist be fixed at £50 per annum.
>
> – 3rd. That it not yet having been decided by the parishioners whether they would have an organist at all, the Vestry was not in situation to decide which salary should be paid.

After some argy bargy, the meeting was eventually dissolved 'on account of the lateness of the hour, it being four o'clock, and there was little probability that the votes could be taken till a very late hour'. The immediate thought which springs to mind is that they were probably hungry and wanted their afternoon tea. It is more likely, however, that at 4pm on a cold November night, no Commissioner or member of the public wished to go home from the top of, probably unlit, Church Hill in the dark and in the mire.

Another body regulating the town was the Bench. By 1827, the Magistrates' Bench no longer used the dilapidated Town House or a room in the Poor House, both of which had been in Bartholomews, but used the premises of the Old Ship Hotel. As well as the usual tasks of judging petty criminals, it was the Magistrates who regulated licences.

> There is a bench of Magistrates, who hold their sittings daily, at the Town Hall, at eleven o'clock. These sittings have been found extremely beneficial here — as petty offenders are checked, kept in awe, or punished, and the good order and peace of the town thereby well preserved.[67]

As today, residents wishing to preserve the peace and quiet, or perhaps more importantly, retain the resale value of their homes, often objected to a new licence for a public house being granted:

66 Henry Wagner, Vicar of Brighton 1824–70.
67 Sicklemore, 1827.

Licensing Day

The first application for a new licence, was that of Mr. Thomas Lower, some years a servant of Mr. Bates. This application was for a house situate at 30, Russell Street, to be called the Pelham Arms, there was also an application for a licence for No. 50, in the same street, to be called Blossoms, by John Barnett, coal merchant and brewer. Mr. Lower's application was opposed by several of the inhabitants of houses adjacent, who, to a man, considered that the licensing of the house in question would materially deteriorate the value of their property in that street, and one of the opposing party, Mr. John Gallard, was put on his oath by Mr. Bates, with a view to ascertain the number of licensed houses in the immediate vicinity; and from his replies it appeared that there were already three within 80 yards of the proposed new house. Mr. Poune, Mr. C. Shrivell, and other owners of property in the street and neighbourhood, also opposed the granting of this licence. In favour of the licence, one person only, Mr. Collins, a respectable fisherman, was examined, the sum and substance of whose opinion was, that as the neighbourhood had declined in gentility, from the introduction of butchers', green-grocers' and even ballad-shops no great evil could arise from another public-house. Mr. Poune wished Mr. Collins to be asked whether there was not, in his opinion, an ample supply in the neighbourhood already? The question, however, was not put.

Mr. Lower's application was then reserved for the after-consideration of the Bench.

Some observation was then made from the bench to Mr. Barnett's application, which we could not hear clearly, but we believed it amounted to a denial.

Brighton Herald, 8 September 1827

It seems certain that no cub reporter in the twenty-first century would get away with such sloppy reporting as in the last paragraph. It is delightful to think that a 'respectable fisherman' might consider that the opening of a 'ballad-shop' selling sheet music was evidence of the first signs of a decline in the respectability of a street. As there is no trace of Blossoms in the contemporary Directories, it is likely the licence was not granted.

What excited the political animals in the town? On a national level, it was the 'Catholic question'. The Protestant backlash of the seventeenth and eighteenth centuries had begun to wane in the late 1770s when Catholics were at last allowed to own property, inherit land and join the army – as long as they swore an oath of loyalty to the Protestant monarchy, an oath which must have gone much against their moral principles. However, the fundamental problem was that Catholics were very largely disenfranchised.[68] At the time of the Regency, Brighton had been a Whig (both liberal and Liberal) town. With age and the monarchy on his shoulders, George, and Brighton with him, drifted somewhat towards the Tories. The late Prime Minister, George Canning, had been a moderate Tory and it is revealing of George IV's continued Whig sympathies that he had chosen as his first minister, Canning a supporter of the Catholic Emancipation Bill, rather than the more conservative Duke of Wellington or Sir Robert Peel. This schism between opponents and the supporters of the Bill is quite evident in the pages of the local newspapers.

Letters appeared from 'A Blue'[69] or 'A Protestant'. The writers of these letters use expressions such as: '…enough has been said [*in this letter*] to show how *politically dangerous* the tenets of the Court of Rome are. […] It is absurd to say the Catholic Church has some partial advantage over other churches, while her main design has been to establish despotism, and that a despotism of the See of Rome.'

The population of Brighton consisted of three distinct groups of people: the inhabitants (fishermen, trades people, wealthy homeowners and their servants permanently living in the town); property owners (who visited their Brighton

68 It must be stressed that it was not only Catholics who were discriminated against: Methodists, Presbyterians and all other non-conformists could not be elected to the British House of Commons until 1828 and Jews not until 1858. However, nothing has ever prevented the oppressed from attacking each other, as is clear from the Brighton correspondent of *The Times* newspaper: 'An anti-Catholic petition has been got up here, but it is not publicly known, and is, I believe, confined to a few individuals among one or two sects, and those most rigid ones of the Dissenters'. Friday 2 March 1827

69 In the 1820s, the Tory party was represented by the colour blue; the Whig party by the colours orange, buff and blue.

home only occasionally) and visitors (who owned no property in the town). Of the inhabitants, very few owned enough property to be able to vote in the Sussex elections and none was eligible to vote for the Lewes MPs, although as has been seen above, Thomas Read Kemp, one of the two Lewes MPs, was a man who had invested massively in Brighton and must have had the affairs of Brighton very much at heart. The good folk of Brighton were not, therefore, entirely forgotten. However, the relatively small town of New Shoreham, some seven miles to the west of Brighton, also boasted two MPs, one of whom, Sir Charles Burrell, in a speech to the House of Commons, betrayed the resistance to the Catholics in the Sussex area:

> Sir C Burrell
>
> expressed a hope, that if any concessions were made to the Catholics, they would be accompanied by such securities for the Protestant Church and Hierarchy as would allay the fears which might be entertained for the preservation of religious and general liberty in this country. Any minister, let him be who he might, who should come down to that House and propose a relinquishment of the securities necessary for the preservation of the Protestant Church, would do an act which was unworthy of a minister, and disgraceful to a public man.
>
> Hansard, May 1827

Auguste was amazed when, on trying to find the Catholic church on Sunday, he was shown the way by a most sympathetic and Christian Protestant. Clearly the Whiggish town did not always agree with her more Tory neighbours.

On a far more parochial level, the battle between the 'incomers' and the fishermen continued unabated. By 1827 the focus of the conflict revolved around capstans. It has already been seen that the Ranters and other speakers with an axe to grind used the capstans as their soap box. More importantly, the capstans were at the heart of the conflict between the Brighton equivalent of Town and Gown: the Fisher-folk and the Gentle-folk.

In her account of her father's childhood,[70] Maude Egerton Hine King writes of the early years of the 1820s:

> The fisher-folk were quite able to stand up for their rights in those days, and fought sturdily against any encroachment of the growing

70 Henry George Hine (1811–95) Brighton-born landscape painter, watercolourist and illustrator for Punch.

> health resort on the old fishing-town; and on the strength of their ancient right to draw boats up to the Steine in rough weather, granted them, they claimed by Queen Elizabeth, they made but short work of the railings which the Town Council, with an eye to the more private promenading of fashionable visitors, planted around the greensward. They had their way for the time, but they could not prove their claim; and so in the end the railings were replaced and one by one the other improvements came in and thrust aside the old fishery.[71]

The ferocity of this conflict of interests was revealed by the *Brighton Gazette* on 20 September 1827:

> LOCAL NEWS
>
> The Commissioners for some time past have resolved on removing the capstans opposite the Star and Garter Hotel, where they have long been a great obstruction to the thoroughfare and on Tuesday morning, the Town Surveyor, with a posse of Constables, attempted to put their orders into execution. Being met, however, by a determined opposition on the part of the fishermen, it was thought advisable to return to the Town Hall, till a sufficient number of Special Constables could be sworn in by the Magistrates, to secure the peace of the Town. The Magistrates, on being informed of the turbulent spirit of the fishermen, with the greatest promptitude, rendered every assistance in their power.

The fishermen later came to a grudging compliance as far as capstans were concerned, but there is no doubt that there was a continuing and distinct split between the two social groups within the town:

71 Hine King: *Round About a Brighton Coach Office*, 1896.

(COPY)

"We the undersigned owners of certain capstans now standing on the East Cliff, in Brighton, do consent (without prejudice to any rights which we possess,) on condition of the said capstans being permitted to stand until Tuesday, the 25th day of September inst., to give up to the Commissioners quiet possession of the same, in order to them being taken down and removed, pursuant to an Act of Parliament passed in the 6th year of the reign of his present Majesty intituled, An Act for the better regulating, paving, improving, and managing the said town.

(signed)

GEORGE HOWELL

HARRY TAYLOR

CORNELIUS SHRIVELL

MARTHA SMART

STEPHEN MARCHANT

Dated 18th day of September 1827. Witness, George Vallance – and Lewis Slight, Clerks to the Commissioners.

A desultory conversation then took place as to the price to be paid to the fishermen as remuneration for the capstans, and for the soil on which they stand [...] Sir D. Scott addressed the men at some length, and prevailed upon them to promise that two or three of their body should be deputed to wait upon the Commissioners, to confer all matters in dispute. Thus ended an affair which at one time had assumed a serious aspect.

BRIGHTON HERALD, 22 September 1827

Despite this dispute being settled, the *Brighton Gazette* was clearly no respecter of the fisher-folk:

> Herrings have been sold here this week, at thirty and forty for a shilling. They are brought, we understand, chiefly by the Hastings and Worthing boats, without which we should have almost none, our own fishermen being in general too lazy to go to sea for them.
>
> Brighton Gazette, 29 November 1827

The one other matter of national importance was the rise of working men's organisations. A Mechanics' Institute had existed already in 1825 but was not a success and closed in 1828. These Institutes 'failed to meet the educational needs as well as the economic and social aspirations of the working class clientele for whose benefit they were established, [*the cause being the*] domination of the movement by middle class sponsors, who attempted to impose their own values', according to critics such as Collins,[72] or simply because 'extravagant expectations were quickly disappointed' and 'enthusiasm flagged'.[73] However, a more significant social advance was being made in 1827:

> We are informed that a society, called the Brighton Co-operative Society, has been formed in the town, the ultimate object of which is, the establishment of a community on Mr. Owen's plan, setting aside emigration. We have not heard of the intended site.
>
> Brighton Herald, 20 October 1827

The Mechanics' Institute and the Co-operative Society were largely, although of course not entirely, the result of the work of Dr. William King, physician and social activist. The Brighton Co-operative Benevolent Fund Association was to help the poor manage their little money in the best way they could, helping others out if necessary. Just as importantly, Dr. King oversaw the setting up of the Co-operative Trading Association which was established in July 1827 and opened for business on 1 January 1828 from the premises of the Institute at 31 West Street. The main importance of this food outlet was that the co-operative could

72 'The Mechanics' Institutes – Education for the Working Man?' Michael Collins in the *Adult Education Quarterly*.

73 'The Galashiels Co-operators': http://www.makers.org.uk/place/galacooperators.

sell unadulterated food to those who no longer had even the tiniest plot of land on which to grow their own. The Co-operative even rented some 28 acres of land outside Brighton to produce wholesome foodstuffs. Of all this, Auguste, Comte de la Garde-Messence saw nothing.

Auguste might not have seen the long letter on deflation from the ardent socialist Robert Owen, for it was published in the *Brighton Herald* on 15 September, just a few days before Auguste arrived in Britain, but he must have seen this item in the *Brighton Gazette* on 9 November:

> It ought to be noticed that, owing to the depression of the times, Mr. Hyram Lewis, pawnbroker, who is about to submit his unredeemed pledges to auction, very considerately declined doing so last year, in order to give the parties a longer opportunity of redeeming them.

The snippet must surely have aroused very mixed feelings within Auguste. Just six days previously, any anti-Jewish prejudices Auguste might have had were reinforced by watching a performance of 'The Merchant of Venice', and now here is a Jewish pawnbroker, who has made every effort to be considerate to his clients; on the other hand, did Auguste have any idea of the slump which England had gone through in 1826 and was to some extent was still going through? Perhaps the cheaper pound was a main reason for his visit. We will never know. Auguste was not a political animal. He was a social animal, so let him tell his own tale in his own way.[74]

74 Auguste's spelling of English names has been retained from the original text; for example, *Wedgewood* for *Wedgwood; Brummel* for *Brummell*. All variants are indexed under the modern spelling of the names.

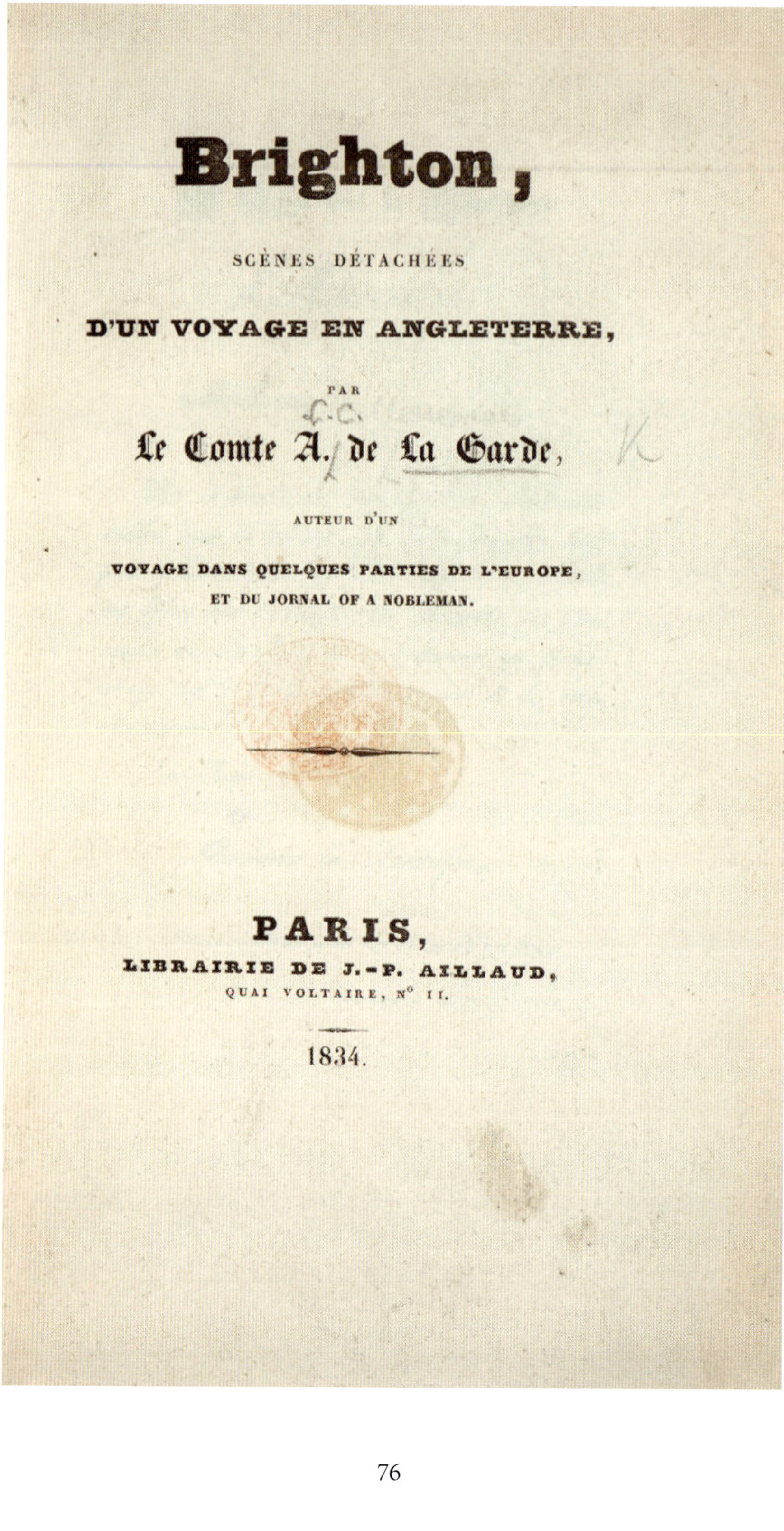

Brighton,

SCÈNES DÉTACHÉES

D'UN VOYAGE EN ANGLETERRE,

PAR

Le Comte A. de La Garde,

AUTEUR D'UN

VOYAGE DANS QUELQUES PARTIES DE L'EUROPE,
ET DU JORNAL OF A NOBLEMAN.

PARIS,
LIBRAIRIE DE J.-P. AILLAUD,
QUAI VOLTAIRE, N° 11.

1834.

To Her Ladyship the Duchess of Abrantès

Madam,

I am both proud and touched by the name of brother with which you have been so kind to honour me. It is in this quality that I place this Essay on England under the auspices of your fine talent. I am happy that I have now been granted the opportunity to express to you publicly my admiration and my devotion.

I have the honour to remain Lady Laure
Your humble and most obedient servant
Auguste, Comte de la Garde

Chapter 1

Departure from Dieppe – Arrival in Brighton – the Glocester Hotel – A room at the inn – To the hunt – The King's Pavilion – Meeting with a compatriot – Sir Robert Wilson – The hunters return – English good manners – General Sir Charles P***[75] – An account of the hunt

Chapter 2

Miss Wilson – A word on Bolivar – The appearance of Brighton – The reading rooms – Lady Hotham – The playhouse – Shylok, Kean and Talma – My first visit – A novel by Lady Morgan – Lady authors – The songs of Thomas Moore – The education of English girls – Lady Haywarden – Lord Southwel's family – The use of the French language in England – An English dinner – An evening with the author of Hadji-Baba – An evening stroll and memories

Chapter 3

Lord Holland – Brighton journalists – Pitt's brother – Lord Canning's home – An auction sale – A gift from the Duchess of Devonshire – A sketch of manners – Mr. McKinnon – Tuppen's Library – A book tombola – The nightwatchmen – An heir – A boat trip – Sketch of a family

Chapter 4

Sunday – Religious tolerance – A Catholic church – The English Madame Maintenon – The walker and betting – A walk on the cliffs – Dieppe and Brighton – Emmett – An episode from the Irish Revolution in 1803 – Charles Butler – Sacred music – The organ and hymn singing

Chapter 5

Lady Holland – The Duke of Bedford – Politics – A glimpse of the North and the Orient – Mr. Fox and Lady Holland in Paris during the Consulate – Madame Récamier – The Duchess of Abrantès – The pageboy and the letter – An invitation to the country – Sea bathing – The new districts of Brighton – The squares – The lay-out of houses – A Gypsy encampment – The fortune-teller – Glees – An evening at the theatre – Madame Vestris

Chapter 6

A morning walk – A traveller's reveries – Brighton's church and cemetery – The devastation of Brighton – Tattersall's grave – Charles II at Brighton – An incident in 1650 – Epitaphs – The German Spa – Clubs – A visit to the Royal Pavilion – Inside the Chinese palace – The sleeper awakes – The King at supper – The blacksmith and the miller from Sans-Souci – Worthless favourites *or* Brighton and Versailles.

75 Many of the names marked with asterisks have been identified by the translator and details of those people given in footnotes to the main text.

Chapter 7

Excursion to Kemptown – The young girl – A state dinner – Cooking at table – The town's developer – Return to Brighton – An excursion to the Devil's Dyke – Memories of Dresden – The last moments of General Moreau – Moreau's observation on Bonaparte – The whims of fortune *or* The unexpected legacy – The Abbé Thirty-thousand-men – Fortune and misfortune

Chapter 8

A grand-dame and the newspapers – The Duchess of St. A*** – The fate of an actress – Sir Francis Burdett – A lady patroness – An old acquaintance – The Congress of Vienna – The Prince de Ligne – A walk to the chalybeate spa – A day in the life of an English lady – The Brighton club – The gazettes – Gambling

Chapter 9

A soirée at Lady S***'s – The anniversary of the Gunpowder Plot – Mohamed's Baths – Colonel Fa*** – Conversation among young English ladies – Princess Esterhazy – The Duke of Devonshire – Prince Koslowsky – Napoleon's niece – Mr. Brummel *or* A King's friendship – Prison orphans – The rescued child.

Chapter 10

Mme de Stael's quip – The Almachs Ball – English ladies – A society review – Contrasts – An heiress – Mr. Thelusson's will – Dancing in England – The lover and the penalty – Young girls and the law – Supper – The bogus Shakespeare.

Chapter 11

Tea – A boat chase – Bets – The Houses of Orleans and England – Falconry – A luncheon with the Duchess of St. A*** – The Saxon hunter – Exercises – A Director of the East India Company – A family concert – A ball for a stranger.

Chapter 12

Preparations for leaving – Public conveyances – The Master of Ceremonies – Mr. Henry Colburn – Conversation – Literary reputations – A luncheon at the inn – Atop the stage coach – Meeting with a publisher – Bears and horses – Roads – Appearance of the countryside – Outskirts of the capital – The Elephant and Castle – Arrival in London.

Preface

'I do not teach, I tell!'
MONTAIGNE

Since Voltaire, who was amongst the first to make England and the English known to us, it would seem that all has been said about that kingdom and its inhabitants. Distinguished writers, especially those of our own times, have treated the subject in so many varied ways, in letters, travels, commentaries, descriptions etc., that in France today we flatter ourselves that we are conversant with all matters pertaining not only to their constitution and their form of government, but also to everything relating to the customs and habits of the different classes within English society: we are peculiarly mistaken. Our ideas on these points are almost all inaccurate, distorted by vague or misleading reports. At this point, allow me to make a remark which is, no doubt, not original, but which I have seen stated nowhere else and which, in my opinion, strikingly depicts the character of our two nations.

Recently, some English authors have published works on the manners and the customs of France. Having been admitted into our clubs and into the privacy of our homes, that is where they have found the models for their tableaux which they have sketched with painstaking accuracy: we have benefitted from their criticism which lends all the more weight to their praise. No-one in England has censured these flattering accounts: it may be that in France some peevish or dullard minds have been offended by them; but the higher ranks of society, which are impartial by their very position, have given them a favourable reception, without in the least being surprised that it is possible to commend merit and customs other than their own.

This noble example has not been emulated by those travellers to England who have published their observations: be they French, Italian, German or of any other nationality, they have nearly all assumed the right to censure and even to insult the country which received them; and yet the majority of these visitors had been offered asylum or assistance.[76] They have used every form of bitter criticism, inspired, no doubt, by the desire to please the large number of readers who, in the tid-bits designed to satisfy their curiosity, expect to find satire and trenchant wit. In a word, it seems that both writers and readers are doing their utmost to be churlish; it is as if a book on England could be a success only in proportion to the number of slurs it casts on the country it describes.

I, too, have visited England. I, too, have been admitted into the most distinguished circles. I, too, have observed some of the eminent men of whom England is so proud. Having been afforded the most cordial, the most open hospitality, I was easily able to study the manners and the customs which I met there. I will not say it was without difficulty that I overcame my prejudices; being a traveller practically from birth, I had learnt that, in order to judge, one must see and compare; I have seen, and now I believe I know: and the praise which I have felt justified in bestowing seems to me to be based on foundations which, being entirely sound, will not excessively surprise those too readily inclined to savour the cheerless pleasure of criticism. Even were this admiration to be held against me, I take the liberty of believing that this is a form of exaggeration which I am, in a way, to be permitted; and when it is about a nation where I have met with so much charm and so much elegance, I much prefer to be thought of as a flatterer

76 *TN La Garde is no doubt referring to the 'asylum and assistance' afforded not only to the Huguenots who arrived in England in the eighteenth century and to the aristocratic émigrés fleeing the post-Revolution Terror, but especially to the French royal family. Louis XVIII 'held court' in exile at Harwell House from 1809 until the restoration of the French Monarchy in 1814.*

than as an ingrate.[77] I have tried to represent, I admit, the brilliance of the picture I am painting, but in such a vast setting, my task was neither difficult nor taxing: others should do as I have done, only better than I have done, were it only to foster the bonds of understanding which already existed at the time which these memories recall, but which have since become closer, even amongst the lowest classes: this has come about through political concord, an interest in our mutual future and a culture shared by our two peoples. These are sentiments expressed so splendidly by my erudite and admirable friend Mr. Bowring[78] in the words of his inspired speech in Nantes: 'The happier you are, the more powerful you will be; the freer you are, the more we will be united.'

No doubt, in my Essay, more stories than observations will be found; but so many observations have been made on England that I have preferred the hasty style of a gazette, in which each page is a day in my life: I believe that the individuals who people my writing might thus become better known and more warmly esteemed. If it is reproduced in such a manner and sent on its way, English society would be of no less interest. My readers will judge without it being necessary for the author, who has interspersed his observations with his portraits, to impose his way of seeing and his mode of thinking.

My readers will also forgive me, I trust, for dwelling in detail, possibly of the most minute kind, on private life as well as local and national customs. The further races live apart, so it is said, the more interesting and valuable the tableaux of their manners become; to my mind, this a false premise, for England and France are near neighbours and seem to meld, the one into the other, thanks to the ease with which they communicate, and yet they know each other no better for all that.

---

77 AN Moreover, would I not have to fear that a remark as severe as that which appeared in the *Quarterly Review* on Baron Haussez' work might remind me of that very fair axiom of Montaigne's: 'To exercise ones critical faculties, one should have both *science* and *conscience*.'

> 'Indeed it seems to us somewhat presumptuous, and certainly not in very good taste, that a person, just expelled from his own country for knowing *nothing about it* – for having mistaken her laws, her wants, her wishes and her temper – should – *pour passer le temps* – elevate himself to be the judge of the temper, wants, wishes and laws of another people, to whose shores he escaped as a fugitive – with no one individual of whom he had any previous acquaintance – one word of whose language he does not understand – whose manners he has not learned – and whose merits and whose errors he is, and ever will be, equally incapable of appreciating.' *Quarterly Review 1834*

TN Charles Lemercier de Longpré, baron de Haussez (1778–1854) published: 'La Grande Bretagne en 1833'. This book appeared either just before, or at the same time, as le Comte de la Garde's book. The article attacking Haussez' book ran to over 25 pages of closely printed text. La Garde's text does not seem to have aroused the same ire.

78 *TN Sir John Bowring (1792–1872). By 1834, Sir John had already had a distinguished career as editor of the* Westminster Review *in which he advocated free trade.*

By first kindling the desire to compare and to judge, the traveller's conscientious reports will then persuade the reader to embrace everything useful and agreeable that has been described, thus multiplying life's pleasures.

In sketching a series of scenes taken from life in England, it was natural to start with Brighton. It is, as it were, the gateway to the kingdom as well as being one of its most interesting places. It is to London what Versailles was to Paris, not only for its royal residence, but also because it is there that the crowd of fashionable people, who, on pain of being expunged from the social register, is obliged by the dictates of convention to show themselves at set times of the year. If my tableaux are to the taste of the public, they will be followed by several others which I have composed during my sojourns in these watering places so sought after by this elegant and nomadic throng which pitches its tents, at the requisite time of year, in Brighton, Tunbridge-wells, Bath, Cheltenham and Harrowgate: this is the constant round which it slavishly follows, until the day the London season recalls it to the capital for the opening of Parliament.

Opposite page: Plan of Brighton with the latest improvements (1827)
Image reproduced by kind permission of Brighton Royal Pavilion, Museums and Libraries

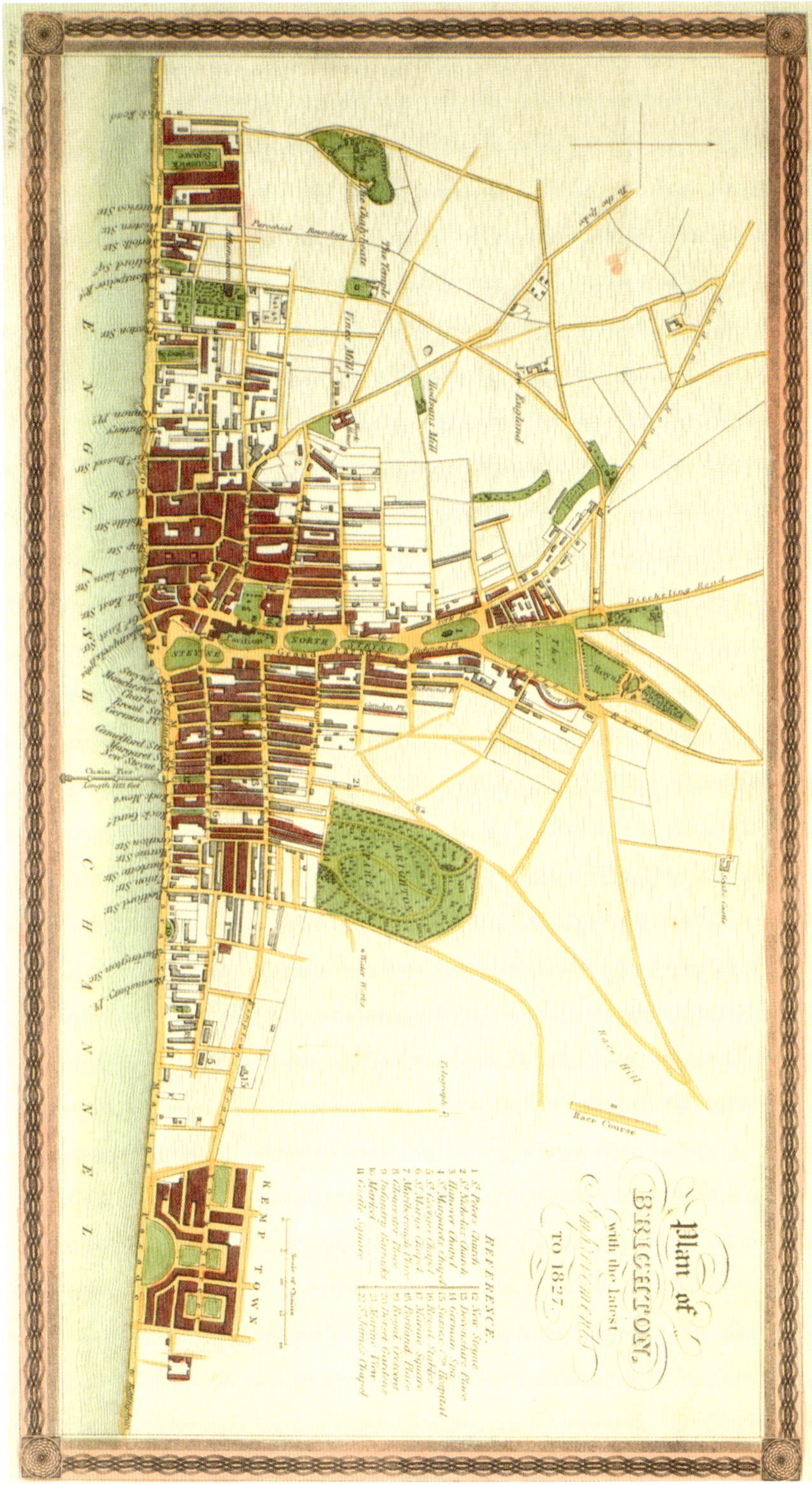
Plan of BRIGHTON with the latest Improvements TO 1827.
REFERENCE.
KEMP TOWN
ENGLISH CHANNEL
Chain Pier
STEYNE
NORTH STEYNE
Pavilion
Parochial Boundary
Ditchelling Road
Race Hill
Race Course

Chapter I

Departure from Dieppe – Arrival in Brighton – The Glocester Hotel – A room at the inn – To the hunt – The King's Pavilion – Meeting with a compatriot – Sir Robert Wilson – The hunters return – English good manners – General Sir Charles P*** – An account of the hunt

That which comes from the heart is not flattery!...
Flatterers do not have one!...
Le Chevalier de Boufflers[79]

Often, in my presence, in many a Parisian salon, my compatriots have complained of the difficulties experienced by a foreigner wishing to make the acquaintance of distinguished English families. Even once you are admitted, the atmosphere, they say, is so systematically cold and reserved that no foreigner can establish that intimacy and that mutual trust which are the source of so much delight on the Continent.

These complaints are then followed by comparisons between the welcome afforded to a Frenchman in London and the reception the English receive from us. We French reproach the English for their lack of warmth, whilst at the same time, attributing our courtesy to our genial and insouciant character. This latter might be better characterised as that form of excitability, which we can hardly deny and which prompted the duc de Ligne's witty remark[80] that: 'the English were the only

79 *TN Stanislas-Jean, chevalier de Boufflers 1738–1815 French statesman, soldier and writer.*
80 *TN Charles-Joseph, Prince de Ligne 1735–1814 Field-marshal and writer. A member of the princely family of Hainaut (present-day Belgium) but an Austrian citizen who lived mainly in Vienna.*

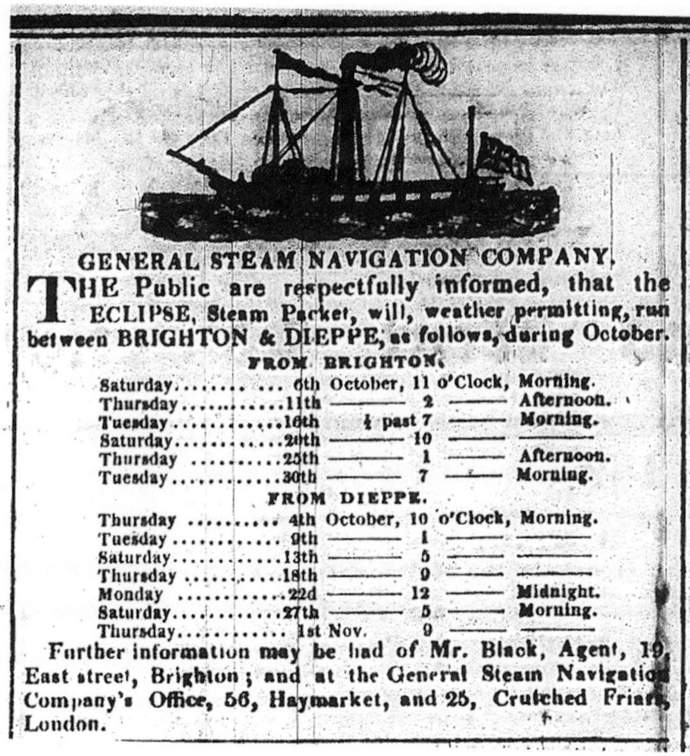

GENERAL STEAM NAVIGATION COMPANY.

THE Public are respectfully informed, that the ECLIPSE, Steam Packet, will, weather permitting, run between BRIGHTON & DIEPPE, as follows, during October.

FROM BRIGHTON.

Saturday	6th October,	11	o'Clock,	Morning.
Thursday	11th	2		Afternoon.
Tuesday	16th	¼ past 7		Morning.
Saturday	20th	10		
Thursday	25th	1		Afternoon.
Tuesday	30th	7		Morning.

FROM DIEPPE.

Thursday	4th October,	10	o'Clock,	Morning.
Tuesday	9th	1		
Saturday	13th	5		
Thursday	18th	9		
Monday	22d	12		Midnight.
Saturday	27th	5		Morning.
Thursday	1st Nov.	9		

Further information may be had of Mr. Black, Agent, 19, East street, Brighton; and at the General Steam Navigation Company's Office, 56, Haymarket, and 25, Crutched Friars, London.

individuals who, once having left their own shores, divulge their biography simply by stating their nationality.'

I was always wary, I confess, of these circumstantial accusations and I did not share those opinions, found in the anecdotes of certain travellers or self-styled eyewitnesses, or indeed of any these people who, from their lofty vantage point on the luggage wagon, imagine they have seen much from their ring-side seat. The majority, having set off with no introductions whatsoever, flatter themselves that the short-lived glory they have enjoyed within their own little coterie in Paris will have cast its bright rays to the other side of the channel. A minority, on the other hand, preceeded by regrettable reports of their foolhardiness and of the error of their ways at home, appear surprised by the mistrust that their former conduct arouses. So it is that the greater number, having visited England for no reason other than to be able to say that they have been there, confine their observations to the state of the pavements in Leicester Square or Piccadilly, limit their essays on manners to those English citizens who frequent Hyde Park or theatre lobbies and, having made no attempt to combat their own prejudices, return to France with a few weary platitudes about the vagaries of the climate, the excessive price of wine and the lack of entertainment on a London Sabbath.

'Let us not judge; let us be circumspect,' I say, espousing the wisdom of Zoroastre, 'It is but disappointment which provokes all these accusations.' And now, being better able to appreciate English manners, since facts speak louder than arguments, I have tried to draw this sketch based on conscientious observation. If the truth of my remarks does not entirely dispel the allegations made by our citizens, it will, I hope, lessen the reliance we still place on certain reports which have been too readily accepted.

Having left Dieppe on the steam ship,[81] I was buffeted by a stormy sea for twenty-four hours: I can compare the pleasure I had in seeing the coast of the County of Sussex only to that I felt when, following a squall in the Black Sea, I glided into the Bosphorus of Thrace under full sail and continued my way in all serenity to Constantinople, between the entrancing shores of Europe and Asia.

And so it was, as my delighted gaze lingered on the long lines of an elegant, picturesque palace, itself the epitome of Brighton as I am told, that a cannon-signal greeted our arrival on what had, for so long, been enemy territory. We came ashore on the Pier, which is a sort of bridge suspended on chains and which juts out nearly 1,200 feet into the sea. It is the very model of elegance and solidity, so very worthy of acting as bridgehead to the graceful amphitheatre before which it stands.

The Chain Pier in 1824. The Royal Pavilion can be seen in the distance between the darker buildings. The parish church of St. Nicholas is perched above the tall dark building to the left of the Pavilion.

Alas the prediction of the comic poet and caricaturist came true in the storm of 1896 when the Pier was destroyed:

But, tell me, Captain; read you ne'er
Of one who built on sand?
When, like the toll, the wind is high,
Your iron fabric, Brown, rocks so, I fear, that by and by,
'Twill, with the toll, come down!

---

81 TN The Eclipse. *Le Comte de la Garde arrived in Brighton on Thursday 11 October.*

Image reproduced by kind permission of Brighton Royal Pavilion, Museums and Libraries

Resignation, the only remedy for moral distress, is also the only one that can be brought to bear for seasickness. Any traveller who has suffered this affliction knows the relief it is to arrive and that rest is essential after this form of torture which crushes your limbs as if they had been turned on the rack. He will also understand my joy at arriving at the Glocester Hotel which my kind friend,

---

St. Peter's Church; The Gloucester Hotel is on the far left of the engraving.

No. 27 Gloucester Place was opened as the Gloucester Hotel in about 1819. It was a four-storey building with bows, balconies, verandas and a Doric doorway, but it was considerably remodelled and enlarged in 1925 when the Gloucester Mansions flats were added. At the beginning of this century it was a night club. In 2010 the property was empty and semi-derelict. By 2014 it had become a thriving pub, entertainment venue and micro-brewery.

"THE GLOUCESTER HOTEL, Gloucester-place, conducted by Mrs. Brierly, is very agreeably situated immediately opposite the delightful shrubbery and garden of the North Steyne, and is frequented by a class of visitors of the first respectability."

From THE WATERING PLACES OF GREAT BRITAIN, *1831*

Image reproduced by kind permission of Brighton Royal Pavilion, Museums and Libraries

Count Zabiello,[82] had recommended to me before I left Dieppe and that I now recommend to travellers who desire comfort in every sense of the word: there they will find a courteous landlady; conscientious servants and, something which is rarely to be found in Brighton, modest prices.

I was served a good dinner consisting of excellent fish, which is plentiful in Brighton, some mutton which is said to be the best in the whole of England and which is attributed to the salt meadows on which the sheep graze, there were vegetables, delicious despite being boiled, various puddings and some rather heady Portuguese wine.

82 *TN Count Michel Zabiello: Polish general active in the late eighteenth century against Russian influence in Poland. Imprisoned in 1794 as an insurrectionist, he was later allowed to live freely in Dresden.*

Here with choice food earth smiles and ocean yawns,
Intent alike to please the London glutton,
This, for our breakfast proffers shrimps and prawns,
That for our dinner, South-down lamb and mutton.

From Horace in London by James and Horace Smith 1828

Given the meal and the perusal of some newspapers of truly phenomenal dimensions,[83] I soon found it was time for bed. This was when the Boots[84] approached myself and my fellow guests, with the offer of bootjack and slippers. Then, candle in hand, he showed me to my room, where my luggage had been carefully deposited.

The staircase was elegant and carpeted despite being so narrow; the bed was extremely good and so big that it would have made three in any German hostelry. Its carved, solid mahogany columns supported an elegantly swathed canopy. The base heaped with a great pile of mattresses topped with a thick featherbed. Once I had clambered, aided by a stepladder, atop this pacific citadel and drawn its white muslin curtains around me, I found myself in a sort of chamber, as sizeable as that of any monk. The certain knowledge of having reached my haven and the expectation of the many new prospects which were soon to pass before my eyes made me forget, in the solace of a deep slumber, the exhaustion and the nausea of my short crossing.

The following morning the sun showered its golden rays on the casements of the hotel, thus giving the magnificent lie to Ambassador Caraccioli's pronouncement to Charles II that in England the sun was 'like the moon at Naples'.[85] It convinced me that this was not so. I took advantage of the sunlight to examine my room in detail; I found scrupulous cleanliness which was most pleasing to the eye. First there was a soft rug laid on the floor despite the mild weather, then a fireplace, its

83 AN Some idle minds have entertained themselves with trying to estimate the content of a single edition of *The Atlas* newspaper; they found out that it could fill two large in-8vo volumes.

84 AN This is the name given to the hotel servant in charge of shoes: I must point out here that the post of *Maître Jacques* (*TN major domo*) is unknown in England and that each servant has his own well-defined role which is his alone at all times.

85 AN This was the same Caraccioli who had claimed that, in England, the only polish was to be found on marble and the only ripe fruit was stewed apples. It is often on such perverted wit that the common mortal judges a nation and that prejudices become deep rooted. Thus, it is only with great difficulty that time and reason can overcome them.

shallow marble mantle decorated with a quantity of charming little knick-knacks; the polished steel fire irons in the hearth revealed the daily attentions they received and the iron scuttle, on its raised foot, was filled with black, shining coals like chunks of jet; among the most useful items of furniture was a large dressing table supplied with all that is necessary for early morning ablutions: there were bowls of all sizes in china and Wedgewood earthenware, small lead crystal bottles, cotton towels, linen flannels and scented Windsor soap, and all this in a simple room at an inn. A moment later, a clean and tidy servant came in with hot water and to take my order for breakfast. I noticed one custom, which is not without its advantages, namely; however many times you ring, the servants never enter a room without first announcing their presence by knocking at the door. I went down to the dining room of the hotel which looked out over the street. Several *gentlemen* in red jackets had already gathered in the room and as they waited for the foxhunt to set off, they were breakfasting, as should any prudent huntsman. My tea was served at a separate table and I could divine the inordinate pleasure the English take in the hunt by the great enjoyment that even the preliminaries gave them.

> Brighton Harriers.– The hounds are to be on the ground at a quarter before eleven, each hunting day, viz., Mondays, near Patcham; Wednesdays, near the race Course; Fridays, near the Dyke.
>
> Brighton Gazette, 22 December 1827

From time to time, other hunters came to join their friends; several carriages, of which some drawn by horses, were making their way up to Ryegate Hill and a few ladies, as daring as they were skilled in handling their hunters, were dashing up from this direction and that to take their part in this perilous enterprise, thereby obeying, no doubt, that natural feeling which Horace Walpole recognised so succinctly when he said: 'it is in our character to take our pleasure from danger'.

When this noisy band had galloped off towards their rendez-vous, I left the Glocester and, walking through the main part of Brighton, I made my way towards the sea. The modestly named Pavilion, built by George IV while he was still Prince of Wales, was the first thing to attract my attention. Its Moorish architecture, its

A contemporary engraving of the Royal Pavilion with Castle Square to the left and St. Peter's Church being the white building in the distance.

elegant domes topped with their eccentric, ethereal spires, the pretty little modern buildings surrounding it and the striking contrast between the two divergent styles, could all lead you to believe that here a great Khan from the Land of the Tartars had pitched his tents, or, more accurately, that the Tzar of all the Russias had whisked his Asian Kremlin into the midst of this newly-built city.

When I requested permission to visit the interior, I was told that this was possible only on the orders of the Lord Chamberlain, the Marquess Conyngham:[86] I at once made up my mind to write to him.

As I crossed the Steyne on my way to the sea, I turned to my right towards the Westcliff which, following the King's-way, leads to Worthing. Having arrived at the Regent's Place, where the sea laps at its foot, I sat down on one of the circular benches on the promenade to enjoy the sight of this fine stretch of water, as calm today as it had been rough yesterday, reflecting in its great mirror the blue of the sky and the racing clouds.

86 *TN Henry Conyngham, 1st Marquess of Conyngham. His correct title was Lord Steward of the Household. It was the Duke of Devonshire who was the Lord Chamberlain of the Household. Was Conyngham's exalted status due in any measure to the fact that his wife was George IV's final mistress?*

This view of Regency Square, drawn in 1823 by William Daniell is incorrectly called 'The Regent's Place' There is no sign of the Chain Pier, although it would have been under construction at the time. Mahomet's Baths project right on to the cliff top. The Grand Junction Road, from the bottom of the Stein along the coast, was not constructed until 1827.

Despite the splendid morning, there were as yet very few people on the promenade; there were but two ladies sitting on the same bench as myself; the younger lady, of captivating face and modest demeanour – the precious birthright of young English girls – held a book in her hand; the other lady attended to her embroidery. A child, whom I had not at first noticed, was playing a few feet away from us at the edge of the waves; she ran up the beach, with the exuberance of her age, to show her sister a newly-found shell.

This caused the book the young lady was reading to slip from her hand. I hastened to retrieve it; and was most agreeably surprised to hear the older lady gently reprimand little Pauline, in French, for having bumped so roughly into her sister.

'Pray allow me to excuse her, madam, since she has afforded me the pleasure of hearing French spoken in a land which is not my own. Having been absent from

It was not until the 1950s that children's clothing was 'invented'. Children in the 1820s wore simpler clothes than their parents; for example, the large 'gigot' or mutton sleeves of the mothers are pared down for the girls and the dresses were less decorated. The girls wore short skirts with trimmed pantelettes beneath them.
Image reproduced with the permission of the Mary Evans Picture Library

France for no more than two days, I now perceive that neither time nor space are necessary to make the memory of it dear to us.'[87]

This lady answered with all the benevolence of a compatriot; and in the course of our conversation, I learned that she had in her charge the education of the daughters of Lord Southwell.[88] For two people far from their homeland, I feel that a shared memory can take the place of earlier bonds, so Madame Lebrun and I were soon chatting like old acquaintances. A tall man of engaging appearance approached the group of ladies: having asked after his Lordship's family, he talked most enthusiastically about the benefit performance which was to be given the

87 AN It was then that I felt the full force of that notion which the heart of a woman alone could render in these words: '*Physical presence is not necessary for friendship, but essential for happiness.*' Those who have lived close to Countess B de S will have recognised this as being one of those many thousand epigrams which she constantly uttered and which were the expression of her very soul.

88 *TN The Southwells were a leading family of English Catholics. See Chapter 2*

following evening at the Brighton Theatre[89] on behalf of the Spanish and Italian refugees.

'It is more successful than I had hoped,' he added. 'All the tickets have been sold; people are even travelling great distances to attend; everyone has offered to help us, and most graciously at that.'

'It seems to me, sir,' I said to him, 'that in England you pay less attention to opinions than to distress?'

'It is to be hoped,' was his immediate rejoinder, 'that our example might be followed the world over: unfortunately, "indulgence for myself, severity for others", is the rule that is the most frequently applied, particularly in politics.'

He then took his leave of the ladies and went off to examine the improvements being carried out on the promenade, for which he himself had drawn up the plans and which would soon be one of the chief adornments of the town.

> The terrace in front of Regency Square is now completed, and is a delightful promenade. We should be pleased to see the same continued on to the Battery, as it would not only be a beautiful esplanade, but remove the present unsightly appearance of the cliff.
>
> Brighton Herald, *15 September 1827*

> Workmen are now employed in setting back the rails on the Kings-road from the Battery to Brunswick-square. By this alteration, the road will be considerably widened and a great improvement affected.
>
> Brighton Gazette, *15 November 1827*

89 *TN The Theatre Royal was built in 1806 on land purchased from the Prince Regent. The first night of the play in question was 3 November.*

The Esplanade now carrying on from the Battery to Brunswick Town is, we hear, designated the "Royal Esplanade". The works are now in a state of forwardness, and reflect great credit on the taste and the spirited projector, Mr. Robinson of Regency Square. Mr. R. [*sic*] has made an application to our Directors and Guardians, for one of the paupers to be stationed on the esplanade, to prevent the intrusion of improper persons, and the ingress of vagrants into the town. We are glad to hear his application was successful.

BRIGHTON HERALD, *17 November 1827*

No sooner had he moved away, than I took the liberty of asking the ladies who was this person who interested himself so greatly in the misfortunes of strangers and works of national importance.

'That is Sir Robert Wilson,' Madame Lebrun replied.

Sir Robert lead an adventurous life as a soldier, as a friend to Napoleon and to Napoleon's persecuted supporters under the reign of Louis XVIII. Sir Robert was a Radical Member of Parliament for Southwark for several years between 1806 and 1836 and a philanthropist. Despite his obvious popularity with the local press in Brighton in 1827, he must have raised strong feelings when he was a younger man. The following comments were all published about him:

A slippery character, *Wellington, 1804*

A man of enthusiasm and of violent passions, *Napoleon.*

That harum-scarum personage, Sir Robert Wilson, *The Spectator Magazine 1839.*

Sir Robert Wilson, 1777–1849.
© National Portrait Gallery, London

Much later, in 1865, his former aide recalled that 'Sir Robert was a tall, slight man, of wiry form and strong constitution, handsome both in person and features, with the singularly soldier-like air that we read so much of in books. In those days of fervid and hopeful youth, the story of Sir Robert's chivalric and successful efforts to save the life of Lavalette naturally touched my heart, and if I had remained in his service, he would have had no more devoted follower.' *Sir Robert was quite the dandy. He clearly delighted in his military regalia, as is clear from several portraits of him in the National Portrait Gallery.*

Sir Robert! ... the man I had so long wished to meet, and yet seemed destined to miss wherever I went! I arrived in Constantinople just as he was leaving; when I was at the allied camp, he was temporarily absent; I reached Paris on the day he left, having just been released from detention for having helped Comte de Lavalette[90] to escape: it is, indeed, most true when it is said that chance is the sequence of effects, the causes of which we do not see: I was far from believing that Sir Robert would be the first Englishman to whom I would speak in England.

'But, madam, may I ask, exactly what is this performance that is to take place tomorrow?'

'It is an act of charity, sir, thanks to the enthusiasm and the energy of Sir Robert Wilson,' young Miss Southwell told me. 'As a foreigner, you would find it of interest to attend. You will see the whole of Brighton society and one of Shakespeare's masterpieces, *The Merchant of Venice*. An amateur actor will be playing the role of Shylock.'

I thanked the kind young lady for her advice and promised that I would follow it if I could obtain a ticket: soon after, I bade farewell to the ladies and took my leave of them.

Continuing my walk by the sea, I passed a few schoolchildren, girls and boys, all out for a walk: their rosy features and all the signs of their having both health and strength seemed to justify the words of one Holy Father (whose name I forget): 'The children of England would be angels, were they not heretics.' Indeed,

90 *TN At the Restoration of the monarchy in France in 1815, Antoine Lavalette (see page 250) was imprisoned and condemned to death for his support of Napoleon Bonaparte. He escaped on the eve of his execution wearing his wife's clothes while she remained in the cell. Several days later, Sir Robert Wilson and two other English men were able to smuggle Lavalette out of France to safety. Sir Robert and his English companions were caught and imprisoned for three months.*

the dazzling complexion of the girls was a reminder of what Diderot said of his own daughter's face: 'Rose petals scattered on a pitcher of milk.'

On returning to the hotel, I noticed that it is the custom here never to lock bedroom doors; what is more, as I walked along the corridors, I found nearly every door wide open, often revealing valuable items left on tables, but with apparently no harm done, for the habit still prevails.

I wrote to Sir Robert: I told him of my desire to contribute to this highly commendable charitable event and solicited him to secure me tickets for the following evening's performance.

> The gallant Sir Robert Wilson has, during the week, been actively engaged in furthering a most benevolent and praiseworthy design, now in contemplation, viz. an amateur performance at the theatre for the benefit of those distressed patriots, the Spanish and Italian Refugees. Saturday next is the day fixed, on which occasion, will be performed, *The Merchant of Venice*, the part of *Shylock*, by Mr. B. Gregory, who received the highest applause in sustaining that character in our theatre last year. It is intended to raise the pit to box prices for that night; and we learn with pleasure that nearly the whole of the tickets are disposed of. Mr. Russell has, with great liberality, granted the free use of the house for the occasion. Among the distinguished personages, who have taken places, are the Marquis Thomond, Lady Susan Hotham, Mrs. St. John, Mr. Bonham, Lady Tierny, Lady Scott, Lady Mary Sheppard, Mr. Weston, M.P., Mrs. Judd, Col. Blake, Mr. Butler, Mrs. Cullen, Hon. Mrs. Burke, Mr. Boldero etc.
>
> BRIGHTON HERALD, 27 October 1827

His reply was not long in arriving; he informed me that, not having any tickets at his disposal, he had entreated Lady Susan Hotham to admit me to her box and that the lady had given him two tickets which he was immediately sending to me.

Lady Susan Hotham was born Susan-Maria O'Brien, and was daughter of the 2nd Marquis of Thomond. She had married Rear-Admiral the Hon. George Frederick Hotham in 1824. She moved in the highest circles of society, having been present in 1834, for example, at a 'Queen's Drawing Room', a social event to celebrate the birthday of Queen Charlotte.

In the nineteenth century, disease and death in battle spared the upper echelons of society only slightly less than the working classes. In 1827 Lady Susan had just given birth, in July, to her second child, George. By 1854, not only had George died, so had his older brother William aged 27, his younger sister Augusta aged 18 and his younger brother Beaumont aged 15. Three remaining children survived to outlive their mother.

Our own French courtesy could not have been more considerate or more swift: kindness and the desire to oblige are useful shrubs which burgeon in all climates: happy the man who is fated to meet them often on his way!

At 6 o'clock the hunters returned to the hotel. To them, dinner was doubly relished from their having got the better of the fox. Their conversation was all of sightings, running to ground, checking and drawing blanks, in short, of all the rules of hunting to hounds which are more or less unintelligible to those who do not know the code.

One of the men seemed to be highly knowledgeable about this noble sport and was twitting, rather artfully, the young sprigs who, with their full purses and their moderately empty heads, have escaped for the space of a week from their offices in the City or from the cruel benches of their Chambers at the Temple and who are managing to convince themselves that a red jacket with brass buttons, a hired hack and boots with superbly shining reveres constitute the perfect huntsman. However, once they have been unseated two or three times going over gates or have left part of their obligatory frock-coat in a thicket, they retreat, leaving to the next horde of hotheads the good fortune of being able to return to London the following week with their bruised limbs wrapped in the shreds of their jacket.

Lord Chesterfield was always amazed that a man in his right mind should hunt for a second time, given that the first time there was a ten to one chance that he would break his neck: but our scatterbrained young people take comfort from their misadventures in knowing that they will soon be recalling their exploits for the benefit of their friends' clerks and juniors; and, along with that, the honour of being able to boast, for the rest of their lives, that they had hunted the fox or the hare with their Graces the Dukes of Rutland and Beaufort, or their very noble Lords Fitz-William, Cleveland and Alvanley.

'These young madcaps look not very unlike certain two-legged animals which walk with their head held high, who squawk very loudly and make everyone laugh when they try to fly. Do you understand what I mean, sir?'

My table companion, General Sir Charles P****,[91] one of the hotel guests, enlivened our glass of Bucelas[92] wine with these entertaining remarks. He continued with some very proper anecdotes about French military men against whom he had for so long fought in battle: he ended the evening by regaling us with some lively observations about different packs of hounds, breeds of horses and the naming of game animals in the Old World and the New, for he had, so to speak, hunted far and wide. Sharing the tastes of those whose fierce passions attach them to a given subject allows us to be taken speedily into their confidence; thus it was that from Sir Charles that I gleaned some absorbing insights about foxhunting, with which the English appear to be so infatuated: for example, here are some details for which I am indebted to him:

'In the past, our ancestors,' he told me, 'used to hunt the wolf, the boar and the bear; they ran down stags, hinds and roe deer; but nowhere, even in the earliest treaties on hunting, do you find any mention of fox hunting, apart from in the reign of Richard II when the ill-fated monarch granted permission, by charter, to the Abbot of Peterborough; until that time foxes were generally caught in traps or with nets placed outside their holes.

'Melton-Mowbray, in Leicestershire, which until just a few years ago was no more than an insignificant little village, is now a famous meeting place for hunters of the fox. That is where our young lordlings go to be educated in the ways of the hunt and to spend, year on year, more than five thousand pounds sterling in order to earn the privilege of being admitted to the Jockey Club and thus to become undisputed judges of the ring and the turf.[93] The town's stables usually house two to three hundred hunters, all pure bred animals (in English we say "thorough bred") or at least half-breed beasts ("cock tail").

'There are few foreigners visiting our country who do not rhapsodise over the excellence of our foxhunting establishments. That of Mr. Osbaldeston,[94] for example, is cited as being amongst the best we have of the kind, as much for the quality and the quantity of his horses and hounds as for the skill of his stable boys and his grooms: but more importantly, he rides to hounds six days of the week

91 *TN General Sir Charles W Pasley KCB, FRS, DCL (1780–1861), Military Commander and Engineer, served with distinction under General Sir John Moore of Coruna in the Peninsular War. He subsequently founded the School of Military Engineers at Chatham.*

92 *TN A light white wine produced in the Loures region of Portugal*

93 AN 'The ring' is the circle formed by those laying wagers on the race. 'The turf' is the race track.

94 *TN George Osbaldeston (1786–1866) Passionate sportsman and ladies' man. Indifferent politician.*

and rests on the seventh, and then only because, as you must no doubt be aware, it is strictly forbidden to hunt on a Sunday.

'What gives our hunts their pre-eminence is the quality of our horses and of our hounds. Mr. Meynell,[95] who was undoubtedly the most skilful hunter of his age, and you may believe me on that point, for a great number of his sayings have become universally accepted today, summed up his idea of the perfect hound thus: "it has a short back, deep chest, straight legs and compact feet". Those who do not hunt will find it difficult to comprehend that such a dog, free of defects, might fetch up to two hundred pounds sterling, and that the annual cost of hunting paraphernalia is in excess of six thousand pounds sterling, but that is the truth of the matter. As for our horses, it is a fact that they are constantly being improved by their interbreeding with Arab bloodlines: the English horse is, and I dare to say so, of all European horses the one in which the original ancestry is most clearly discernible. From that point of view, England may be called the Arabia of the North. The Persian horse had been brought to these shores in the reign of Elizabeth I; but later James I imported from the Barbary coast a number of mares which, when they interbred with indigenous animals, produced these sturdy, courageous and spirited animals which are, in short, perfect for the use to which, it appears, they are mainly put: hunting and racing.

'You can have proof of the remarkable speed of these thoroughbred horses from the account of a criminal trial which, some time ago, was brought before our assize court.

'Not far from London a famous highwayman carried out a theft at six o'clock in the morning and, that very same evening, at five o'clock, he was betting on a cock fight in Duncaster: when he was arrested for the crime, he produced an alibi based on the statements of witnesses against whom he had laid bets. The verdict of the court was that it seemed impossible that this man could have ridden eighty-five miles (nearly forty leagues[96]) in so little time; the upshot was that he was acquitted. When he was condemned to death a few years later for a quite different felony, he confessed that he was the perpetrator of the crime of which he had been accused and asked, as a final indulgence, to be able to see, one last time, his

95 *TN General Pasley is recalling Hugo Maynell (1735–1808). Maynell is reputedly the 'father of foxhunting'. Amongst his many other innovations, he bred a new type of hunting hound.*

96 *TN London to Duncaster (Doncaster) is 170 miles, purportedly ridden in 11 hours. A 'league' is generally considered to be three miles – so none of these distances is very convincing.*

excellent horse for which he had been offered two hundred guineas during his imprisonment; his horse was brought to him; he patted it affectionately, then he plunged a stiletto into its head, striking it down dead on the spot, for he could not bear his fleet and faithful companion to survive him.'

Sir Charles was about to pass on from these sketches to some no less interesting ones about racing, but it was late and he wished to put off the rest of his homily[97] to another day. And thus, I said to myself, as I took leave of him after we had warmly shaken hands, this morning's simple courtesy acted as an introduction; without knowing me, an Englishman has taken the trouble to be of service to me in the most obliging manner in the world; another has discoursed most considerately on France, poked fun at the shortcomings of his fellow countrymen and informed me of certain facts which seem to be of the greatest moment: until now, nothing has borne the least similitude to the image drawn by our own sullen social commentators.

If they had wanted to depict the English at home, they should have borne in mind the maxim already quoted: 'To be a critic, one must have both science and conscience'. We will see whether what is to come will justify my observations: be that as it may, my first day seemed to me to bode well and will, I hope, serve as a preamble to my rebuttal of their arguments.

97 AN When the English discourse on one of their favourite subjects, their conversation is a veritable homily, so devoutly are they caught up in it.

Chapter II

Miss Wilson – A word on Bolivar – The appearance of Brighton – The reading rooms – Lady Hotham – The playhouse – Shylok, Kean and Talma – My first visit – A novel by Lady Morgan – Lady authors – The songs of Thomas Moore – The education of English girls – Lady Haywarden – Lord Southwel's family – The use of the French language in England – An English dinner – An evening with the author of Hadji-Baba – An evening stroll and memories

I have always been happy to be considered a foreigner, no matter where I have found myself: a Frenchman in Russia, a Pole in Paris, yes, I am a cosmopolitan. I have found the secret of being content anywhere and of being dependent nowhere.

The following day, I hastened to pay a visit to Sir Robert to thank him for his obliging conduct: it did not take me long to find his home for it is customary for the name and the title of the inhabitant of a house to be engraved on a small brass plate fixed to the door.

According to the Sussex Gazette, Sir Robert lodged at 72 King's Road. At some time after 1827 No. 72 was renumbered and became No. 116 King's Road until the house was demolished in 1887 to make room for the building of the Metropole Hotel.

"Among the recent departures are Col. FitzClarence, Lord and Lady Holland and Sir Robert Wilson and Family"

Brighton Herald, 29 December 1827

72 King's Road, 1827, the left-hand house of the small group of grey houses.

Image reproduced by kind permission of Brighton Royal Pavilion, Museums and Libraries

---

Sir Robert seemed to be exactly as several of our mutual friends had described him to me. He and I had met so many of the same men, frequented so many of the same places, had been present at so many of the same dramatic events that our shared reminiscences soon made us old acquaintances.

He introduced me to his daughter. Her glowing complexion, framed by pretty blonde curls, reminded me of those portraits of the Madonna as immortalised by Raphaël. She had been brought up in Paris and appeared to me to combine French ease and elegance with the well-bred disposition of the women of her country – a felicitous combination, which, since I have been here, I have been able to admire on more than one occasion.

Despite my visit to Sir Robert being short, it was not without interest: that very morning he had received news from his son, an aide-de-camp to General Bolivar.[98] The details the young man gave of South America, and which Sir Robert was eager to pass on to me, I found most fascinating. He told of the interview between the liberator and General Paez. When the two met, the former had in attendance only his aide-de-camp whereas the latter was accompanied by a contingent of five hundred horse. It was in the most vivid colours that the young man sketched this striking scene in which General Paez, overcome by the superiority of his erstwhile leader, fell at his feet and resumed his place as Bolivar's lieutenant and his friend. The letter ended with these words:

'The fragile links which attached the vastness of America to the Old World are broken; on all sides the cry of freedom is to be heard from Mexico to Peru. Now that America has reached maturity, she has broken free from an agèd mother, just as a sturdy child will emerge from the tutelage which shaped its early years.'

A few similar sentences sufficed to persuade me that a similar desire for glory and liberty was just as likely to be an hereditary trait in Sir Robert's family.

Sir Robert asked me to arrive at the theatre early as he wished to introduce me to Lady Hotham before the performance. I promised to be punctual. As I left his house, I asked Sir Robert to grant me his friendship: 'It will be all the dearer to me,' I said to him, 'for being the fruit of an act of kindness on your part.'

His only reply was to shake my hand in the English manner, and I know of no more vigorous interpretation of a kindly thought, nor of a quicker way to one's heart. It is more readily understood than those empty offers of assistance which fill men's pockets but which are no more than mere trifles, to be given away without the least loss to the donor.

To occupy my time until dinner, I wandered the various districts of the town: the width of the roads, the granite pavements which ensure the easy movement of pedestrians, the elegance of the grand buildings as much as that of the plainest houses, everything proclaims that Brighton is a watering place dedicated to fashion. The closeness of London (for you can indeed call it close when you are separated from it by a distance which the public conveyances cover in five hours) makes Brighton a stylish epitome of the great metropolis: here you will find the same opulence; the same sparkle but without that frenzy

98 *TN Simon Bolivar 1783–1830 One of the leaders in the struggle against the domination of Spain over South America.*

of commercial activity which, in London, seems to leave neither place nor time for private pleasures. Here the shops are well stocked and varied; those in which fruit, meat and fish are sold are remarkable, above all for their fastidious attention to cleanliness, which others elsewhere would do well to emulate. These shops seem to fear intruding upon the senses in a place where good taste alone should prevail.

Half a century ago, Brighton was of no importance; there were barely a few fishermen's huts to be seen. It was the patronage of the King, who at the time was Prince of Wales, which elevated the town, on a whim, to the status which it enjoys today. He it was who made the town fashionable and to whom it owes its subsequent expansion and embellishment. One can easily tell in which period each square or each new neighbourhood has been built, according to whether the construction of the buildings is more or less recent. Facing a great number of houses are well-tended lawns, or little gardens with thriving flower-beds. The windows have large glass panes and are always open, for the inhabitants like fresh air and are not afraid of being seen: this enables the passer-by to catch sight, inside,

Image reproduced by kind permission of Shirley Veater

of a profusion of furnishings and a domestic opulence which the English so aptly call *comfort*. But what enchants above all are the *Verandas*.[99]

These are akin to wrought iron bowers, of varying forms, which project out as a balcony on each floor and are topped with a sort of zinc tent painted in stripes of various colours, the majority being wound around with roses or flowering vines. These decorations, replicated from warmer climes, give Brighton houses that pleasing, diaphanous atmosphere characteristic of Indian cities: everything about these homes seems fitted out for steady, serene happiness, and yet these are homes for but such a short while.

My next calls were to several reading rooms, 'dispensaries for the human spirit', as they have been called by the Prince de Ligne. They are much like intimate clubs where people can meet in spacious rooms to converse or to read: to subscribe costs no more than 30 shillings per year;[100] for this modest sum you can obtain the main political and literary gazettes from London and the provinces as well as several periodicals. You will also find a vast collection of first-rate books.

I entered my name in the register of subscribers at Tuppen's Library. This list is published in the town's newspapers and thus, by the very next day, your Brighton friends will learn your address, and in the same manner, you will learn theirs. This eliminates much tiresome research.

Tuppen's Library was situated on Marine Parade between Manchester Street and Charles Street. Sicklemore points out the advantage of the spot.

'Marine Library.

—Tuppen's, though not immediately situated on the Steyne, is but a very few paces from it; and here such a disadvantage, if such it may be termed, is most amply compensated by its open, salubrious, and agreeably commanding marine views. Lucombe's and Turner's may boast of the splendour of their Steyne situation, and its envied approximation to the Palace and grounds of his Majesty; but the attractive diversities of ocean are Tuppen's, including the whole sweep, from Beachy-head eastward, to Selsea-bill westward; and now and then, at particular tides and seasons, the Isle of Wight is interestingly

---

99 *TN both words in italics in original*

100 *TN Despite the lowering of prices after the conclusion of the Napoleonic blockades and wars, 30 shillings would represent nearly a year's wages to a lower servant.*

Image reproduced by kind permission of Brighton Royal Pavilion, Museums and Libraries

> visible. Not a floating object of any description, within sight of the town, can pass up or down the channel, therefore, but the Marine Library includes it in the extensive beauties of its prospects. As may be imagined, the telescopes, under such inducements to employ them, are seldom out of hand here, and to this requisite and agreeable species of accommodation, particular attention is paid.'

On 1 November 1827, the Brighton Gazette *reported:*

> 'Tuppen's Library continues to be well attended, notwithstanding the lateness of the season. Miss Corrie is still the vocalist there, and possesses the undiminished favour of the public.'

The Library was closed for the winter on Saturday 10 November. The season had ended.

Having arrived at the theatre at the agreed time, I found Lady Susan Hotham with her sisters, the Ladies O'Brien,[101] daughters of the Marquis of Thomond. Sir Robert introduced me to these ladies, in whom were combined beauty and refinement – the universal language of European salon society.

101 *TN Sarah, later Lady Stanhope Taylor and Elizabeth, later Lady Bucke, Viscountess Berehaven.*

After seating me next to herself, Lady Susan asked me if I knew the play that we were about to see.

'No, madam, but I have heard it mentioned as one of Shakespeare's greatest and that makes me regret that I do not have a sufficiently adequate mastery of your language to be able to grasp the beauties of the performance.'

'But perhaps you read English?'

'I do indeed.'

'In that case, I have here a volume of Shakespeare's works: in it you will find this tragedy. I brought it with me, thinking that it would make it easier for you to follow the dialogue. However, if you find certain passages too difficult, I will explain them to you.'

Small though the playhouse was, it seemed to me to be functional and well laid out; the overall decoration did not lack style, all the boxes being swathed in red fabric: the chandelier, lit by gas, and a whole multitude of candles in candelabras, fitted to every tier and between each box, gave out a dazzling light which set off perfectly the glowing colour of the upholstery.

The tragedy of the Merchant of Venice is based on an implausible story by Bandello, an Italian writer of the sixteenth century. Despite applauding the creation of the character, moneylenders the world around cannot but think ill of the ending.

A few scenes from this work are most movingly tragic; others are spoiled by those frivolities from which not a single play by Shakespeare is exempt. In a word, this dramatic work bears the stamp of its author's genius: it is sublime and uneven – like Shakespeare's teacher, nature herself.

The amateur who took the role of the Jew seemed to me to play it with a great deal of feeling, and I said as much to Lady Susan.

The 'amateur' was Barnard Gregory 1796–1852.

The Brighton Herald, *the rival newspaper to the Brighton Gazette which Gregory edited, was very fair in its appraisal:*

> The Shylock of the Amateur (Mr. Barnard Gregory) was the leading feature. It was the best performance of an Unprofessional that we have ever witnessed – still, in a critical point of view, it was very imperfect. This arose from a poverty of voice in the actor, which is particularly observable in the upper tones, or in the expression of violent passion;

> and from his action being too studied. His conception of the character was accurate – many of his points were excellent, and drew forth warm and deserved applause; and, we repeat, that altogether it was the best amateur performance we ever saw.

In his 'History of Theatres in Brighton' Porter[102] paraphrases this somewhat laconically as: 'a gentleman of literary talent, editor of the Brighton Gazette, *unevenly acted Shylock.'*

Gregory was far from making himself popular either on or off the stage. Even ten years after Gregory's death, in 1862, John Erridge still had uncharitable thoughts of him:

> 'Gregory, ... — who was the manager of the concern [The County Bank on the south-east corner of Castle Square], — being the noted Barnard Gregory, who alternately was a banker's clerk — at Masterman's, London, and Wigney's, Brighton, — wine merchant, chemist and druggist, editor of the *Brighton Gazette,* chapel building speculator, theatrical performer, manager of the Sussex and Brighthelmston Fire Insurance Company, and finally, as a public man, proprietor and editor of an infamous London newspaper, the Satirist, for a frightful calumny published in which, on the ex-Duke of Brunswick, he was incarcerated one year in Newgate.'

The chapel Barnard had built in 1824 was St. Margaret's in St. Margaret's Place. This chapel was demolished in the early 1960s and replaced with the tower block called Sussex Heights.

'When you are in London,' she replied, 'I insist you go to see Kean[103] in the role; he is our Talma;[104] he will give you an idea of the excellence of our theatrical talents in England. I also recommend that you hear him in the roles of Richard III and Sir Giles Overreach, both of which he does to perfection; but time and time again, it is as Shylock that I see him with renewed pleasure. You will be able to appreciate his study of the human heart, which he reveals intuitively through his art, and by which he conveys every subtlety; by which he gradually intensifies the feelings of resolute vengeance which prompt Shylock to place the horrible condition upon

102 Henry C. Porter: *The History of Theatre in Brighton*, 1886.

103 *TN Edmund Kean 1787–1833 English actor, noted as much for his tempestuous life off stage as for his portrayal of villains on stage.*

104 *TN Francois-Joseph Talma 1763–1826 French actor, noted for his realism and simplicity.*

the loan of his money. In the scenes of the third act, between the Jew, Solanio and Tubal, you will see him move from the anguish of despair to savage joy, a contrast which will not fail to make you shudder. In short, at all times and in the most delicate situations, Kean identifies so intimately with Shakespeare's genius that it is impossible not to apply to him these few lines by Pope on Macklin,[105] a famous man of the theatre:

"This is the Jew
That Shakespeare drew".'

'This study of nature, madam, which has raised Kean[106] so high in your good opinion is also the distinguishing characteristic of our own Talma. He was less fortunate than your actors, for he found the theatre plagued with specious taste and by the abuse of melodramatic style; by dint of hard work and single-mindedness, he managed to impose simplicity, truth – or in other words, beauty: but what he had felt instinctively as right, he saw employed only for the first time in England; it was during his travels as a young man, as a pupil of the great talents that London possessed at the time, that he studied and appreciate their delivery which was both plain and vigorous, and which he introduced so successfully into our theatres. I have not yet set eyes on Kean, but what I find admirable about Talma, and what makes him incontestably the best actor of our time, is that he has always been natural on a stage where human nature is nearly always suffocated by bombast.'

The play ended with much unanimous applause from the select audience which seemed thereby to be rewarding the actors for their very real talent and above all for their readiness to take part in such a praiseworthy endeavour.

Between the tragedy and the burlesque that followed, the director of the theatre, Mr. Russell, came on and recited poems full of gusto and sensibility which were perfectly tailored to the circumstances.

---

105 *TN Charles Macklin 1710(?)–1797 Macklin was the first contemporary actor to play Shylock as written by Shakespeare rather than as a comic figure.*

106 AN The famous tragedian Kean died in London on 15 May 1833. Nothing depicts the inflexibility of English morals more clearly than the way in which the English public wilfully deprived itself of his fine talent following a lawsuit during which it was proved that Kean had carried on an illicit liaison with the wife of Alderman Cox; he could no longer appear on stage without being excessively hissed. He submitted to this warning and so spent several years in America. Finally the London public called him back and, chastened by his exile, he reappeared in the same theatre where he had had his first success and this time with greater brio and to greater acclaim than ever.

The following address was delivered by Mr. Russell on the above evening, and was well received:

Who can behold this scene, and coldly gaze?
What sage refuse his tributary praise?
Sweet Charity, endow'd with heavenly grace,
Here find an altar, here her holy place;
No narrow ties her bounteous gifts confine,
All tribes all nations, may approach her shrine:
Nor yet must Misery woo, and pine her aid,
She flies to rescue, ere the prayer is made.
Heard you that sigh? uttered with such restraint,
As if the spirit had rebuk'd the plaint:
As if it told the tale of dire distress,
A generous pride still struggled to suppress;
It was a stranger's voice – which seemd afraid
To own the sufferings craven want betray'd;
Yet hot from conscious guilt that wanderer seeks
To hide the grief his soul, unwilling, speaks.
No social crimes on him have cast their brand,
He fled, no culprit, from his native land;
His aspirations soar'd with noblest aim,
To share the glories of Britannia's fame,
To keep that oath with freemen sworn and sealed,
In Saragossa's walls, and Talavera's field.
The world had seen this little Isle contend
In Freedom's cause, alone, without one friend,
Against the world's confederate hosts, and owe
That freedom, countless triumphs o'er the foe.
- The flame was kindled in each virtuous breast,
And Britain burst the chains which man oppress'd;
She made him think of rights by laws assum'd,
And envy thrones by subjects' love secured.
The patriots strove in vain! proscribed, oh where
Could the poor Exile refuge find, but here?
And here that refuge he has found; each hand
Was stretch'd to aid him as he touch'd the strand;
Unwearied still, Benevolence sustains,
And Beauty toils to sooth the Exile's pains;

To dress the sorrowing heart with grateful smiles,
For woman's pity every grief beguiles.
Oh! may such mourner every solace meet.
May England ever thus misfortune greet;
So – shall she win the blessing of mankind,
And trophied brows with wreaths celestial bind.

BRIGHTON GAZETTE, 8 November 1827

'Sir Robert wrote these lines,'[107] Miss Bruce whispered to me. 'What do you think of them?'

'That poetry is a respite from more serious occupations, and that the lyre can sound most melodious in the hands of the warrior,' I replied.

Towards the end of the performance, Sir Robert returned to the box, which he had left to congratulate the ladies on their good deed. Soon after, we took leave of Lady Susan, having obtained her permission to call on her in her own home to thank her for the kindness she had shown me.

It was at this lady's house[108] that, under the auspices of my obliging guide, I started my round of visits the following morning.

As I arrived at the front door, I showed some surprise at the way Sir Robert hammered on the brass plate. I did not yet realise that the different social classes

107 AN This poem no doubt prompted the quatrain about Sir Robert published the following day by the *Sussex Gazette*. It had been sent to the editor by a Spanish émigré:

Brighton, 10th Nov 1827

To the Editor of the Sussex Advertiser

Sir,

If the enclosed lines on Sir Robert Wilson, dictated by a sincere admiration for his exertions in the cause of charity, are deemed worthy of appearing in your Paper, I shall feel obliged by your inserting them in your earliest number.

Sir Robert Wilson
Il sait penser, négocier, écrire,
Brave soldat, éloquent orateur,
S'il prend l'épée, ou la plume, ou la lyre
C'est pour servir la cause du malheur.
par un Espagnol Refugie
Brighton, ce 8 Nbre, 1827

Sussex Advertiser 12 November 1827

TN *Thinker, negotiator, writer*
Brave soldier and eloquent orator
He takes up the sword, the pen or the lyre
But to serve the cause of the martyr.

108 TN *55 Brunswick Square, later renumbered as 57 Brunswick Square, Hove.*

in English society announce themselves by each knocking in a different manner. He observed my amazement.

'Our fashion is very unlike the diffident way you knock at the carriage entrance of your grand houses in Paris; there are fine distinctions in our habits which will give weight to your observations on us, for you know the saying: seeing is believing! Thus, the postman knocks twice, ordinary people three times and those from the upper ranks of society, seven or nine times in quick succession; as for tradesmen and suppliers, they may not knock more than once; servants of the house ring the bell and never knock.'

As he was concluding, the door was opened to us. Lady Hotham received me with a benevolence that was easily discerned in her features. With her were her sisters and a few of her lady friends. As we entered the room, the conversation was running on the new work by Lady Morgan. Her novel recounts, in particular, events relating to the Hotham family as is revealed by its title: *The O'Briens and the O'Flahertys*. The discussion was thus doubly of interest to me. The company wished to know my opinion of the book and of its author. As I had but dimly heard of either I therefore declined to comment on the merits of the work.

'This novel outlines, in the main, events before the time of the Irish rebellion,' Lady Susan explained to me, 'and although there is no denying that its wit sparkles and that its events and characters are most skilfully portrayed, we may censure the author, for the colours of her descriptions are too garish and her political opinions are too harsh. We may also criticise her for constantly bringing into her work the matter of religion, which is more suited to the realm of the chronicle than of the novel. As with several other of her works, she tries too hard for effect.'

It is not easy,' I rejoined, 'to please all and sundry; it is a rare privilege which belongs to genius alone. We ask much of it, because it promises much; but inferior talents often make intellect pay a high price for the fruitless glory of a hard-won reputation. I have seen, in my dealings with some lady authors, that the path to fame is not always a felicitous one; the price of prominence is in the struggle to maintain it, and the laurel crown, which according to the ancients served to safeguard them from thunderbolts, all too often draws those very thunderbolts down upon their heads; in short, it has seemed to me that talent, for these ladies, is close to being a misfortune. I enjoy Rivarol[109] who,

109 *TN Antoine de Rivarol 1753–1801 Writer and epigrammist.*

when speaking of the lady who was his companion in happier times, said:

"She has the taste of sound fruit and the wit of a rose.'"

Never having met Lady Morgan in society, I could only conjecture about her; nevertheless, the reputation she enjoyed fired me with a great desire to make her acquaintance.

'For that, sir, you will have to go to Dublin where Lady Morgan usually resides; beside the attraction of seeing one of the finest towns in Europe, you will find a select circle of people in the birth-place of our modern-day Anacreon,[110] Thomas Moore.'[111]

'Ah, as far as Mr. Moore is concerned,' I went on, 'him, I do know and admire. The only thing that can equal the charm of his poetry[112] is his witty, unassuming and diverse conversation.'

'It is true,' said the youngest Lady O'Brien, 'that he justifies Lord Byron's opinion: "Moore is one of those writers who will outlast the century which he has enlightened, and his songs, which deserve to go down in posterity, will last for as long as Ireland, music and poetry exist".'

As I showed a lively desire to hear one of these Irish songs, Lady Susan's youngest sister, demonstrating that delightful simplicity which increases twofold the value of a favour, sang, accompanying herself at the piano, in her pure, sweet voice, the song which begins with these words: (*She is far from the land*).[113] To my mind, the music suited perfectly the words: I was singularly struck by the strange, elusive inflections which give Irish music its unique and melancholy character. Sung with the expression and the feeling which must have inspired the author from the outset, the poignant lines and the mysterious words seemed to evoke, in the minds of many of the assembled company, their common fate. At my request, the young lady was kind enough to sing a second song and I promised myself that I would translate a few of these beautiful poems which, with their admirable undertones, reflect the pain, the remorse and the hopes of an ill-fated people.

---

110 *TN Anacreon 570–488 BC Greek lyrical poet.*

111 *TN Thomas Moore 1779–1852 Irish singer, poet, musician and song writer. Moore wrote nearly 100 full length works (collections of poems, satires, biographies, memoirs etc, including a 4-volume History of Ireland). He was considered by many to be the national bard of Ireland. He championed Catholic emancipation and the Irish cause. La Garde is credited with translating many of Moore's verses into French.*

112 AN Since writing this, I have had the good fortune in London to strike up an intimate acquaintance with Mr. Moore. I will talk more about him, as well as about other famous persons with whom I have contact, in the course of my further observations on England.

113 *TN The brackets and the English appear in the original text.*

I said as much to my obliging vocalist who offered to furnish me with Moore's ballad as well as some others, if I so wished.

'Do not be surprised, sir, by our enthusiasm or by our manner of expressing ourselves when we sing Thomas Moore's most outspoken songs: the patriotic tones, the poetic yearnings of these hymns to independence have nothing seditious about them; here, the authorities are vigorous – but so is liberty.'

At that very moment, the ladies were told that their *fly*[114] was waiting: we extended our visit no longer and set off for the house of Lord Haywarden whose exertions, along with those of Sir Robert, had made the previous day's performance possible. He was away from home, but Lady Haywarden was gracious enough to receive us and we were shown into her daughters' schoolroom.

The Hawarden (pronounced Harden) family consisted of the head of the household, Lord Hawarden. His full name was Cornwallis Maude, 4th Viscount Hawarden (1780–1856). He had married, Jane Crawford Bruce in 1811. Lady Hawarden had been born in about 1795 and she lived until 1852. Their three children were 15 year-old Augusta, Isabella, aged 13¾ and Maria Adelaide aged 7. Little Florence Pricilla Alicia was only 2 at the time and would still have been in the nursery. Their Brighton address was 58 Regency Square.

She was supervising their education herself, with all the affection of a mother and all the authority of a woman of consequence. At her request, the young ladies showed us, with becoming eagerness, extracts from their history and geography manuals, their instrumental and vocal music books and their sketches, in watercolour as well as pastel. I commented, not without astonishment, that nothing in their plan of work had to do with household duties or with the supervision of a home. This insight convinced me of the essential difference which exists between the education given to young English girls and that received by girls in France and in Germany. In this latter country, especially, skill in domestic economy seems to be not the adjunct but the goal of girls' education, no matter what their social class: they learn everything appertaining to needlework, embroidery, netting and even,

114 AN *Fly*: This is the name given to a small, very low carriage, either enclosed or open, mounted on four wheels and drawn by one single horse. *TN 'Its name is a contraction of "Fly-by-night", and it was, of course, the occupants of the Pavilion who were credited with putting these vehicles to the use suggested by their name,' according to Margaret Barton and Osbert Sitwell in* Brighton, *published in 1935.*

in the minutest detail, all that pertaining to the pantry and the kitchen. Thus they develop habits which do not allow them to remain without occupation for one single moment. In Saxony and almost everywhere else in Germany, I have seen ladies bring their netting to the most fashionable evening gatherings, or else invite each other to tea parties where the fare consists of great quantities of cakes, cordials and sherbets, that is, what they call dainties, everything having been made by the ladies themselves.

Young English ladies do not occupy themselves solely with producing ornamental work or acquiring serious, practical skills; they all learn music and very many of them learn to draw: these skills are the means of combating boredom; nature has made them a necessity, society a duty and habit a pleasure, and it is these which perhaps they will find indispensable in the retired lives which is to be their lot when they are married. One may never see a woman working, but that is not to say that she is ever idle: it is only at certain times of the day that she is busy with her children or making and receiving calls: thus she finds that her talent for decorative handiwork is an indispensable distraction not provided by plain needlework which often leaves rather too much freedom to the active imagination of the young.

We spoke of the previous day's performance and of its pecuniary outcome, which had already exceeded three hundred pounds.[115]

'That will no doubt be a good example to other provincial theatres,' said Sir Robert, 'and if we have shown how it is done, we will necessarily find imitators.'

'So we must hope,' added Lady Haywarden. 'Charity is a universal language; few people speak it, but everyone understands it.'

From the help being extended to the Italians, our conversation naturally turned to Italy, and in particular to Tuscany. Her Ladyship had lived for many years in Florence; she spoke of it as of a friend whom you might miss and who might miss you in return. When, as with Lady Haywarden, sound judgement is combined with wide ranging knowledge, demonstrating that one has observed much and observed well, one must leave in one's wake as many regrets in those left behind as one carries away in memories.

115 *TN Perhaps la Garde was privy to more information than the* Sussex Herald *which had announced an income of £200 from the benefit. The sum given by the author may have included the donations listed by the* Herald *on 8 November. The newspaper gave report that: 'Mr. Marshall, MP for Yorkshire, has forwarded to Sir Robert Wilson a subscription of £20, for the Spanish and Italian Refugees. Mr. A. Baring £10 in addition to a large sum given in London, and General Sir H. Cook.'*

As we were taking our leave of Her Ladyship, Lord Haywarden returned with his sister-in-law, Miss Bruce. Sir Robert informed him that we were going to call on Lord Southwell. Taking advantage of the easy manners of social intercourse in Brighton, where ceremony is banished, Lord Haywarden accompanied us.

Lady Southwell is the mother of the young people I had met on the esplanade with their governess; I therefore immediately found myself on familiar territory and in truth, for a moment, I could have believed myself in France.

Thomas Anthony, 5th Baron and 3rd Viscount Southwell, lived from 1777 until 1860. His wife, née Jane Berkeley was born about 1780. She died in 1853. The lady's official title was Jane, Viscountess of Castle Mattress, Lord Southwell being the landlord of Castle Mattress (or Matrix) in County Limerick, Ireland, at the time. The family was Catholic, as was the Count de la Garde. The 'young people' Auguste had met the previous day were little Pauline aged 12 and her older – and presumably long-suffering – sister, Matilda, by then a sophisticated teenager. Lady Southwell's other children (Thomas, 26; Sophia 24; Laura 21 and Charles 20) were, no doubt, too old to be seen in such frivolous occupations on the promenade.

The mother, the daughters, the son and Lord Southwell himself all spoke such flawless French and had so thoroughly adopted our manners and nearly all our customs that I felt as if I were entering a Parisian salon. It is ever a matter of amazement, mingled with a feeling of pleasure, that I see our language so universally adopted; I believe that our national pride has every reason to be flattered by this innovation, so recently introduced into English practice, thanks to the peace and to the mutual esteem in which the peoples of these two nations hold each other. Twenty years ago, Madame de Staël could rightly say that, if he were to be well received in England, a Frenchman must stand on his dignity, speak but little, and speak the language of the land; today the English are eager to speak to a Frenchman in his mother tongue; I would even venture to say that he is encouraged not to speak English. At least, this is what one notices amongst the upper classes, and even amongst those whom we call the middle classes. The other languages of Europe are much less in vogue: Italian is learned for singing, and German, despite being the native language of the ruling dynasty, is known by no one. This success, or rather this privilege, afforded to our native tongue is more gratifying to us than the decision made at Aix-la-Chapelle where, by mutual agreement, the nations of Europe chose it to be, from that time on, the one and only language to be used in diplomatic transactions[116] for, truth to tell, it was more difficult to overcome the resistance which seemed to stem from the prejudices of Old England than to force twenty nations to use a language which was not their own, but which, by its clarity and precision, cried out for such an honourable distinction.

I was too content with the good fortune I had met with in my first encounter not to attach great value to a renewal of the pleasure. I therefore asked for and was granted, as I was in every other house, permission to continue my visits. This affability proved to me how unfounded were those ideas, such as were given credence in France, relating to English aloofness and reserve and how illogical it was to think that, by being seen to be considerate in England, one gave every appearance of being from foreign parts.

Sir Robert took me to dine at the home of one of his comrades in arms, Colonel Black, where I was welcomed with a very military forthrightness. I found there were many guests. Dinner, elegantly served, afforded me the chance of noting the differing customs that the English have adopted for their meals. These customs they observe wherever they go, even in Brighton, where they stay only briefly and in rented houses: as these customs are founded on fastidious adherence to routine, they are to be found even where the household is in temporary residence. For each course, the cutlery is replaced, as are the various silver serving spoons and forks. There is one thing, however, which seemed to me to be a polite convention which is far too restrictive, and this is the trouble the host and the hostess take to serve the fish and to carve the fowl and the joints themselves; this prevents them from taking part in their guests' conversations; it seems to me that leaving this tedious task to the servants, a custom which is accepted everywhere nowadays, would better suit the guests and the hosts.

When the cloth had been removed, the servants placed before us glasses for various kinds of wine, each guest having no less than six. Finally, we were brought earthenware Wedgewood plates on which were depicted flowers, fruit and, above all, vine leaves, all so perfectly reproduced that they rival the porcelain of Sevres

116 *TN The 3rd Congress of Aix-la-Chapelle was held in 1818 and drew together representatives of Britain, Russia, Prussia and Austria to discuss the withdrawal of their joint occupying forces from France and to negotiate their own future relationships with each other.*

and Saxony. On these plates rested, next to the silver gilt knives and forks, brightly coloured little napkins with embroidery or trimming. There is one custom which is widely respected during the meal and which gives rise as much to affability as to increased intimacy between those present. One after the other, the diners inveigle each other into finding an excuse to drink a toast. Thus when a gentleman hears himself named, or, if he is too far away to hear, is informed of such by a servant, he waits for you to indicate your choice of wine; the glasses are filled and you acknowledge him with a nod, he will then immediately reply and drink at the same time as yourself. I was not spared such ploys. What appears regrettable as far as the ladies are concerned is that they must wait until a toast is proposed to themselves before they may drink; but English courtesy leaves nothing to be desired in that domain.

As soon as the lady of the house had given the ladies the signal to withdraw, all the gentlemen rose, as one of them hurried to the door to open it for them to retire. The gentlemen then sat down again with the Colonel taking the place at the head of the table which his wife had just vacated. Cut-glass carafes filled with various wines began to be passed round; shortly after, the conversation took a serious tone and turned to questions of politics and national interests; but alas, despite all these matters being discussed in French, it would have required a far longer stay in England for me to have been able to take part.

I will only hint at the custom which takes each gentleman, in turn, one after the other, into a corner of the dining room, for it belongs to an outmoded form of manners which is so very contrary to the delicacy of our modern French ways: what seemed to me to be most bizarre is that, as soon a gentleman has left, however briefly, the table, a toast is inevitably drunk to him, and as his occupation does not hinder his hearing the toast, he must take the trouble to prepare a short vote of thanks, which he delivers, in all seriousness, before seating himself back at table.

We ended the evening at the home of Mr. Morier, brother of the English envoy in Dresden.[117]

117 AN With Mr. Morier I attended a dinner in the 'Swiss-Saxony' fashion, at which each of the eight guests came from a different country: Mr. Morier from England, Count Tolstoy from Russia, Mr. Doulski from Poland, Count Enseidel from Germany, Count Pozzo di Borgo, Spanish envoy to Berlin, Mr. Hupsh, born in Constaninople, Prince Cariati, a Neapolitan, and myself.

© The Fitzwilliam Museum, Cambridge

James Justinian Morier was born in Smyrna in 1780. His childhood was exotic as was his later, business career as he moved between Smyrna (present day İsmir in Turkey), Constantinople and England. While still a young man, he was taken up by the British diplomatic service and served in Persia (modern Iran) for 7 years. In 1827 he had not long returned from a diplomatic mission to Mexico. He was finally to retire 1831 and died in Brighton in 1849. He enjoyed writing throughout his life and published popular travel books in between 1812 and 1818. His most famous work was, however, a novel set in Persia: 'The Adventures of Hajji-Baba of Isphahan'. His other novels have disappeared more or less without trace.

Mr. Morier is the author of a charming, provocative work disguised as a novel and in which he allows a barber from Isphahan to comment, with unaccustomed candour, on the customs and manners of Persia. Mr. Morier's long sojourn in Isphahan, as English consul-general, enabled him to study the character of the inhabitants and to observe important events within the country. He conversed with us about the Orient, which he depicted with all the colourfulness of an imagination that has been powerfully stimulated; and then he entertained us with the episode from *Hadji-Baba* relating to the beautiful Zenar, one of the Shah's wives, whose sufferings recall to mind the perplexing cruelty of Asian despots.

During the evening, I encountered Mr. Mansfield,[118] brother-in-law to my friend Mr. Hughes,[119] American envoy in Holland. Together, the two Misses Gent, accompanying themselves alternately on piano and guitar, sang a few of those Scottish ballads which, as with almost all vernacular music written in the minor key, communicate the charm of melancholy reverie.

Towards eleven o'clock, a tray was brought on which was a light supper of fruit, conserves, cheeses and sandwiches: this last delicacy consists of two slices of bread spread with butter and mustard between which very thin slices of veal, tongue or ham are placed. On a separate tray there were hot water, sugar and brandy with which to prepare grog. Mrs. Morier had presided her gathering most graciously; to my mind she was a credit to the distinguished man who had taken her to himself as his life's companion.

It was quite late when I left the house; but the night was so fine, the air so pure and so still that instead of making my way back to the Glocester Hotel I wandered aimlessly and without direction through the already deserted and silent streets, illuminated, nonetheless, with pools of light shed by the bright gas lamps; at infrequent intervals I saw in the distance a carriage or two as they rushed along, they alone disturbing my intense solitude.

I ventured onto the esplanade from where I could glimpse the Royal Pavilion. There is nothing of the artist about any traveller, any mere lover of art, who, in the course of his peregrinations, be they scholarly or simply born of idle curiosity, does not halt awhile at night to contemplate, as it gleams in the moonlight, the monument that he has admired during the daylight hours. It is only at night that the impression, which has captivated him in the morning, grows and gives food for thought; only then are revealed to him the charms and the impressions that had escaped him. So, in Rome I delighted in stopping, now at the foot of the massive ruins of the Coliseum, now before the magnificent dome of St. Peter's; I loved to contemplate the uncertain light which embellished the elegant arcades, or

118 *TN John Mansfield was the English husband of Mary B. Smith, sister of Christopher Hughes' wife Laura.*
119 *TN Christopher Hughes, American Ambassador to the Netherlands 1826–30.*

those magnificent shadows flung far across the landscape. Ah me! I must make my confession: the Royal Pavilion with its Moorish arches and its stonework tracery; with its domes, some rounded, some pointed, like the minarets on a mosque, struck me as no more than curious and, as it were, fantastical, for my mind was still full of those other, more striking, images: I could do no better than compare it to a chessboard covered in its pieces. I hurried away.

Instead of following the cliff top, I walked down onto the beach and started to stroll along the shore where the water lapped peacefully at my feet; here, at least, as if to make amends, nature solemnly unfolded before my eyes, grand, harmonious, manifold vistas such as no monument could produce.

To my right,[120] the chalky rock of the high cliffs, stretching away into the distance, rose to over 300 feet above my head and threw a pallid gleam onto the water; to my left, the wide ocean deeps stretched out like meadowlands of sapphire and silver. All this, with the moon the only companion of my walk, and the gentle murmur of the evening breeze, seemed to have an indefinable hold on me. It was not long before memories started to echo in my thoughts: suddenly I felt myself transported to other shores where, at so many different periods in my life, I had seen similar seas, not peaceful and silent like the one I could see at present, but wild and menacing; I have roamed the harsh Swedish coast, escaping the storm which dashed our ship to pieces on its rocks; I have blundered along the shores of the Adriatic, lead on by countless lanterns set alight to guide us after a terrible gale had tossed us, with neither masts nor rudder, into the port of Ancona; I have ranged the inhospitable shores of the Black Sea, being only too happy to come to rest on them when our ship was the last remaining of the fleet of sixty which had set sail from Constantinople, and when cold and hunger threatened to annihilate the few that the waves had spared; and finally, I have wandered the seashore of Odessa when night granted a few moments solitude free from danger, amidst the plague which was ravaging the ill-fated city.

Happiness is no more than a fleeting state of mind which casts its spell upon our life; but conjuring up the memory of these past ordeals shed an even greater charm onto the cheerful tranquillity which surrounded me like an enchanted aura. Here, I was not on my native soil, that is true, but how many reasons there were for not dwelling upon the fact! So many pleasures of all kinds came to my mind;

120 *TN* [sic]. *In Brighton, the cliffs run away to the east – Auguste therefore had the cliffs on his left and the sea on his right.*

the hospitality, the friendship even, with which, after my many travels, I had been met when I had very first arrived here in Albion; this land that I was visiting after knowing so many others.

For me, all apprehension was at an end, I had cast it aside the moment I reached Brighton, as a bird will shake the raindrops from its storm-drenched wings. But it was more than that: the sweet-scented coastline of Provence; the sinuous banks of the Bosphorus bordered with verdant turf and gently lapped by an imperceptible swell; the golden sands and the azure sky of the Bay of Naples – I had seen them all and they too had been beautiful, unsullied, tranquil – they all seemed so far away from me now. Now I was living entirely in the present, I could dismiss from my imagination these vivid, fleeting memories of my turbulent life just as the ripples of the rising tide were obliterating the clear imprint of my footsteps.

I could not relinquish these emotions, which I owed to the fascination of a fine night, I could not bear to tear myself away from this shore, from these cliffs, from this sea, from everything which had just awakened in me images of the past and produced these long, bewitching reveries.

At last, I returned to my hotel; but I will not soon forget that solitary walk on the shore at Brighton.

Chapter III

Lord Holland – How news comes to Brighton – Pitt's brother – Lord Canning's home – An auction sale – A gift from the Duchess of Devonshire – A sketch of manners – Mr. McKinnon – Tuppen's Library – A book tombola – The nightwatchmen – An heir – A boat trip – A sketch of a family.

Brighton is not only a town of courtiers, frequented by the elite, to whom is reserved the privilege of being admitted to the Pavilion; strictly speaking it is more an immense inn to which, in turn, flock the various ranks of the leisured classes with their own various objectives: in summer it is for sea bathing, in winter, for the hunt and at any time of year it is for fashion and pleasure; for fashion in particular: whether one owns a sumptuous town house in St-James Square or an enchanting estate in Devonshire, it is imperative, at the precise moment decreed by the fashionable world, that you abandon your citadel in London, or the shady and verdant lawns of your park or your country seat, to come and inconvenience yourself within the elegant confines of a house in Brighton. This is a town where a shrub is a luxury and it is the verandas alone which give an inch or two of shade: but no matter; fashion so dictates! Fashion, which reigns so tyrannically in this land of liberty.

'I have come,' Sir Robert announced as he entered my room the following day, 'to suggest an interesting walk which is that along the esplanade leading to the Pier; there we will find Lord Holland,[121] the nephew of our famous Mr. Fox: it is his custom to ride in the vicinity between one o'clock and two. He is a man whose acquaintance you will find charming, I have no doubt.'

121 *TN Henry Richard Vassal-Fox, 3rd Baron Holland of Foxley (1773–1840) English Whig politician, nephew of Charles James Fox.*

The entrance to the esplanade with the Chain Pier in the background (1824) Image reproduced by kind permission of Brighton Royal Pavilion, Museums and Libraries

'I will be most eager to renew my acquaintance with him,' I replied, 'in the hope that his lordship may perhaps have some memory of a very young man whom he no more than glimpsed in Paris many years ago.'

A gentle slope led us down to the gated esplanade.

We paid the nominal entrance fee of one penny (two 'sous' in our French money): 'This toll, small as it is, suffices,' Sir Robert told me, 'to give a decent return to the shareholders whose finances were invested in erecting this structure, for beside being both useful and elegant, it has one rare advantage for us: that of having cost very little. Thanks to the talent of Captain Brown, the engineer who was already famed for having invented the iron chains, this masterpiece cost no more than £27,000 sterling, and as the crowds in Brighton are far from waning, the shareholders can count on a considerable profit.'[122]

122 AN This magnificent construction has just been almost entirely destroyed by the storm of 15 October 1833. The town has thereby been deprived of its finest ornament. The news of this disastrous event was immediately conveyed to Captain Brown, the engineer responsible for this elegant phenomenon, and already a subscription has been opened for procuring the funds necessary for the prompt reconstruction of this important masterpiece which will no doubt be rebuilt on a more solid basis.

We found Lord Holland riding very slowly up and down on a small black horse and surrounded by a few friends; to us the conversation looked most lively; some men were listening attentively, others were speaking avidly. There was barely time for me to be introduced to him and even less to renew our acquaintance, for he had just received the news of the battle of Navarino,[123] and this turn of events, which could well have such a great influence on the peace in Europe which the hostilities had so recently disrupted, was leading to many a wild conjecture. This was, however, an apt moment for me to be able to judge the extreme ease with which the English broach a discussion and take it up. The subject was of a nature to give rise to lively debate. Lord Holland handed Sir Robert the letter containing the official details of the battle; the latter read the letter aloud, and, despite the importance of its subject, I could not prevent myself from reflecting on how many times the general had had to read similar dispatches when, as attaché to the armies who were attacking France on all fronts, it was he who had had the task of announcing any victories; victories which, at the time, were a novelty for his exultant listeners.

As for this naval skirmish, the details and the outcome were so precise and Admiral Codrington's[124] report so modest as to the details concerning himself and so dazzling at to what concerned others, that the first reaction was entirely focused on national pride, and allowed of but one feeling; that of enthusiasm. The flattering manner in which the English admiral depicted the conduct of the Chevalier de Rigny[125] caused Lord Holland and his friends to heap upon me congratulations, which my recollections gratefully transferred onto the person to whom I was indebted: but, I must confess, at that moment I was proud to be able to call myself a fellow citizen of the man who, so it was said, had carried himself in the affair like a valiant knight of yore, or like a courageous warrior of our modern times. And so our opinions were suddenly in sympathy with each other; this was, indeed, such a strange novelty to see two nations, rivals for so long, fight and win beneath the same banner, that it seemed to us that this victory should serve as the footing for a sound alliance; I welcomed the good omen with delight.

---

123 TN *The naval battle of 10 October 1827: As part of the war of Greek Independence, a naval force of the British, French and Russian fleets combined to fight the fleet of the Ottoman Empire in the Bay of Navarino to the east of Greece.*

124 TN *Admiral Sir Edward Codrington (1770–1851) The imposing facades of Codrington Mansions, on the north side of Western Road in Brighton have been obscured by the shops built in their front gardens during the nineteenth century. On Tuesday 29 September 2009, a plaque to the memory of Admiral Codrington was unveiled by His Excellence the Greek Ambassador at 139 Western Road.*

125 TN *Rear-Admiral Henri de Rigny 1782–1835*

The Chain Pier, built in 1823, was the only pier in Brighton at the time. Designed by Captain Samuel Brown, who had already build similar chain-borne structures in Scotland, it cost £30 000 but proved to be a great success both as an embarkation pier and as pleasure attraction. However, the pier was also a working structure. The steam packet has drawn up to embark passengers – and the three gentlemen on the left clearly have business matters, or gossip, to exchange.
Image reproduced by kind permission of Brighton Royal Pavilion, Museums and Libraries

Soon after, Lord Holland's friends took leave of us, some to check the details of this battle which so interested them, since they had relations who were in the fleet, others to hurry off with the news to anyone who did not already know it: bearing news always gives one a certain importance; it is as if one has all the merit of being party to what has happened. Besides, one is all the more easily inveigled into the need to repeat the slightest rumour by the certainty of being listened to in a town where, be it the debates of the town commissioners or speeches by influential members of the two Houses of Parliament, everything is deliberated, weighed and analysed with just that meticulous diligence you might expect to arise from the idle moments of a bathing party; for these foundlings which bear the name '*They say*' and who are never wrong, are sure to find on each and every street corner some corroboration or some confirmation.

Lord Holland dismounted; Sir Robert and I followed him in his footsteps. He went to take a seat on the landing stage at the far end of the Pier, which, extending 200 feet from the shore, producing the illusion of a ship at anchor in the bay.

I will not dwell on Lord Holland's merits; he was brought up in the ways of Fox, the man whose genius has shone so brightly on England, whose genius prompted Napoleon to say that all a nation required to make its moral fortune was half a dozen Foxes. It is easy to see that Lord Holland took advantage of what he had learnt and capitalised on it through his experience and his studies. His travels put him in the position of being able to judge men and of being able to compare them; he is a scholar without being a pedant and to his superior intellect he allies such a kindly heart as cannot fail to command respect and inspire affection. It is not surprising that so many combined qualities should have won Lord Holland numerous friends; and if he has acquired detractors, is that surprising? Mediocre minds attempt to humiliate worthy men in order to lessen the huge disparity which separates them from their superiors. His family motto is: *Deeds not words*. But it is neither to his uncle nor to himself that these words really apply; it is through their words that they have done so much good! What revealed to me Lord Holland's brilliant qualities was his courageous perseverance in championing Napoleon during his captivity on the island of St. Helena; and as for Lady Holland, her discreet attentions went far to temper the odious austerity of his imprisonment! Both received their reward in the illustrious victim's appreciative recollection of them on his deathbed.[126]

We conversed about Spain, Italy and Paris; his manner of recounting a whole host of anecdotes relating to each country or about prominent persons was so lively that his conversation seemed to bring each tableau to life. What a wide education! And how well he talked about the arts, literature, politics and even society tittle-tattle! No one is better proof of Quintilian's assertion: 'It is the heart which renders man eloquent.' I spoke to him of his uncle and the great kindness he had shown me when, during his visit to Paris, I was introduced to him by my childhood friend, Madame Récamier.[127]

---

126 TN *Despite being an ardent supporter of Napoleon, Lady Holland met the Emperor in person only once. However, during his captivity on Elba and St. Helena, the Lord and Lady Holland ensured that the prisoner received a constant flow of newspapers and books. In his will, the Emperor left to Lady Holland a gold snuffbox.*

127 TN *Jeanne Françoise Julie Adelaide Bernard (1777–1849). Julie married at the age of 15 and became a famous society hostess under her married name. See Translator's introduction.*

The building, Royal Crescent Mansions on the corner of Burlington Street, incorporates the much smaller, former home of Tory statesman George Canning who lived here while Prime Minister in 1827. He is said to have had a room soundproofed with baize – the felt used on billiard tables – where he could practise his speeches without being disturbed.

'Lady Holland[128] will be delighted to receive you,' he told me, 'and if, tomorrow, you would like to spend the evening at our home, it would give me great pleasure to tell her that you will be there.'

Sir Robert undertook to accompany me later to his lordship's house;[129] Lord Holland then mounted his small horse whose modest appearance seemed hardly suitable for such a famous parliamentarian. Thereupon we walked away from the pier along the lower esplanade and, by means of a stairway cut in the cliff-face, we reached Marine-parade and continued our stroll along the terrace which towers so majestically above the sea. There we found Lord Chatham;[130] Sir Robert accosted

128 *TN Elizabeth Vassall Fox (1771–1845) was famous as a society hostess in her home at Holland House, Holland Park, London where she received the elite of the Whig aristocracy and literary world. In 1797, she had been divorced for adultery by her first husband and was able to marry Lord Holland whose son she had just borne. Her skills as a hostess become clear in Chapter 5.*

129 *TN 30 Old Steine.*

130 *TN John Pitt, 2nd Earl of Chatham,(1756–1835) elder brother to William Pitt the Younger*

him. The Lord's noble bearing and his open face, set off so well by his white hair, the laurel wreath of advancing years, enhanced the appeal of his exquisite courtesy. The reports from Navarino immediately gave our conversation both purpose and significance but the news was so recent that no one had yet been able to conjecture upon either the effects or the causes of the battle. I greatly regretted not being able to discuss the matter more comprehensively; I confess that I would have found it most stimulating to be able to judge whether Mr. Fox's nephew and Mr. Pitt's brother were of the same mind regarding a fact which was of such vital importance to English politics.[131] We were nearing the house in which Mr. Canning[132] used to live:

> MARINE PARADE, BRIGHTON
> BY MR.CREASY
>
> At the Old Ship Tavern, Brighton, on Monday 22d of October, 1827, at Twelve for One o'Clock precisely, unless an acceptable offer is previously made by Private Contract.
>
> **A** Freehold Mansion, situated on the preferred part of the marine Parade, encompassing unusual advantages, with the most admired and extensive sea views, – Comprising on the *Basement* every requisite and necessary Office; on the *Ground Floor*, a Spacious Dining Room or Library, Parlour, Principal Stair Case, and Water Closet; on the *First Floor*, an elegant Drawing Room, opening under a Stone Portico, a Breakfast Parlour, leading to a Splendid Banqueting Room, Nine principal Sleeping Rooms, Dressing Rooms, Water Closet, and Five Attics; the Residence of the late
>
> **RIGHT HON. GEORGE CANNING**
>
> This desirable Mansion has a Tunnelled Walk under the Road leading on to the Sea Beach. May be viewed by tickets only, which with full particulars, may be had of the Auctioneer, North-street, Brighton; at the place of sale; and of Messrs Blunt, Roy & Blunt, Solicitors, Liverpool-street, London

131 AN In comparing these two great men, Napoleon said that in Fox it was his heart which roused his genius, whereas with Pitt it was his genius which doused his heart.

132 AN George Canning, was born on 11 April 1770 and died on 8 August 1827 in Chirswick [*sic*], the country house of the Duke of Devonshire, in the same room as Fox had breathed his last twenty years previously. And there was a further fell twist of fate: a few weeks before his death, Canning had kissed his mother and said to her as he left the house: 'Whatever happens, we'll see each other in August': his mother died suddenly in July and Canning in early August.

that very morning auctioneers had started a sale of his effects as well as of part of his library.[133] As I was eager to acquire a memento of this illustrious man, I asked the gentlemen their permission to take my leave.

The room in which the sale was being held was already full of buyers, amongst whom were to be found a great number of persons of distinction; amongst others, Colonel Dawson, who is nephew by marriage to Mrs. Fitzherbert,

---

Captain the Honourable George Dawson, commanded a troop of the 1st Dragoon Guards. He fought at Quatre Bras and Waterloo, where he was wounded. His tribulations came later, when he wanted to marry Mary Georgiana Emma ('Minnie') Seymour, the sister of Captain Horace Seymour. Minnie had been raised by Mrs. Fitzherbert, the consort of George IV, who had settled a dowry of £20,000 on Minnie. Both Mrs. Fitzherbert and the King opposed the marriage; Mrs. Fitzherbert because she thought Minnie could do better socially and George IV because he did not want the dowry to go to 'a penniless soldier'. However, George Dawson's tenacity won the day. The couple were eventually married on 20 August 1825, after Mrs. Fitzherbert had excluded him from Minnie's settlement and imposed a series of long separations. The son of George and Minnie became the 3rd Earl of Portarlington when he inherited the title from George's older brother. George died in 1856.

---

as well as the Dean of Ossory,[134] Sir Henry Rycroft,[135] Lord George Lennox[136] and several Members of Parliament. The smallest trinkets were fetching very high prices. The books were not to be sold until last; as I waited, I wandered through the rooms where, undoubtedly, so many admirable schemes, so many noble thoughts had been engendered. What a difference between the desolation I now found in these rooms and the crowd which aspiration, ambition, but perhaps also friendship, had drawn to them when the minister was at the height of his powers! How many feelings of loyalty must he have inspired in this place! It was here that he could pour out his heart surrounded by his family who adored him! here that

133 TN *This places the events on 9 November 1827.*

134 TN *Lord Holland had succeeded his uncle Lord Upper Ossory in 1818. The Dean may have been purchasing on behalf of Lord Holland*

135 TN *Sir Henry Rycroft (c. 1766–1846) the last Knight Harbinger, a post which he held from 1816 until his death. 'The task of the Knight Harbinger was to ride one stage onward before the King on his progress, to provide lodgings and provisions for the court.'*

136 TN *Possibly George Lenox Conyngham II (1796–1887), younger half-brother of William Lenox Conyngham of Springhill and for many years First Clerk in the Foreign Office.*

he would reveal to his friends the plans he had drawn up for the prosperity and the happiness of his country; here that he devised such momentous acts of his ministry as the recognition of the South American States and the resurgence of Greece. Now, everywhere was silence and melancholy. These impressions crowded in on my mind. 'And so,' I said to myself, 'even he, whose life is the most fulfilled, will, in an instant, cross the narrow boundary between two eternities and find himself at the grave, just as the absent-minded man will suddenly find himself at his own home.'

I returned to the drawing-room; the sale of books was just starting; a few were sold at very high prices, especially those bearing the name of the late lamented minister.[137] A young Mexican, a relative of my excellent friend Garcia del Rio, the Peruvian Minister to London, pushed the price of one such volume several guineas above its real value.

'You have paid a great deal,' I said to him, 'for a signature, my dear sir.'

'It is nothing to what the memory of this noble friend to my country is worth,' he replied. 'Beneath his name I shall write:

Nominatus est usque ad extrema[138]

and I shall bequeath the book to the National Library of Mexico.'

A magnificent copy of the Aeneid, translated from the Italian and illustrated with fine engravings, was next for sale. Lord Lennox and Colonel Dawson overbid considerably; the volume was knocked down, at a very high price, to the latter. It was a seemingly insignificant circumstance which had made it so precious to the two bidders; on the first blank page were written, in pencil, these simple words: 'Presented to the Right Honourable George Canning by the Duchess of Devonshire'. The auctioneer had not failed to draw attention to the charming dedication in order to raise the value of the book. Other bidders showed the same eagerness to try for a collection of the weekly periodical *The Microcosm* on which Canning had successfully worked since the age of sixteen; for single copies of *The Anti-Jacobin*[139] and *The Quarterly Review*, both of which contained articles written by him at the time of the French Revolution; for two brochures containing *The Knife Grinder* and *The Loves of Mary Pottinger*, satirical poems ascribed to him; and

137 AN It was much at this time that a subscription was opened in England for the erection of a monument to the glory of this famous man, and several thousand pounds sterling were raised in a very short time. The most solid testimony of the national spirit of a people is revealed by the importance it accords its great men and the honours which it pays to their memory. At the death of Mr. Canning, I was able to appreciate the truth of the nation's deep and unanimous sentiments. *TN A monument to Lord Canning was erected in Parliament Square, London, in 1832.*

138 *TN His name reaches the highest realm.*

139 *TN Also known as The* Weekly Examiner.

finally for an engraving depicting him being carried in triumph by his constituents following his election to Parliament for the town of Liverpool in 1816.

FURNITURE, LIBRARY OF BOOKS, AND EFFECTS
By Mr. Creasy,

Upon the premises, Marine Parade, Brighton, on Thursday, the 8th November, 1827, and the following day, at Eleven o'Clock, by order of the Executors of the late

Rt. Hon. George Canning,

All the Splendid Household Furniture, consisting of capital goose feather beds, large Witney blankets, wool and horse-hair mattresses; Marseilles quilts and bedding; field, tent, and French bedsteads, with appropriate furnitures; elegant four post bedsteads, with rich chintz hangings; mahogany chests of drawers, dressing tables, &c.; dressing glasses, chamber chairs, &c.; drawing room furniture, comprising couches, sofas, and chairs; rosewood and mahogany card and sofa tables; rosewood cheffoniere, French clocks and time-pieces in or-moulu, a brilliant chimney glass 72 inches by 60 inches, alabaster and painted vases, Brussels carpeting, suite of chintz window curtains, brass fender, &c.; mahogany dining-room chairs, tables, sideboard, &c.; a set of mahogany chairs stuffed in green morocco, with sofa ensuite, window curtains, &c,; and all the kitchen utensils.

Also the Library of Books, which include the Spectator, Life of Buchanan, Old Plays, Court of St. Cloud, James' Naval History, Goldsmith's Works, a *black-leather Bible*, in excellent preservation, the Works of Ben Johnson, the Bulletins from 1793 to 1823, Buffon's Histoire Naturelle par Sonnini, in 127 vols., Antiquités Nationales par Millin, Voyage de Humbolt, a splendid Mvsevm Florentinvm, Annali di Tacito, L'Eneide di Virgilis, Le Decamerone, &c. &c.

May be viewed two days previous to the sale with catalogues only, which may be obtained at the Office of Mr. Creasy, the Auctioneer, North Street, Brighton, at one shilling each.

BRIGHTON HERALD, 27 October 1827

Being expected for dinner at Baron Dimsdale's house,[140] I had time to purchase only a few trifling works, but works to which the place of sale and the memories

140 *TN 29 Marine Parade, lodgings of Robert Thomas Dimsdale, 4th Baron Dimsdale (1796–1865).*

associated with them gave great value in my eyes.[141]

I made my way to the baron's home and he welcomed me with that hospitable courtesy for which he is so well known. It would appear that he has inherited his courtesy, just as much as his title, from the court of Catherine II to which his grandfather[142] had been so long attached.

After dinner, more guests came in and a little concert was devised: the baroness sang some pieces of English music that she had chosen with taste, and among which was this Irish melody by Thomas Moore: *The Minstrel Boy to the War is Gone.*

The minstrel boy to the war is gone,
In the ranks of death you'll find him;
His father's sword he hath girded on,
And his wild harp slung behind him;

'Land of Song!' cried the warrior bard,
(Should) 'Tho' all the world betrays thee,
One sword, at least, thy rights shall guard,
One faithful harp shall praise thee!'

The Minstrel fell! But the foeman's steel
Could not bring that proud soul under;
The harp he lov'd ne'er spoke again,
For he tore its chords asunder;

And said 'No chains shall sully thee,
Thou soul of love and brav'ry!
Thy songs were made for the pure and free
They shall never sound in slavery!

---

141 AN One of these works had a curious binding and was called: *Letters to the Right Honourable William Pitt on the use of wig powder*. The author, John Donaldson, attempts to prove, by a long litany of facts, that the use of wig powder is one of the main causes of the high price of bread; he shows that there are 50,000 wigmakers in the kingdom and that if one supposes that each used one pound of flour per day, in one year, that would add up to 18,250,000 pounds or 5,314,284 four-pound loaves; then, if by adding the number of people who powder their own wigs or who are powdered by people who are not professional wigmakers, he proves mathematically that the quantity of wheat and fine wheat flour used in the manufacture of starch and powder amounts to the sum of no less than 2,292,000 pounds sterling.

142 *TN The Baron Dimsdale of 1827 owed his title to his grandfather's skill in inoculating Catherine the Great and her son against smallpox in 1768. So high was the first Baron Dimsdale's renown as a physician that he was called back to Russia to inoculate Grand Duke Alexander. Both Frederick the Great in Potsdam and the Emperor Joseph in Vienna received him in their court.*

I must confess I find those ladies much to my taste who love music, and even more so, those who practise it; it is a safeguard against idleness, and a woman who does nothing, thinks too much. English girls seem to be thoroughly conversant with the truth and the importance of this principle: they nearly all, despite the enormous cost of lessons, which is never less than one guinea, learn to sing and to play the piano and the harp. Their diligence in the matter enables the vast majority of them to compensate for what English endowments deny them, namely, musical ability; and if at times their voices lack range, they do seem to me to shine at least in being accurate and versatile; in short, they bring so much sensitivity and elegance, especially to their interpretations of these ballads from their homeland, that they seem to be motivated by Shakespeare's notion: 'no person is so callous, so insensitive and so arrogant that their nature cannot be eventually changed by music.'

I had imagined that gambling was rife in England; I had already received invitations to gambling evenings (*cardparties*[143]) for the following days. Brighton, so I had assumed, must surely resemble many of the spa and bathing towns in Germany where gambling invariably forms the main entertainment; yet one rarely sees, in the corner of a drawing-room, any table set up for whist, and even then there is often a lack of players. I remember that in Vienna, the majority of gatherings in good society were devoted entirely to games of chance; if there was a drawing-room with one hundred guests, twenty-five card tables would be assembled and fully occupied; there would even be a three-cornered table for a game of *L'Hombre*[144] if there were not enough players for one of the tables. I have always regarded Whist as a useful invention: it prevents those who know nothing besides gambling from boring themselves and from imparting their boredom to others. When I expressed my surprise at seeing so little liking for cards, I was told that in London drawing-rooms I would find our tedious game of *écarté*[145] all the rage; moreover, it was added, when men are gathered together in their clubs, and notably in the one in Brighton or in Crockford's in London, or during the hunt or the races, games with very high stakes materialise: at the end of every evening the losses amount to several

143 *TN In English in the original text.*

144 *TN 'L'ombre' was a fast-moving game for 3 players. It originated in Spain in the seventeenth century and was one of the first card games to involve bidding.*

145 *TN A trick-taking card game for two players, similar to Whist. The players used a French 32-card pack (all cards between two and six being removed).*

thousand pounds sterling. At supper, I found myself seated near Mr. Mackinnon,[146] Member of Parliament and of the Royal Society in London and whom the baron had pointed out as the author of a most interesting work 'on the progress of public opinion'. His conversation, which was full of shrewd remarks, made me extremely eager to further my acquaintance with him; he anticipated my request by handing me his card and inviting me to come to visit him often in Brighton and in London, which I promised to do with a lively desire to keep my word. The evening ended early – a boon from which one occasionally benefits in Brighton, thanks to that flouting of fashionable rules condoned by the coteries of bathers.

As soon as darkness fell, I was astounded yet again by the long garlands of lights which lit the streets and breathed new life into them. Here, the gaslight glows with a purity which it is truly impossible to imagine, even when you have seen towns on the Continent where this form of illumination is adopted more widely. This light owes its excellent properties to the quality of the coal from which it derives. I stopped every few paces, almost against my will, to gaze at the opulent shops with their gold work, crystal-ware and fabrics; at their counters artistically laden with merchandise and lit with a myriad of lights reflected in a multitude of mirrors: these shops, I was assured, were in no way inferior to those in London.

Gas light may have been attractive, but even in 1822, it could be dangerous:

> There was an explosion of gas in the shop of Mr. Allison, tobacconist, (next to Lucombe's Library), on Monday evening last. It appeared that the gas had escaped from the pipe under the counter, and concentrated itself therein, and that while Mr. A., who was apprised of the circumstance by the disagreeable smell, was trying to discover the aperture with a lighted candle in his hand, the gas exploded with a loud report, inflicting some slight injury on Mr. A's face.
>
> Brighton Gleaner 4 November 1822

By 1827 Brighton streets had been lit by gas for some six years. The gas was piped from works at East Brighton (at the bottom of the present day Wilson Avenue) and from Hove (immediately west of St. Andrew's Church).

146 *TN William Alexander Mackinnon became thirty-third Chief of the Clan Mackinnon in 1808. He sat as a Westminster M.P. for most of the parliaments between 1819 until 1865. The 'interesting work' Auguste refers is Mackinnon's* The History of Civilisation and Public Opinion, *published first in 1846 by Henry Colburn, Auguste's own publisher.*

Auguste may be exaggerating the brilliance of the gas lighting. Four years later, in 1831, John Docwra Parry was still not satisfied:

> Brighton is lighted with gas, but very indifferently; the individual lights are large and handsome, but much too 'few and far between' and in some parts the illumination is confided entirely to the private lights of the shops, consequently when these are shut up, there is almost total darkness. In some localities, as in Regency-square, the inhabitants have voluntarily incurred the expense of a double number of lamps.

However, La Garde was ever a flatterer and indeed, there had been recent improvements in the system:

> The lights of the New Gas Company have been greatly improved, at which, we must say, we greatly rejoice, inasmuch as we cannot forget that to this Company we are indebted for the lighting of our street lamps. The defect hitherto has been, we understand, a want of sufficient pressure.
>
> Brighton Gazette 29 November 1827

A throng of strollers, most of whom were strangers to the town, give the scene the lively feel of a fair.

Following the crowd of idlers, my walk took me to Tuppen's Library and Reading Rooms.[147]

> The unpropitious state of the weather in the evenings this week, has tended to thin the gay votaries at the Marine Library. Lucombe has closed his evening amusement for the season. Tuppen still retains Miss Corrie, who will continue with him until he closes, which will be in about a week's time.
>
> Brighton Herald, 27 October 1827

At the far end of the main room was a stage; several musicians took turns to perform songs and instrumental pieces. The crowd was large: there was no entry fee, but the owner of the establishment had, nevertheless, found a most ingenious

---

147 *TN See pages 109–110.*

Image reproduced by kind permission of Brighton Royal Pavilion, Museums and Libraries

way of more than recouping his expenses: in the interval between a sonata and a ballad, a handsomely bound volume was put up as a lottery prize; each ticket, of which there were rarely more than twenty-five or thirty, cost only one shilling. When this sort of subscription had been completed, which normally took but a few minutes, the prize ticket was drawn; in this way a large number of books came to be sold at prices which were much to the benefit of the proprietor.

Odds Bobbs! cry'd my Lord, there's a raffle on foot,
That's good, said my Lady – so off they went to't.
You'd have laugh'd to have seen them, or amble or hop
With a heart full of glee to the bookseller's shop.
The Bookseller's shop is the change of this place,
From Sir Timothy Traffic e'en up to his Grace.
In a corner sate little Miss Tittup, a-leering,
And old Lady Wishfor't sate opposite sneering;
Sir Christopher Croaker, with spindles so taper;
Sat squinting thro' spectacles over a paper.

from THE BALNEA *by George Saville Carey*

Returning to my hotel, I came across the *watchmen*: these are officials employed to safeguard and to police the town; to this end, they are armed with a long, iron-tipped stick and a rattle with which they can alert each other as soon as there is an arrest to make; it is very rare for anyone to escape them, for upon a signal they all rush *en masse* from every street corner and prevent the offender from escaping. These men are living clocks and barometers: they announce their watchful presence by crying out, at regular intervals, the time of night and the weather conditions. Here in Brighton there is at least, of necessity, some variety in their call, thanks to the frequent changes of temperature, and, unlike the watchmen in Madrid, they are not condemned to shout time after time *Sereno* (fine weather), the word which has given them their name.

> The safety and good conduct of our rather rowdy little Brighton was left at nights in the care of the watchmen. Old Charlies, as we called them, who during their perambulations round the town, crying the time of night and the kind of weather, were frequently claimed as lawful prey by the practical jokers who roamed the streets in the small hours. But it must be confessed that, as a rule, these scatter-brained gentlemen paid up very handsomely though anonymously for the privilege of playing their silly pranks. One old fellow I could name had five guinea-pieces left at his lodging the morning after he and his box were so mysteriously carried away into the churchyard and left high and dry on a steep granite tomb.
>
> Maude Egerton Hine King: *Round about a Brighton Coach Office* (1896)

The next day an elegant carriage drawn by four horses stopped at the door of my hotel: a young man got out, entered the dining-room where the other travellers and I were finishing our breakfast and, sitting at the table next to mine, ordered tea to be served. I observed him carefully; his elegant attire, the striking carriage and four which had brought him and his whole appearance of opulence and wealth were all those of a dandy, such as I was constantly seeing; and yet he seemed to me to lack somewhat that ease, or rather that self-possession which characterises the true dandy. I soon learned the cause: one of my fellow guests told me that this young man called N***[148] had inherited the sum of 50 million francs from his uncle, the jeweller, Rundell,[149] who had died a little while previously, leaving no children. It was impossible not to ask my friend to repeat several times, the enormous amount of the capital sum involved, for it was so immensely disproportionate to the sums inherited in other countries that one might be tempted to believe that there had been a gross exaggeration; however, nothing was truer. To give an idea of the colossal fortune belonging to the firm of Rundell and Bridge with which the testator was associated, one merely has to recall their earnings at the time of the king's coronation: this ceremony occasioned a host of receptions and dinners. The quantities of jewellery and plate which they loaned to the government as well as to corporations and individuals, was so great they made more than a million francs in hire fees in one period of just twenty-four hours. From that alone, one can judge the accumulation of pieces to be found in their stores. I looked on in amazement at this tradesman's nephew who, only yesterday was merely one of the crowd and who today can walk as an equal in fortune to the richest princes in Europe; and in truth, I admired his unassuming manner which he has kept despite that common adjunct to fortune: self-satisfaction.

'That young man,' my companion told me, 'is still suffering under the effects of surprise; he has borne the first shock well; let us wait to see him in six months.'

Indeed, we will have to wait, I said to myself as I left the hotel: all men are alike; and who has ever been able to resist the intoxicating effects of unexpected prosperity! In six months, perhaps, he will be surrounded by a swarm of toadies and be sovereign over an obsequious mob; through the miraculous medium of this coveted metal, he will know everything, be on tap for everything and be right about everything, for the folly of the rich is legendary! And how could it be otherwise? Our forefathers decreed that '*poverty is no sin*'; modern society proclaims: '*it is worse, it is the crime of penury*'; the indigence of the pauper is so contagious that everyone flees from him; it is not this rejection which is perhaps the one which he might find the most humiliating, for his condition may sometimes force him to expose himself to a gratitude even more horrid than his destitution; but life was smiling on our heir, thanks to the simple merit of having an uncle who knew how to calculate the magnetic force of one guinea upon another; soon, blighted like a sound fruit on contact with a rotten one, contaminated as it were, this young man,

148 *TN Joseph Neeld (c 1789–1856) grandson to Rundell's favourite sister.*
149 *TN Philip Rundell (1746–1827). Rundell, with his partner John Bridge, became Royal Jeweller in 1789.*

who today is so unassuming, will perhaps be no more than the very embodiment of that insolent vanity so common to parvenus in every land.[150]

As I mused over these unexpected turns of fate, less uncommon here than anywhere else, I took myself off to the edge of the ocean, from whence has come the immense wealth of this island. Having made my way down onto the beach, I had a whim to find out more about one of the great pleasures much in vogue in this town and which is a miniature version of the grander form of being under sail – that is to say, the exchange of commodities, vices and blazing guns between nations; so I hired an elegant little sailing *boat* for a few hours and in it I tacked up and down the coast several times. I delighted in gazing at the string of mansions and charming houses which adorned it with such style; my elderly pilot was a man whose labour it has been for several years to serve as guide to any enthusiast for this kind of entertainment, townspeople and visitors to Brighton alike; he gave me a fine speech about the ever increasing prosperity of the town. He had known it, so he told me, before it had a name, before it had a reputation, before the king's inclination had made it the liveliest destination in his merry kingdom. Even today he could see, in his mind's eye, the strand as it was thirty years ago, occupied by a few fishermen's cottages; now he saw it adorned with substantial structures which, stretching from Kemptown to Brunswick-square, vied with each other in elegance along the whole three miles. He also informed me of a bizarre practice, namely, that all the fine fish caught along this coast is sent to London, only for it to return immediately to stock Brighton's market. A wealthy company has obliged their contracted fishermen to sell nothing locally, but to send everything immediately to London, from where it is dispatched to the various corners of the country. Thus the sea is, in a manner of speaking, shackled, and any food connoisseur in the provinces is at the mercy of a trading company.

Pay well, and on good things you'll dine, They've good bread, white or brown;
Good beer, good mutton, and good wine, And famous fish—from Town!

Robert Cruikshank BRIGHTON: A COMIC SKETCH *(1830)*

150 AN The system of checks and balances soon came about for this young heir; he wished to ally himself with a social class to which he was not born; he married the daughter of Lord S***. In France, we have a comedy by Moliere which so well depicts the tribulations of such an alliance, that I refer my readers to it; our young man proves the case: *He brought it upon himself!*
TN Probably a reference to Moliere's play 'Le bourgeois gentilhomme'.

The sky became overcast and the sea stormy. The wind was starting to freshen. Any foolhardy fellow from the *Funny Club*[151] would have taken great delight in confronting the peril and braving the storm. I deemed it sensible to cut short my nautical perambulation, for I called to mind the drawback of squalls, of which the hardened mariner so truly says: 'if you wish to learn to pray, take to the sea'.

Having been invited to dine with Major S***,[152] I seized the chance to observe in detail the private life of a family belonging to that intermediate class within English society which can be regarded as one of the true mainstays of the might and of the prosperity of the nation. This authentic portrait of innocence from a far distant past, set amidst the decidedly modern social life of Brighton, seemed to me, inevitably because of the very contrast it made, to invest with great charm and appeal the innate virtues which it represented.

At six o'clock I had gone to the Major's house in Oriental-place, the new part of town called the West-end.

In London, the district bearing this name is entirely given over to fashionable society: the West-end of Brighton is by no means exclusive. There are no grand districts and consequently, no humble districts – everywhere is elegant and prosperous, as you would expect from a watering place.

The Major is a retired soldier. He is very bluff and very kind. At the conclusion of a large number of campaigns in various parts of the world, he retired from service in order to devote himself to the education of his large family, settling in Brighton where he lives all year round in a delightful house, for in general everyone occupies his own, and it is unheard of to share, as is done in Paris, where within one house several families are piled one atop the other, separated by nothing but a simple wall, and destined never to know each other.[153] The Major's family consisted of five girls and five boys, a number which might seem remarkable elsewhere but which here is no more than average. The regular features and glowing complexion of his daughters confirms Madame de Staël's observation that 'the beauty of the women in England instantly attracts admiration'.

---

151 *TN A group of rowing enthusiasts which, once a year, awarded the prize of a fine little fishing boat and all its paraphernalia to the most skilful boatman on the Thames.*

152 *TN Major Phillip Stewart. He died in 1837, in Brighton, at the age of 72, probably at his home, 28 Oriental Place* (Pigot's Directory 1832). *His son, M.P. Charles Stewart, lived in the same house.*

153 *TN Here the author does show himself a little ignorant of the social structure of a large part of Brighton. Firstly, the grand squares that had already been built by 1827 (Lewes Crescent, Sussex Square, Russell, Regency and Bedford Squares) were surrounded by far more modest building for the tradesmen. Secondly, many of the houses in the grand squares were built as lodging houses and did not always house just one family of visitors at a time during the season.*

Oriental Place is the turning with the carriage going up towards the newly completed Sillwood House at the top.
Image reproduced by kind permission of Brighton Royal Pavilion, Museums and Libraries

Each of the five sons has taken up a different profession. Three are in the East Indies, serving as soldiers or administrators for the Company; another trained at the Woolwich School,[154] which is somewhat akin to our own École Polytechnique, and passed out as an officer in the light artillery and the fifth, the only one still living at his father's home, is a Member of the House of Commons. Two of the daughters have married well; and the final three will soon do so. These details, which I discovered from my host, persuaded me to congratulate him on the success which had crowned his paternal attentions. Yet it seemed to me that there being such a large number of children could well have diminished the chances for happiness that might fall to the lot of each of them.

'Far from it,' he replied. 'In general, we see all our large families prospering. The ministrations of a good father is no more likely to wear thin if they are extended to many children than if they were to be directed and focused on just one. Each one is a buttress which supports the vault. Each profession reaches out a helping hand to the next and gives the other mutual support. What they require is connections: each child brings his own into the equation. Contacts are established, simply and without fuss; and these are continually strengthened by the family bond. The same is true of the girls: the families into which their

154 *TN presumably Woolwich Naval Dockyard.*

brothers have been received, and the in-laws of the girls who are married, all establish close relationships. And as marriage is less likely here than elsewhere to be a financial transaction, once you are accustomed to agreeable intimacy with your wife, you soon pass to the stage of being accustomed to being in love. I regret that I am not able to introduce you to the whole of my family at once, but I am separated from three of my sons who are scattered in far-flung places. One however, a judge in the Resident's Office in Bombay, should soon be restored to me. He has obtained three years' leave from the Directors and will be spending them here with us. Such an extended leave of absence whilst in the public service may well surprise you; but bear in mind that the journey home and back again will in itself take more than one year, and that after such a long separation, two years fly past all too rapidly. Moreover, my son is making his journey overland.'

'My goodness! Overland, sir?'

'Yes, it is the best way to avoid the monotony of such a long journey, and an even better way of making it shorter, for it can be done overland in less than two months, and it will be possible to do it in even less if the plan to establish railways across the greater part of the route is carried out. In the last few days I have received a letter telling me that he has arrived in Cairo: he will soon be setting sail from Alexandria and once he has reached land again, it will not be long before we see him here on our island.' Our conversation was interrupted by the arrival of a servant bringing to the Major's son several letters to which his friends wished him to affix his stamp. He asked us to excuse him whilst he performed this necessary duty imposed upon him by his status as a Member of the House of Commons. The address on each letter had been left blank: he wrote them in his own hand and signed them, having first inscribed the day and the date.

'I understand,' he turned to me and said, 'that your *deputés* in France do not enjoy the same privilege. Here in England, every Member of each House of Parliament has the right to receive, at no charge to himself, fifteen letters per day and he may send ten such letters: however, no letter may weigh more than one ounce. Everyone is eager to solicit a share in this privilege. This trifling exemption, or I should say, this facility which we are allowed and which, each day, enables us to perform a few small favours – not to mention the opportunity of being elected at the age of twenty-one – are no recompense for the fatigue suffered by Members of Parliament and for the disagreeably late hours chosen for parliamentary debates. How often, night after night, have we listened to the disadvantages or the advantages of the Reform Bill as it hangs in the balance, and yet we are not excused the obligation of being present in our various committee rooms at 11 a.m. sharp.'

'However, sir, I have heard that this fatigue is as much sought after as the sweetest of slumbers: I have been assured that the expense of contesting an election, and often unsuccessfully at that, may run to the substantial sum of twenty, thirty or even forty thousand pounds. If this is done out of sincere devotion to the public good, it must be admitted to be most honourable.'

'You are not mistaken as to the amounts, sir, and indeed, you fall a little short of the real figures. A few years ago, an election for the County of York was fought between the families of the FitzWilliams, the Hareswoods and the Wilberforces: it is a fact that the total amounts spent on this election, which was won by Lord FitzWilliam, surpassed the astonishing sum of ten million francs in your money. It is not unusual, therefore, in the wake of such electoral struggles, to see the fortunes of the wealthiest families encumbered for a great many years.'

When the ladies had left the table to retire to the drawing-room, we continued to talk on many subjects which were of the greatest interest to me as differing from our own habits. Thus it was that I learned that Mr. S***, who was a mere Major, would no doubt have been made Lieutenant-General, had he not, at the time of the Treaty of Amiens, decided to sell his commission as Lieutenant-Colonel for a few thousand pounds. When the war broke out again, he bought back a commission as an Ensign and started on his way up the ladder of this wearisome profession which is particularly harsh on its lower echelons. This is something of which French soldiers cannot conceive and is no doubt justified by the word 'custom', which is an answer to everything. If we had entered into a discussion on the matter, we could well have fallen into disagreement, but a servant came to tell us that coffee was waiting and we hastened to join the ladies.

During the evening there was music and the two oldest girls skilfully blended the tones of the harp and the piano whilst the youngest ones went about their handiwork with needle, brush or card. These delightful trinkets were rendered doubly precious by their intended use. 'In a few days time,' Mrs. P*** told me, 'a grand bazaar is to open and this type of work, made by a large number of the ladies of Brighton, will be on public sale in aid of the town's hospital. The stalls will be kept by the most distinguished inhabitants who, by joining fashion to charity, have reconciled two concepts which seem mutually exclusive. Thus they manage to do good, which is both their motivation and their goal.'

Next, Mrs. H*** entertained us with lengthy details on the probable financial outcome of these generous thoughts and on the advantages which would result for the sick and needy. Carried along, no doubt, by her fascinating subject, she spoke with a liveliness which revealed all the charms of her inner soul:[155] she gave herself up to a sort of febrile excitement which surprised me, for I had previously noted that English girls and young ladies take as much trouble to hide their education, their efforts and their studies and to remain silent, as ladies in every other land do to flaunt them. Young English women would not be soon forgiven for speaking up with the intention of impressing a salon audience and it would seem that they attach no importance to receiving the compliments of society. They withdraw effortlessly into this virtuous, contemplative placidity, which cannot fail to remind us that still waters run deep.

At nine o'clock, tea was served. At eleven, there was supper before the guests left. The whole of the proceedings were accompanied by music and constant conversation carried on with an easy intimacy that made the hours agreeably short. From time to time I was asked to inspect a multitude of trinkets from India and from China, all beautifully worked, some in pure gold, others in ivory or tortoiseshell; I was then shown a collection of decorative ladies' adornments from those same two lands, and finally, gold-threaded brocades embellished with silver flowers called Kinob[156] with which Indian women dress their hair; a style which has been adopted by the English ladies. The whole of this elegant souk was credited to the three absent brothers whose generous intention it was to enrich their young sisters' collection year by year.

Often in the course of my journeys, the impossibility of fully apprehending the sensations that I have felt at the sight of a painting or of a view, has evoked in me an indefinable feeling of regret. Such a situation was now upon me and I

155 AN The charitable exhibition put on by ladies of the aristocracy for distressed foreigners, is proof of the veracity of this assertion. In the exhibition there are drawings done by the Duchess of Kent and by her daughter, Princess Victoria, as well as some fine works by the Queen of Belgium. Twenty-nine ladies from the Court of Hanover have sent a worked rug for which 60 pounds sterling has already been offered; the Queen and Princesses of France and those of the royal families of Prussia and Sweden have also made contributions. *TN Princess, later Queen, Victoria was aged 8 in 1827 and still firmly under the thumb of her German mother, the Duchess of Kent.*

156 *TN This was a silk brocade made in Benares and known as kimkhab. It was usually known as kincob in Europe, but the Count seems to have misheard the Western mispronunciation.*

was near to feeling that same melancholy impression when, at midnight, I left this haven of such kind-hearted warmth; but I had had the happiness of glimpsing and of fully understanding this calm, industrious existence which nurtures unsullied affection and which leaves in its wake unvarying serenity as well as a taste for domestic pleasures that fear no rivalry from frivolous worldly distractions. So, as I took leave of this family, so kind and so close-knit as they are, I could feel content with myself once again and sanguine of my future; I felt I had found some clues as to a possible inner happiness which, in this imperfect world, we all create for ourselves and picture in our sweetest dreams.

Chapter IV

A Sunday – Religious tolerance – A Catholic church – The English Madame Maintenon – The walker and gambling – A walk on the cliffs – Dieppe and Brighton – Emmett – An episode from the Irish Revolution in 1803 – Charles Butler – Sacred music – The organ and sacred music

That a man should have a religion does not surprise me; what surprises is that he should believe himself strong enough to not have one, for without falling into the impiety of d'Alembert and calling it 'the great maybe', I would concur with Byron that 'amidst doubt, he who believes has the advantage', or as the prisoner of St. Helena[157] has said: 'religious feeling is such a consolation that it is a blessing from Heaven to possess it.' So let us worship those principles which forbid hate to endure a single day and which stipulate that love be eternal.

To Stern's most perceptively drawn cast of characters in his *Sentimental Journey* we could add the 'critical traveller': that morose spectator who travels to escape the world-weariness of his own spirits and the aridity of his own heart and who dwells endlessly upon that subject which is ... the tedium of an English Sunday. I concur that this day, given over as it is to religious observances and family gatherings, leaves little hope of amusement for the foreigner. Doubtless the austerity of conduct is in striking contrast with the disorderly distractions in Germany, Italy and France; in such countries the array of entertainment in theatres, public gardens and assembly rooms offer, in diverse forms, repose to the industrious classes at the close of their labours for the week: whereas here, the enchanting solemnity, even during a walk on the brightest of Spring days,

157 *TN Napoleon Bonaparte, imprisoned on St. Helena from 1815 until 1821.*

would appear to repel any notion of pleasure. Yet if we consider the spiritual aspect of this state, we will be convinced that it is to this inner life, to this very real piety, which is evident in all social classes, that England undoubtedly owes her prosperity. His zeal to do his duty, on religious grounds, makes the workman industrious, the manufacturer diligent and the farmer energetic. These qualities, as they are passed from generation to generation through the ages, along with the Englishman's innate integrity, secures for his children an ease which is, nearly always, its own reward, being, as they are, imbued with the same principals.

I had been warned against one particular sort of religious intolerance; not that religious intolerance sanctioned by the law of the land, but that sustained by individual prejudices: I was able to convince myself how weak the basis of these admonitions were by an event, trifling in nature, which was more conclusive for me than any homily. As I was leaving the Glocester Hotel I had asked for directions to the Catholic church; I was told it was in High-street,[158] off St James's- street. By the time I was half way along the latter, I could no longer remember the name of the former. All the shops were tightly shuttered, not only because it was Sunday, but more importantly because it was the hour at which services were held and during this time, so that one should be devoted entirely to prayer, any form of activity is forbidden upon pain of a heavy fine. I accosted a lady accompanied by a liveried attendant and asked her, as well as I could, in English, directions to the street I was seeking.

'You are, no doubt, going to the Catholic church?' said the lady.

'Indeed, and I would be most grateful to you, madam, if you could point the way to me.'

'Follow me, sir, I will take you there.'

I was in no doubt that I had found, as my guide, a fellow Roman Catholic and so I walked beside her, chatting about Brighton and about France, a country she did, however, not know.

Once we had reached the corner of High-street she said:

Go straight along here and when you reach the end of the street and see a small green door, you will have arrived.'

'I fear, madam, that from your directions, I will still have some difficulty in

158 *TN Before the opening of St. John the Baptist Church in 1837, Catholics worshipped in a chapel in High Street. This Chapel was built in 1805 but demolished in 1835. A twentieth-century block of flats stands on the site.*

finding the church, but I will, indeed, ask.'

'No, sir, that will not be necessary. I will take you there myself.'

'I do not wish, madam, to abuse your kindness.'

'Not at all. Your mass starts at ten o'clock and our service at ten thirty. I will be able to return in time.'

'So you are not Roman Catholic?'

'No, sir, I am Protestant.'

'And tolerant, madam. It is that which must be the first law of any religion.'

We had reached the door of the church and I went in after having thanked my obliging guide and, by now, in the wake of such an example, feeling better disposed to being open to the full worth of the evangelical ethic.

Despite the 'Catholic question' discussed in the introduction, Brighton has always been a very tolerant town, as Sicklemore points out:

> 'In the true spirit of universal tolerance, no civil nor political interest, ought to be blended with religious dissentions, the great unerring Deity of the universe having the capacity only of deciding who is right, and who is wrong; we have, therefore, religious edifices of various denominations, to be resorted to, as the dispositions and persuasions of parties may direct, viz.:—the Countess of Huntingdon's Connexion, in North Street; the Independents, in Union Street; the Particular Baptists, Salem Chapel, in Bond Street, and Ebenezer Chapel, in Richmond Street; Hanover Chapel, (congregational) in Church Street; the Methodists, in Dorset Gardens; the Quakers, in Ship Street; the Unitarians, in the New Road; the Huntingtonians, in Church Street, and Union Street; a Catholic Chapel, in High Street; a Synagogue, in Devonshire Place; and a Chapel belonging to Mr. Faithful, in Church Street.'

The Catholic chapel is small. I noticed that the worshipers said their prayers with a reverence and a zeal not often met with in Catholic countries. I was shown to a pew near to Colonel Stonor[159] with whom I was already acquainted and when the mass was over, we left together.

159 *TN According to the* Brighton Herald, *Lt.-Colonel Charles Stonor (1781–1834) must have made frequent visits to Brighton as he is reported as having arrived at the New Steine Hotel in Brighton on 6 October, 15 November and 24 November 1827. Lt.-Colonel Stonor was of a Catholic family which fought for the emancipations of their co-religionists.*

Ireland's Grounds are the maze-like triangular plot of land on the left of the engraving. Hanover Crescent lies just beyond the grounds, and to the left of the crescent are the six original almshouses built in 1795. The parish church of St. Nicholas stands on its hill to the extreme right of the picture and the, as-yet, un-built church of St. Peter's already figures in the valley. The area known in 1827 as Ireland's Grounds, The Royal Gardens or The Royal Cricket Ground where Sutton was walking, just north of The Level in Central Brighton, are now cover by the terrace and gardens of Park Crescent. Sicklemore describes in detail the Royal or Ireland's Pleasure Grounds:

The following is a faint outline of these beautiful and extensive pleasure grounds: two handsome lodges conduct to the cricket ground, at the upper end of which is an excellent bowling green, with raised banks, and a billiard room with a colonnade and rustic seats in front. At the lower end, beyond the fence of the grounds, and totally separate from them, is an excellent range of stabling and other accommodations. Proceeding across the cricket ground, you reach the tea-gardens, at the entrance of which is a commodious bar, with dressing rooms, &c. and over these is an elegant promenade room, thirty feet by eighty. Immediately on entering the gardens, is a second bowling green, somewhat smaller than the first, surrounded by a beautiful lawn and tea boxes; on one side, at a short distance, is a grotto, and on the other an aviary, in which are tea boxes, &c. At the farther extremity of the gardens is a canal, across which a neatly constructed bridge leads to a battery with six pieces of cannon, beyond which is a maze (an improvement upon the plans of those at Hampton Court and Bath) in the centre of which is a Merling swing, &c. The gardens are admirably well laid out, and do great credit to the proprietor, Mr. Ireland. They are under the immediate patronage of His Majesty; and will, we doubt not, become the favorite resort of our fashionable population.

Image reproduced by kind permission of Brighton Royal Pavilion, Museums and Libraries

The weather was superb and he proposed accompanying me to the *Royal cricket-ground* to see a most strange event: a man called Sutton had wagered several hundred guineas that he would walk twelve hundred miles in twelve hundred consecutive hours. On the way, I asked the Colonel about the lady who had heard mass in a side chapel of the church and whose fine, regular features betrayed the remnants of a great beauty.

'That lady was Mrs. FitzHerbert, the English Madame de Maintenon,'[160] he told me. 'The regularity of her features in advanced age, her exemplary piety, the excellence of her personal qualities and the marriage she contracted with the king in his youth, despite such marriage being invalid and unacknowledged – like that of your famous marquise – also make her appear very much like mademoiselle d'Aubigby:[161] however she is, in every respect, worthy of the high regard in which the King holds her and the affection which he entertains for her. As you will no doubt be introduced to her, you will find that I do not in the least exaggerate my high opinion of her.'

We arrived at the grounds where Sutton was performing his feat: the course measured one mile round and we saw him cover the distance twice within forty minutes. He then rested for the remainder of the two hours. He was to continue this same trajectory night and day for fifty times twenty-four hours. He had started almost a month previously and appeared to be suffering very little fatigue; on the other hand, the adjudicators of the wager, who were taking it in turns to accompany him, looked like two ghosts. Sutton told us he was certain to win the challenge, having already covered the same distance in the same number of hours in Milton, near Portsmouth in 1822.[162]

England is not the only country in which one sees these eccentric wagers,

---

160 AN In identifying Mrs. FitzHerbert with Madame de Maintenon, the comparison can be made only in relation to their lives within society: everyone is of the opinion that Mrs. FitzHerbert has as much warmth, as much kindness and as much real integrity as our famous Marquise suffered from selfishness and a hard heart: both now are consigned to history which has judged them.

161 *TN Lt-Colonel Stonor was presumably no expert on seventeenth-century France. Even Maria Fitzherbert's enemies would be unlikely to compare her to Julie d'Aubigny (1670–1707). Mademoiselle d'Aubigny (or Maupin) was an outrageous brawler, swordswoman, actress, serial adulteress, opera singer, lesbian and duellist. A far cry from the staid Mrs. Fitzherbert of the late 1820s.*

162 *TN Richard Sutton was challenged to walk 1200 miles in 1200 successive hours for a purse of 100 sovereigns. His walk started on 29 October 1827. It finished on 18 December 1827. Despite surmounting dreadful winds and rain; swollen legs and hecklers; a small audience and pitiful donations, on 22 December the* Brighton Herald *records the end of the event with these few words:*

'Sutton completed his task of walking 1200 miles in 1200 successive hours on Tuesday last, – at least, so it is said, and, certainly, we are not competent to prove the contrary, not do we presume to doubt the fact.'

Richard Sutton appears to be completely absent from the record books. See article in Appendix A.

so different from our own way of going on; I told the Colonel the amusing yet extraordinary story of a cleric from Kaminiek in Podolia who had the reputation of being the heaviest drinker in Poland. Count Potocki had bet that this cleric would empty, in one draft, a large glass containing four bottles of Tokay wine; and the Count won the bet, which was for four thousand ducats.

'Why were you not anxious that you would make your friend lose his wager?' the intrepid cleric was asked.

'I knew I could do it,' he replied, 'I had practised before dinner.'

'My word,' said the Colonel, 'if that cleric had been Shakespeare's Clarence, he would have emptied his butt of Malmsey instead of drowning in it.' But the Colonel did not seem at all surprised. Being English, he was accustomed to such things, and he then read me an article from that morning's newspaper in which a certain man named Skipper had won a rather similar bet to Sutton's. He had wagered that he could walk fifty miles a day for ten consecutive days by walking just thirteen hours a day.

As we left the grounds, the Colonel pointed out to me a well which, like so many others in Brighton, fills up at low tide and runs dry at high tide: this was a geological conundrum which neither he nor I could solve: we simply marvelled without comment. From there we walked to the cliffs which stretch out over a distance of several miles along the coast: nothing could more resemble one of the dazzling esplanades of a European capital: there was a crowd of carriages, elegantly mounted riders and fastidiously dressed strollers thronging the space as if it were a holiday: barouches, gigs and phaetons were interspersed with a large number of those quite common little carriages called *flys* and which have no merit other than that of being extremely light. These *flys* appear to be peculiar to Brighton. They can be hired, like any other conveyance, by the hour or by the trip and at moderate prices. They are so much in vogue that they always find takers.

A few days previously I had left Dieppe at the height of the season: the bathing had attracted a select and numerous public; there were frequent social gatherings, and although such pursuits seemed to be permitted to the leisured classes alone, I could not prevent myself from placing side by side the scenes taking place along these two shores separated by no more than a narrow stretch of sea: on the one side, an occasional carriage; a few grandly dressed ladies sheltering beneath their umbrellas on their way to the ball; in Brighton I saw a picture of luxury which more than justifies the articles published in France about English opulence, and which are so well founded that one could not possibly apply to it the Italian proverb which so well depicts the strange affinity between luxury and poverty:

Tira la carozza coi denti[163]

As the Colonel was taking his leave, he invited me to dine with him.

'I would be glad to accept,' I replied, 'but this evening I must be at Lady Holland's by nine o'clock and I fear I would have to leave you unacceptably early.'

'I am offering you no more than a family dinner,' he told me, 'at which you will not have what we English call *plenty* but where you will have what you would call in good French '*not too much*' and afterwards you will be free to act as you wish.'

I accepted and we parted at the far end of the promenade where I found the Misses O'Brien, whom I approached.

'I have here for you, sir,' said the elder lady, 'the stanzas of Mr. Moore's ballad which you wish to translate into French: but perhaps you are not aware of the tale which gave rise to the song.'

'Indeed I am not, madam, and knowing the tale would doubtless aid me to discern the composer's thoughts.'

'Although most interesting, the story is quite short, and I shall tell it to you.'

We went to sit on one of the circular benches on the promenade and there she started her account with these words:

'During the troubles in Ireland, young Robert Emmett[164] was accused of high treason and condemned to death: his punishment made a very great impression on the minds of the people, for he possessed in great measure the attributes that are the most admired: courage, modesty, elegant manners and natural talent, all much enhanced by his experiences gleaned from extensive travel; but you are right to say, sir, that genius is often no blessing! He stood before his judges with all his noble virtues clear to see and, indignant to his core, rejecting the very idea of the crime that he was supposed to have committed: that of having betrayed his country. His deathless words, when the sentence was handed down, moved even his enemies, and older and wiser heads indulgently showed compassion for the fate of a young man whose only mistake was perhaps, after all, to be honourable.

'But how can I describe the anguish of the young girl whose love he had won?

163 *TN 'To pull the carriage with your teeth,' Italian proverb implying that poverty and wealth often go hand in hand.*

164 *TN Robert Emmet (1778–1803) Irish poet and patriot, was hung, drawn and quartered in Dublin. He was the last person to receive such a punishment from a British court of law. Thomas Moore had become a close friend of Emmet when they were both students at Trinity College, Dublin in 1795. Moore had tried to dissuade Emmet from becoming too involved in political activities. Once again, La Garde's spelling differs from the correct version.*

Sarah Curran,[165] the daughter of one of the most famous orators in Ireland, loved him as one loves only once in a lifetime.

'Richard Curran, her brother, had been educated with Emmett at Trinity College. After having travelled in Switzerland and France, Emmett returned to his country in 1802 where he renewed his friendship with Richard, his childhood companion and fellow student: his visits to the home of Sarah's father became more frequent and the enthusiasm which the young man inspired in the brother was not long in stirring the sister. Robert loved Sarah and, far from fearing the idea of making her party to his audacious plans, believed he would prove himself to be more worthy of her by sharing them with her. Imagine her alarm! Emmett was going to endeavour to win back Ireland's independence from the thrall of the English. He was counting on an incursion by French troops and believed that a popular uprising would guarantee the success of his venture.

'Nothing could have been more daring and nothing could have been more implausible than his plan: to confide in the daughter of a man who had sworn allegiance to the British government was, maybe, to expect too much of her. Aghast, Sarah wrote several admirable letters, each one full of spirit and good sense, to her lover in an attempt to counter his determination: she pointed out the chances of success and of setbacks; anxiously she drew his attention to the dangers of such an undertaking. Alas! her conjectures were only too correct: the insurrection lasted a mere three hours and no more than a handful of solders was required to repress it: all Emmett's plans came to no more than that. He managed, however, to escape detection and hid in the Dublin home of a faithful friend; it was from this hiding place that he wrote to Sarah one last time, begging her yet again to follow him: "I am waiting for you and you alone," he told her. "The boat which is to take me to America is in the offing and is leaving tomorrow; come, restore to me my life and my happiness." The unfortunate girl, convinced that Emmett would leave without her, replied that her duty obliged her to stay with her father. In despair, Emmett voluntarily gave himself up to the authorities!

'Emmett saw his good name dishonoured; he sank under the weight of the charges brought against him, withered in the face of that rejection which befalls, more than on any others, the victims of a political deed. It was Sarah alone, with more vigour than ever, who took up the cause of her ill-fated lover.'

165 *TN Sarah Curran (1782–1808).*

'Ah, my dear young lady,' I exclaimed, 'it is but women who will never forsake those who are unfortunate: nature has filled their souls with so much love and so much compassion that they have every appearance of being the guardian angels between man and misfortune. Pray continue. I find your story most interesting.'

'No sooner had an ignoble death put an end to Emmett's days, than Sarah's passion became inflamed by the horror of such a fate, and there was nothing which could temper the grief of eternal separation! Banished by her father, who had disapproved of her love, she was obliged to accept the shelter afforded her by Mr. Cowper Penrose and his family. In vain, generous, tactful friends paid her the most considerate attentions; all efforts to moderate her suffering were of no avail. Her distress, as calm as it was deep, permitted of no outward expression; she listened to her heart alone and was turned to ice. A solitary figure amidst the most sparkling galas, to which her friends occasionally managed to tempt her, she appeared to be as lonely as if in the wastelands of the desert; in vain, society laid before her its seductive pleasures; friendship itself was impotent against her incurable malady. Should one risk a question to her? No; for this would lead merely to silence and tears; if, on occasion, she succumbed to the inquisitor, she would utter a few words left to flutter to the ground like dying leaves which had, until that moment, clung to the branches of a uprooted tree. A mutual friend mentioned that he had seen her at a ball in Dublin, where she had created a most poignant impression: at the time she was twenty years old; her beauty was chaste and austere; her figure slim and pliant; her large, black eyes and her sorrowful, piercing gaze revealed an impressive sensibility; her pale complexion lent to her regular features that appeal which will always spring from passion or suffering. Sad and wistful, she would wander like a shadow come to spread gloom at the banquet; her demeanour and her manner revealed the effort which she made to overcome her anguish and forget for an instant her memories; but, as a famous woman once so rightly said: "what tortures us to death is tomorrow's suffering heaped onto yesterday's pain".

'Having drifted though the sumptuous rooms in which the brightness of a thousand candles rivalled that of daytime, she would come to sit on the steps of the musicians' podium: there, as lonely as if she had been on the steep ocean shore, in the confusion of her troubled reason, she would sing a few verses of an Irish song, the naïve, touching expression in her voice drawing tears from the guests in the midst their pleasure, whilst others, who at first seemed to have gathered around her out of curiosity, appeared to turn scornfully from her; for there are certain sorrows that the common mortal cannot comprehend; they prefer to look away than to attempt to assuage them.

'Yet her pain could not but be sincerely felt and shared in a country where compassion is so robust and so prevalent: a gallant young officer, Colonel S***,[166] much taken by such a rare steadfastness and who believed that a soul so devoted to a memory would be more capable of love than any other, offered her his hand, seeking not her love but her respect, not her affection but her friendship: at first she refused the proposal, despite the honourable intentions, which she fully appreciated, in order to remain faithful to the tomb containing the relics of her only love. At last, her position became daily more and more difficult; having no support and no protection and existing entirely on the generosity of her friends, the virtuous, tender-hearted girl finally submitted to their entreaties; touched by Colonel S***'s noble conduct, she consented to take his name and walk through life in his safe keeping.

'Hardly had her husband reconciled her with her father, than he took her to Sicily, in the hope that new horizons and new sights would banish from her memory the recurring image of her unprecedented misfortune: but all his efforts were in vain: *sorrow is a sickness of the heart; sister to a sickness of the body; these two twins are rarely long separated*. This young flower, which the winds of passion had wilted, withered rapidly: by day, forcing herself to smile upon her husband and to deceive him with a semblance of happiness, the forlorn girl concealed her despair in feigned gaiety; and thus were serene days so often purchased at the cost of tear-stained nights! Finally, having only just reached Palermo, she rejected life and, victim to the most ill-fated of passions, sunk into her grave at the age of twenty-one.

'It is upon this sad story that Mr. Moore, a friend of the family, composed his ballad at just the time when the poor girl was leaving for Sicily: that her heart was incapable of a merely fleeting passion, is borne out by her life and her death.'

She is Far from the Land

She is far from the land, where her young hero sleeps,
And lovers are round her, sighing;
But coldly she turns from their gaze, and weeps,
For her heart in his grave is lying!
She sings the wild song of her dear native plains,
Every note which he lov'd awaking

166 *TN Captain Sturgeon of the Royal Engineers.*

Ah! little they think, who delight in her strains,
How the heart of the Minstrel is breaking!
THOMAS MOORE, early nineteenth century

It was with gratitude that I received from Miss O'Brien these verses, so touching in their evocation and their phrasing. I cannot flatter myself that I have managed to reproduce the melancholy elegance of these '*melodious tears*', but the intentions of the author will, I hope, be clear.

I took leave of Miss O'Brien, and went to my engagement with Colonel Stonor. He introduced me to his father-in-law, Mr. Charles Butler,[167] one of the most distinguished lawyers in England and a jurist of some thirty years standing who has tirelessly devoted his talents and his efforts to rehabilitating the Catholics. Soon, dinner was served: before we took our seats, the meal was blessed.[168] In the midst of this family feast, Mr. Butler had the air of one who has maintained the status of patriarch as in days of old; he was a skilful raconteur and his long career had provided him with many anecdotes, so rightly called 'the wit of our elders', that one never tired of listening to him. His arguments, when speaking of the Catholic question, were so very logical that I could no longer doubt that the matter would one day be resolved, to the furtherance of equity, morality and reason.[169]

At table there was a Mr. Parr who, so I was told, was a descendent of Thomas Parr, the English Nestor, who had lived for one hundred and fifty-three years and who, during his long life, had lived though ten reigns from Edward IV to Charles I.

'It was the wish of Parliament,' Mr. Stonor told me, 'that this man, having been spared for so long by the passage of Time, be buried in Westminster alongside the other great men and women of our nation.' A toast was drunk to Mr. Parr which, naturally, bade him emulate his ancestor.

---

167 *TN Charles Butler (1750–1832). When, after the passing of the Catholic Relief Act of 1791, he took silk, he was the first Catholic to be able to do so in over 100 years.*

168 AN In every English family, there is a blessing before everyone sits down and grace is said at the end of the meal: where there is no clergyman present, it is the head of the family who performs the ritual.

169 AN So much consistent effort has reaped its reward: the emancipation of the Catholics, which Mr. Canning had not lived to see, was authorised during the tenure of the Duke of Wellington, and this was the first stage in a political reform which had been so ardently desired and finally obtained. Thus, within a few years, England will benefit from the last remaining elements of those noble and impressive ideals which philanthropy brings about day by day: thus, a monstrous inequality between citizens of the same land has disappeared. The time will soon come, no doubt, when the English will be able to take control of a yet another form of freedom; as soon as the clergy, which holds property worth in excess of five thousand million, has been compelled to return to its original, humble vocation, the children of industry will be able to benefit from this freedom; and then we will truly be able to call the reform 'liberty'.

After dinner, as both dancing and other pleasures were forbidden on a Sunday, it was thought that a little music would do no harm. There were a few pieces by the famous Handel, who is so admired by the English that, in this country, you dare not doubt his genius any more than you would that of Shakespeare. When the pieces were sung by the pure, melodious voices of the Misses H*** they seemed to me imbued with an earnest, solemn harmony which is well suited to this kind of composition. The songs were accompanied by a rather large organ, one of the jewels of the household. I know of no other instrument whose tones are in better harmony with the human voice; there is something gentle, something solid yet vibrant about it and I am surprised that secular music distains the benefits the organ could lend it. It was then that I understood the keen interest which, in Holy Week, drove the whole of Parisian fashionable society to the Abbey at Longchamp to hear the sweet voices of the nuns, accompanied by the sounds of this magical instrument, as they sang the praises of the Lord. These cadences, in such a place and on such a day, must have spoken to the imagination as well as to the heart.

The Colonel reminded me that I was expected at Lord Holland's house; it was with regret that I left this family gathering and took a *fly* pulled by a burly man. Such forms of transport have long been forgotten in France; but whereas the English have made giant strides in industry and in the sciences, it seems to me that they are stagnating in many of their local customs. And so it is that, here, I have come across sedan chairs and two wheeled *flys*, conveyances unknown to us at home except by hearsay.

Chapter V

Lady Holland – The Duke of Bedford – Politics – A glimpse of the North and the Orient – Mr. Fox and Lady Holland in Paris during the Consulate – Madame Récamier – The Duchess d'Abrantès – The servant and the letter – An invitation to the country – Sea bathing – The new districts of Brighton – The Squares – The lay-out of houses – A Gypsy encampment – The fortune-teller – Glees – An evening at the theatre – Madame Vestris

On reaching Lord Holland's house, I found there were very few guests, despite it being nine o'clock, but Sir Robert, with his unfailing tact, had arrived before me.

His Lordship greeted me with his accustomed cordiality and introduced me to her Ladyship who was an old acquaintance. Slowly the drawing room began to fill; the conversations became more interesting. For a moment I could almost have believed myself to be in Madame Geoffrin's[170] salon.

Seated in a rather tall armchair to the right of the fireplace, Lady Holland received the compliments that her guests were eager to pay her. In my mind's eye I could see her at the height of her stunning beauty, as I had last seen her twenty years previously when, at the time of the Consulate,[171] she had come to Paris with her uncle Mr. Fox,[172] and the dazzling charm of the great man's name had cast some of its light on the niece. Even these many years later, her regular features

---

170 AN It was to this lady that, having won all the votes of the Polish diet, Poniatowski said: 'Mama, your son is king.' *TN Marie Thérèse Rodet Geoffrin (1699–1777) took on the role of mother and mentor to many of her illustrious guests.*

171 *TN Napoleon Bonaparte was First Consul of France between 1799 and 1804. He was crowned Emperor on 2 December 1804.*

172 *TN By the time of the beginning of the French consulate, Elizabeth, Lady Holland had already been married to Lord Henry for two years. Her time in France was spent either with her husband or her husband's uncle, but not her own uncle.*

still gave her face that noble and expressive appearance which, in England, nearly always supplants the grace and bloom of youth.

Near her was the Duke of Bedford, heir to a family famous for its liberal principles and the concern it has always shown for the glory and the prosperity of its country; when I was introduced by Lord Holland, the duke, who seems to have appreciated that an affable manner is one of the duties entailed upon the noble name he bears, acknowledged me most cordially. I had known his duchess as a very young woman when she was travelling with her mother, Lady Gordon; Lady Georgiana's elegant manners and her ravishing beauty had captivated Paris. I asked after Lady Georgiana, but the duke replied that she was not in Brighton at present but that he was expecting her within a few days.

> *The Duchess of Bedford (1781–1853) was born Georgiana Gordon. She was the duke's second wife and bore him 10 children. It is said that her beauty also captured the artist Sir Edward Landseer who was reputedly her lover for some 20 years during Georgiana's happy marriage to the Duke of Bedford.*
>
> *The son of the duke and duchess, Lord Charles James Fox Russell (1809–94) is also in the room. At the age of just 20, in this year of 1827, his main claim to fame was his election to the M.C.C. Lord Charles was an ardent cricketer throughout his life.*

To the left of the fireplace were Messrs Baring, de M***on and Labouchère[173] as well as Sir Robert, young Lord Charles Russell, Admiral Sir Edward H***[174] and a few other guests whose names I do not recall. In the centre of the room there was a table laden with books, albums and engravings around which several people had gathered, amongst others Miss Fox[175] the daughter of Lord Holland, and Miss Russell, the Duke of Bedford's niece. Our conversation soon took on the intimate

173 *TN It is not clear if this is a reference to the Whig politician Henry Labouchère, 1st Baron Taunton (1798–1869) or his father, the banker Pierre César Labouchère (1772–1839). Either man would have felt very much at home in this gathering of Protestant Whig financiers. Pierre César had married Sir Francis Baring's third daughter, Dorothy. Pierre César was therefore the brother-in-law of the Baring brothers, Henry was their nephew.*

174 *TN Admiral Sir Edward Hamilton (1772–1851). Sir Edward had made his name in 1799 by having, in a daring naval action, recaptured* HMS Hermione *from the Spanish. The vessel had fallen into the hands of the enemy only because the crew had mutinied and murdered their Captain in the previous weeks. The young Edward Hamilton was seriously wounded in the skirmish, but went on to serve along the North French coast during the Napoleonic wars. As his career declined, he became the master of the Royal Yacht. By 1827 he would have been living in retirement.*

175 *TN The Hon. Mary Elizabeth Fox (1806–91).*

tone that had been familiar to us in the witty banter of Paris salon society, but where, however, the tradition is now barely kept up since politics and card-playing have infested every drawing room.

Señor Mauri, a Spanish author who has lived for many years in France, had just sent Lord Holland a translation into French of the finest Spanish poetry. It was perhaps somewhat bold of a foreigner to publish his own French translations in Paris, for notwithstanding Madame de Staël's adage, 'Nothing is more difficult, or more easy, than writing French poetry,' Señor Mauri's talent has enabled him to slip skilfully between these two pitfalls and has condoned his strange manner of creating poetry: his translation of a Lope de Vega satire on pride, which Lord Holland read to us, seemed to be written with elegance and flair.

'The Spanish poet is right,' said Lady Holland, 'we too often confuse pride and self-respect: *pride is offensive, self-respect is defensive*; they are two very different emotions.'

Lord Holland merited Señor Mauri's homage and is quite capable of appreciating the worth of the Spaniard's work, for his lordship is well versed in Spanish literature which is too little known nowadays: His Lordship, too, has translated several plays and has published a monograph on the life and the writings of Lope de Vega. Monsieur de M***on, who as a figure in the ever changing magic lantern that was the salon of M. de Talleyrand and who was such a good judge of men and things, pointed out the contrasts between some of the recent anecdotes based on Parisian society and other tales from times past. Having the gift of being able to perceive and to reproduce the ridiculous with lively irony, M. de M***on then went on to sketch, in the brightest and most vivid colours, the biographies of the many highly influential people in Europe whose careers he had seen from beginning to end: his manner of speaking justified perfectly Lord Holland's assertion: 'I maintain that your Memoirs would be the least overstated and the most amusing of our times'

As might have been expected, the conversation moved rapidly from this light-hearted, amusing trivia to the increasingly significant topic of the day: the battle of Navarino. According to rumour, the Greek cause, which has until now been so poorly served, was about to gain renewed strength. It was generally agreed that the harsh but valuable lesson meted out by our forces to the Ottoman and Egyptian navies, would put an end to the shameful excesses of the Turks in the

Levant; it was this which would usher in a new era of independence and grandeur for Greece. Admiral Sir Edward did not share this hypothesis, having recently returned from that country and seen it abandoned by the majority of those very foreigners who had rushed to its aid in a fit of fervent nostalgia or philanthropy.

'We will never,' he said, 'make anything other than brigands or pirates out of this race which has been sapped of its energy; it is bloodthirsty but lacks courage, conceited but lacks national pride; no sooner will the Greeks have been freed from their oppressors than they will destroy each other, thus possibly avenging the Turks better than could the Turks themselves by slaughtering them.'

Sir Robert cut in to defend Greece.

'Do not visit upon a whole population,' he said, 'the mistakes of a few individuals; if in the long run, their national character has become perverted, you must attribute it to nothing other than the state of subservience in which they find themselves and the senseless domination to which they are subjected by the Ottomans: allow this victory to bear its fruit; then you will see Greece adopt an attitude worthy of her noble origins. Have not all the major powers become hoarse in exhorting the Turks to return to a system of government more suited to modern-day European civilisation? And since the voice of reason has not been heeded, we have had to have recourse to the gun, the ultimate argument of kings.'

'This supports the opinion of Henry IV,' said Sir Edward. '"*Unjust measures prove only strength, not right.*" But in the end, Time, our master, whose lessons we dare not challenge, will show us the advantage to be gained from this insurrection, both for them and for England. In politics, we have long seen that established power grants legitimacy: why did Mahmut[176] not consider the Greek provinces as an integral part of his empire? Do we have any more reason to intervene in his way of ruling than he would himself if, as leader of a million Orientals, he had asked Russia and Prussia by what right they had eradicated Poland from its place amongst the nations; if he had asked Austria how it came to own a part of Italy and on what grounds it had taken possession of Venice; if he had asked Piedmont who had given it Genoa, if he had asked Holland how it had acquired the Low Countries? The Sultan's reply would be simple: "the right of conquest". And what

176 TN. *Mahmut II (1785–1839). Mahmut was an enlightened Sultan of the Ottoman Empire from 1807 until his death. It was, however, during his reign that both Greece and Egypt fought against him and eventually regained their independence from the Empire.*

would Europe say if Mahmut insisted on seeing Gustavus-Adolphus IV[177] back on the Swedish throne and Saxony back in his fiefdom. Moreover, is it not true that the Ottoman Porte[178] has always been a faithful ally of England?'

'That is a mistake,' said Lord Holland, 'which, by dint of repetition, has become practically axiomatic; but it will not be difficult to override it and give it the lie.'[179]

'And yet,' the Admiral went on, 'in the end, would it not be better for us if it were the Ottomans in the Dardanelles rather than the Russians? Already you can see this northern colossus bearing down on Europe with the combined weight of its fifty-two provinces, most of which are as mighty as a kingdom and have an inexhaustible supply of weapons scattered across their territories; it can be rallied at the slightest call from just one of them, and so quickly that in 1812, Count de Witt, the lieutenant-general commanding the Caucuses[180] was able to muster, not from across the Ukraine, but exclusively from the estate belonging to his mother, Countess Potocka,[181] four regiments of Cossacks, each numbering one thousand men, armed, mounted and sufficiently trained to go into action, and all within six weeks. Even now you can see this mighty power, master of the vast Black Sea basin and of a land where there is an abundance of everything needed to fit out and maintain a navy, sending fleets through the straits of the Bosphorus, with sailors who know nothing of discouragement in defeat and who will echo the words of Peter the Great when speaking of the forces of Charles XII:[182] "By fighting us, they will teach us to conquer them". Inured as they are to everything and impervious to fatigue by their life of hard work and the rigours of the climate, the Russian people will soon become as good sailors as they are soldiers, the determination of the Tsar will see to that: they lacked only stern masters and now they have such men who have learned from Codrington. The ingenious Algarotti used to say that St. Petersburg was the window through which Russia constantly watched Europe; I repeat,

177 TN *Gustavus-Adolphus IV (1778–1837) King of Sweden 1792–1809. Gustavus was deposed by his own troops and succeeded by his uncle, Charles XIII.*

178 TN *A nineteenth-century way of referring to the Ottoman Empire (1299–1923).*

179 AN It was precisely this which Lord Holland's eloquent speech in the House of Lords proved, irrefutably.
TN *In reply to the King's Speech, Hansard reported on 29 January 1828 that Lord Holland had agreed that there was an alliance with the Ottoman Porte but that it was not 'ancient' but rather 'short lived in its duration'. La Garde would have been in London at the time of this speech and would have seen it reported in the newspapers.*

180 AN At present, he is Governor of Warsaw.

181 TN *Greek born Zophia Potocka (1760–1822) had first married Count Joseph Witt. They had two sons, Jan and Kornel. She later married the Polish count Potocki. See Translator's Introduction.*

182 TN *Charles XII of Sweden 1697–1718 was an arch enemy and contemporary of Tsar Peter I of Russia (1672–1725).*

it is preferable for St. Petersburg to be that distant window rather than Constantinople.'

'And yet,' Sir Robert broke in, 'is it not shameful for Europe to suffer the finest parts of her territory to be occupied by barbarians who have neither laws nor principles.'

'But who have their faith,' the Admiral intervened. 'For more than a century now we have been demanding that the Turks be expelled: well, what will happen to those Turks seeking refuge when their lands are laid waste and overrun by Cossacks and Bashkirs; how could Russia then be said to have served Europe? It is not the territorial, but the moral subjugation of Turkey that must concern us: it is her flawed civilisation that must be attacked by instilling a taste for the arts and the sciences: but in truth, does not the strange coalition of the three powers easily call to mind the fable of the 'Oyster and the Lawyer':[183] France and England will have the shell but Russia will swallow the oyster. As for the costs of the trial, yet again, it will be we who cross the judge's palm with silver. Napoleon said: "I could have shared the Turkish Empire with Russia; Constantinople was the great aggravation, the real rub, the city would have given Russia the advantage; she wanted it and I dared not grant it to her; it was far too precious a key and it alone was worth an empire. He who holds Constantinople can rule the world."'

'And you, sir,' Sir Robert turned to me, 'who have lived so long in Russia, may I ask you your opinion of the situation?'

'Such a conundrum, posed in the presence of such arbiters, is not easy to resolve, Sir Robert. The best reply would undoubtedly be Montaigne's "*What do I know?*" But it is true that I have had occasion to judge Russia's policies: as a young man, my position in St. Petersburg brought me into contact with a few of the statesmen who are today its leaders. However, a question so complex would demand such a lengthy exposition that I would, no doubt, weary your patience. Although there is much that is accurate in what Sir Edward has laid before us, his alarming predictions must, I think, be tempered by taking into consideration the moral fibre of Nicholas I:[184] he has been imbued with that system of moderation taught him by the brother who raised him; when there is an attack, his impulsive judgement on the outcome might not be sanctioned by everyone. As things

---

183 *TN In Aesop's fable, the result of a dispute was that the two warring parties each obtained one half of the oyster's shell. The lawyer earned the flesh of the oyster ... and the pearl.*

184 *TN Nicholas I of Russia (1796–1855) had acceded to the throne in 1825.*

stand, Napoleon's prediction on St. Helena that "within ten years, Europe will be republican or Cossack" is far from coming true. It seems to me that, at present, Russia is asking the powers to allow her to take the step, which she promises will be the last, and she declares that, having achieved her aim, she will have no further intentions other than to enjoy peace and to assist others to enjoy it. If we look at the consequences ...'

'Ah! as to the consequences,' broke in Sir Edward, 'it is not so much the consequences which worry these gentlemen from the North; they know full well from experience that no-one will be tempted to venture onto their territory in order to request explanations or reparations. To reassure them that there was little chance of invasion, as if knowing that the result of Darius'[185] expedition, or the war waged by Charles XII were not enough, Napoleon has recently proved that all the might of Europe would shatter if opposed to their icy ramparts or would be blown to dust beneath their steely skies.'

At the conclusion of our discussion, I made my way to Lady Holland's side; we spoke of Paris: her conversation and our mutual memories turned my mind to gentler thoughts. I reminded her of the supper Madame Récamier had held for her after the Peace of Amiens[186] at the Chateau of Raincy, which, at the time, was in the hands of Monsieur Ouvrard:[187] our thoughts returned to those illustrious guests who had ennobled the festivities with their names and their fame. Every one of them had come in all their finery; amongst the women who, with My Lady Holland and our charming hostess, adorned this extraordinary evening I recalled Madame Marmont, Madame Roger, Mademoiselle de Sivrieux (now Madame Michel), the Marchioness de Visconti, Princess d'Olgorouki and Madame Divoff: the beauty of all these ladies recalled one of the most brilliant periods in Parisian life. Amongst the men there were Berthier, Junot,[188] Eugène

185 TN *In the fifth century BC, the Russians had repelled an invasion by the Persian armies of Darius I. At the beginning of the eighteenth century AD, Charles XII of Sweden had attempted much the same feat and suffered much the same fate.*

186 TN *The Peace of Amiens of 1802, between England and France, lasted less than one year. Madame Récamier would have been 25 years old, La Garde in his very early 20s at this time which was one of the most glittering and optimistic of the early nineteenth century in France.*

187 TN *Gabriel-Julien Ouvrard (1770–1846) was a highly successful financier despite attempts by various French regimes to discredit him. He was finally bankrupted towards the end of his life, seemingly through no fault of his own, and died penniless.*

188 TN *General Jean-Andoche Junot (1771–1813) fought in the Napoleonic troops and was awarded the title, Duke of Abrantès. It is to his wife, the duchess, that La Garde dedicated his book on Brighton.*

Julie Récamier could never resist a chaise longue. The 'abbaye' is somewhat more luxurious than the name would imply – no nun's cell for the lady. Julie Récamier retired to the Abbaye-aux-Bois in 1819. In this portrait, she would have been between forty-two and fifty years old.
© RMN-Grand Palais (Musée du Louvre)

Beauharnais,[189] Moreau and several Ambassadors: the Marquis de Luchesini, Count de Cobentzel, Monsieur de Marcoff, Lord Erskine (later the Chancellor of England); Mr. Adair was also there, as was, above all, Mr. Fox, for whom My Lady entertained a strong feeling of tenderness and admiration. Lady Holland talked to me most vivaciously about Madame Récamier and asked me if I had recent news of her. I replied that I had left her only a few day previously, that she was living in the Abbaye-aux-Bois and enjoyed a reputation which had the rare honour of surviving, unsullied, our troubled times.

'When I recently passed through Paris,' added Lady Holland, 'she was so painfully afflicted by the death of her friend, the Duke of Montmorency, that I was not able to see her. I found out, however, that in all other respects, she was happy.'

189 *TN Eugène Rose de Beauharnais (1781–1824), son of Josephine de Beauharnais by her first marriage. In 1806 Eugène was adopted by his step-father, Napoleon Bonaparte. Eugène was an able soldier and received many titles and honours during Napoleon's reign.*

'Yes, My Lady. She has borne a most strange reversal of fortune without complaint; but in the wake of such a successful life, she has, and justly so, acquired the most desirably form of fame for a woman, that of a blameless existence; a fame that is generous as it requires no generosity: her beauty has brought her homage from across Europe; despite all the fevered excitement of her life, she has never turned her back on an unhappy man and today, now that she has lost everything, her noble and touching qualities have allowed her to retain all those friends who held her dear in her more affluent days, and if it is happiness to be loved, what woman could think herself more happy.'

'We can only regret,' continued Lady Holland, 'that her handsome face was the one attribute, however frivolous, on which her reputation rested; the wider world accords us but one pedestal for our fame; it will lavish its praises on but one sparkling feature; had Madame Récamier not been beautiful, it would have been her judgement and keen wit which would have been universally admired: there is not one person in the world who can listen as she; she feels and she understands everything. Remember me to her, and assure her, when you write to her, that not all her true friends are in Paris.'

During our conversation, Lady Holland asked me where Madame Junot was at present.

'She too, lives in the Abbaye-aux-Bois,'[190] I was able to tell her. 'It is a refuge open to all afflictions, a safe haven for all wrecked vessels and gathers to itself many an example of touching resignation and true piety.'

'Her husband was the governor of Paris[191] at the time of the Peace of Amiens, and we have not forgotten his wife's consideration for us, nor Junot's resistance to the orders of the First Consul, which was to lock up all the English residents of Paris as soon as war was declared.'

'The Duchess of Abrantès,' I said, 'also endures, most nobly and philosophically, the loss of high position as far as her wealth is concerned, but she is striving to replace it with one of good reputation by arranging the large number of papers she possesses and which record the events which she has witnessed. It is said that she is going to publish all these authentic documents as her *Memoirs*;[192] this will shed

190 *TN Laure Junot was to die at the Abbaye-aux-Bois in June 1832.*

191 *TN Junot had been Governor of Paris for a short time in 1806, not 1802. Lady Holland is living rather a long time in the past. Her memory does not seem too secure.*

192 *TN The Memoirs of the Duchess eventually ran to eight volumes. They were published in 1832. She also published six volumes of her 'Histoire de salons de Paris' as well as four other volumes of memoirs and several novels.*

a new light on the life of our Alexander for whom her husband played the role of Parmenion.[193] In conjunction with the events of her own life, these illustrious pages, written in the fluid, elegant, often energetic style that her friends so admire, will bring her a renown which may well compensate for all the brilliance of her former distinction.'

'At the time when I knew her,' Lady Holland continued, 'Madame Junot had all the talents given by a polished education. I have seen few women possess so many aptitudes and yet take so little advantage of them: when I was acquainted with her she had not yet become an authoress, but she had all the qualities necessary to become one; wit, imagination, sensitivity. I will read her memoirs with much interest as soon as they are published.'

The inevitable Chinese beverage was then served, along with ices, sorbets and a wide variety of fruits. During this interval, a page-boy brought My Lady a letter which he held out to her on a silver-gilt tray.

'Here we have a deferential custom which is most commonly practised in England,' Monsieur de M*** quickly pointed out to those around him. 'It reminds me of the circumstances to which Monsieur de Narbonne owed his privileges during the Empire; he had arrived from Germany and was bearer of a letter from the Grand Duke of Baden. He went to the Tuilleries, to the Emperor's *levee* and, walking forward to deliver his letter, instead of holding it out in his hand, presented it on his hat. The Emperor, much flattered by such elegant courtesy which his own courtiers had never even imagined, showered all kinds of boons on the new favourite who, by his loyalty, has since proved himself most deserving.'

As Mr. Baring had come over to speak to Lady Holland, I took the opportunity of telling him that I had been entrusted with several letters for him and so hoped to be able to deliver them to him in person when I got to London.

Alexander Baring (1773–1848). Created 1st Lord Ashbourn in 1835. In about 1817 Alexander Baring bought The Grange estate in Hampshire. In the mid-1820s he retired from the banking business established by his father. According to the Brighton and Hove Herald on 3 November 1827,

> "Mr. Alexander Baring was expected last evening
> at 87 Marine Parade."

193 *TN Parmenion was a general in the services of Alexander the Great. La Garde seems quite happy to equate Napoleon I with Alexander.*

Alexander Baring 1838
Alexander (right) and his brothers Sir Thomas Baring and Henry Baring, were the brothers of Frances, Mrs. Thomas Read Kemp. It could not have been inconvenient to T. R. Kemp to have married into such a powerful family of bankers.
Image courtesy of The Baring Archive Ltd

This was very much towards the end of La Garde's stay in Brighton and not near the beginning as is implied by the narrative.

'I deeply regret,' he told me, 'that I am leaving Brighton tomorrow morning with my family and that will deprive me of the honour of receiving you; but if you have no fears of becoming acquainted with the interior of an English country house, come to stay a few days with me in Hampshire, which is where we are going. Mrs. Baring would be flattered to have your company, and if you will allow it, I will let her know that you are to visit.'

'I accept with pleasure,' I replied. 'It will be of great interest for me to compare life in an English country seat with that of the great estates in Poland and Russia.'

'It might not give you a very precise comparison,' he told me. 'However, for our most illustrious families, life in the country may well resemble that in the grand properties you mention. Be that as it may, whatever the state of my house, I would be honoured to receive you in my home.'

When he had gone, the conversation took a more general turn, Lord Holland enlivening it with the full wealth of his recollections, and Sir Robert with the vigour of his imagination. Mr. Allen,[194] an old friend of Lord Holland's house, talked about geology and quoted some most curious facts which he explained

194 *TN Dr John Allen (1771–1843) Dr Allen trained as a doctor in Edinburgh. Between 1802 and 1811 he worked at Holland House as both physician and librarian, but above all he had become a close and trusted friend of Lord Holland. In 1811, he took up the Wardenship of Dulwich College in London and later became the Master of the school.*

with that modesty peculiar to the truly learned. Some young people joined us: Miss Fox and Miss Russell spoke little, but so pertinently that it was regrettable that their shyness prevented them from saying more. The Duke of Bedford, who combines in equally high measure the skill of speaking well and of listening attentively, took little part in our conversation at that moment. However, the hours had sped past rapidly and, fearing to outstay my welcome on a first visit, I withdrew, delighted by my evening. Sir Robert accompanied me to the door and I expressed my gratitude for the constant flow of pleasure which I owed to him.

'I would be delighted,' he told me, 'to play my part in encouraging you to prolong your stay in Brighton, yet I confess you did well to accept Mr. Baring's invitation: let me persuade you not to delay before going into Hampshire. You will see him on his own estate, in the bosom of his charming family where he forgets his enterprising financial dealings and devotes himself to the arts: his fine collection of paintings and sculptures will be ample proof for you of his extensive studies and his taste; and what is more, you may be sure that you will not find a better object for your comparisons than The Grange.[195] I, too, have visited the principal houses of the great Russian and Polish lords; putting national pride aside, I still consider that England has the advantage.'

'In that case, Sir Robert, my curiosity will be of the liveliest. I did not believe, I must confess, that anything could rival the luxury and the grandeur that I saw displayed in Countess Potocka's country house at Tulchin, in Ukraine. To be able to describe it to you I would have to be indebted to a chapter from *A Thousand and One Nights* in order to portray, as those tales do, its enchanting oriental delights. But it is true, a woman who is mistress of 8,000,000 francs and suzerain of more than 600,000 serfs may easily wave her magic wand.'

'That is as may be, but where is *comfort* in all that? Go and look first and then you can judge.'

Once I had returned to my lodgings, I cheerfully made haste to consign to paper the varied memories of my day, in the certainty that if flattery is a perfidious gift, well-earned praise creates a permanent debt.

The season was already well advanced, but the bravest souls were still taking sea baths. Indeed, the weather was very fine, despite it being October; but this

195 AN. The name of Mr. Baring's estate at Northington in Hampshire.
TN The monumental, Greek Revival, building 'improved' by Baring in the early 1820s is now in the guardianship of English Heritage.

Image courtesy of the Wellcome Library, London

is a not uncommon occurrence in England at this time of year. Being curious to compare the bathing in Brighton with that on the French coast, I went down to the esplanade very early the next morning and there, already, a considerable number of bathers had gathered. I saw nothing remarkable about the way the machines were arranged: here, as in Dieppe and Boulogne, a little cabin is perched on four wheels and furnished with everything required before and after the bath, such as linen, oiled silk, flannel, and so on. The bather climbs in; the driver, sitting on a sort of bench, guides the machine across the beach and into the water; once it has reached a point where it is deep enough, he turns his horse around to face the land, and the bather, by means of steps placed at the rear of the machine, makes his or her way down into the sea. If it is just a simple wetting for a lady or a child, two women take the bather in their arms as the individual emerges from the machine and dip the bather three times into the waves. The English place great store in the efficacy of the electrical jolt given to the limbs by the instantaneous shock of the cold, salty water.

After lunch, I continued my walk along the sea front, taking great delight in gazing at the succession of squares and gardens, with, in their centre, lawns and beds filled with flowers and bushes, around which rose, as if by magic, an infinity of houses, or rather palazzos, under construction. And how right they are to create so many of these huge enclosures which, with names such as *Square, Crescent* or *Circus,* bring a welcome interruption to the unbroken uniformity of the buildings. Each lawn is surrounded by slender railings and it is the residents alone of the adjacent houses who have a key and the right to walk in the gardens.[196] A Parisian who has often heard of the delights of such squares in English towns has no idea that the ancient Place-royale[197] could, for very little effort, give him some idea, albeit an imperfect one, of what they look like in Brighton and London. I walked into several houses where the builders were still at work. I returned to some thoughts I had been having: all these dwellings, be they large or small, are built to exactly the same plan, the proportions alone differ. There is no carriage entrance; a small door leads into a passage from where one proceeds into a parlour which doubles as a dining room; a narrow flight of stairs leads to the first floor and two living rooms; one large and one smaller. On the second floor are the bedrooms for the whole family and in the attic, those of the servants. The kitchens are in the basement. Outside you see the same uniformity; the facade never has more than three window openings with sash windows operated by counterweighted cords: the reason for this is the window tax,[198] which everyone makes strenuous efforts to escape. By dint of putting several of these houses together, the overall effect is one of architectural wealth and ornamentation borrowed from Greece, Rome and the Orient and this eventually fuses to become one of these palaces which astound the eye. Not long ago, there was only one building material in use in England: brick. Stone was a luxury, used exclusively for public monuments. Blackened by smoke and smog, brick would quickly take on a murky hue which cast a gloom over everything. But in recent years, the invention of 'Roman cement' has given English buildings a quite new appearance: brickwork is fashioned into columns, capitals and pediments, and is then entirely covered in this stucco which lends itself so well to the most delicate ornamentation; hardened by exposure to the air and carefully painted in light colours, it deceives the eye into imagining the finest Genoese or Florentine marble. All these grand houses, as well as those which have already been completed, will soon be let out to rent. The owner will carpet the bedrooms, add a few pieces of furniture and will then advertise, of his own free

196 *TN In 1887, many of the 'Squares and Crescents' were passed into the control of the Town Council. To date only the residents of Sussex Square, Lewes Crescent and Marine Square still have private central gardens, accessible to residents only.*

197 *TN Already renamed 'place des Vosges' by 1800.*

198 *TN Window tax was first imposed in 1696. By 1827, any house with eight windows or more was subject to this 'tax on light and air'. Many houses in Brighton were originally built with 'bricked up' windows which could be opened up for the first time as and when the tax was repealed. The repeal did not occur until 1851.*

will, for tenants, because, apart from the permanent inhabitants, no one in the town owns his own house, as fashion brings to Brighton the same travellers, at the same time of year, for the same pleasures. No house is rented for more than a week at a time, even if it is solicited for a much longer period; the owners have recognised that a year is made up of fifty-two weeks, thus they gain a whole month's income. This practice applies, in England, to everything which may be hired, be it furniture, horses, carriages and even servants. The rent on these houses is often exorbitant, to such an extent that, in the season, the rent on a house in one week can far exceed the cost of staying in a hotel for a whole year in certain French towns.

> Regency Square, Brighton – to be LET, for the winter, a good FAMILY HOUSE, elegantly fitted up and Furnished for a private residence, and which the owner occupied himself. ... Apply Mrs. Cole, 56 King's-road, Brighton.
>
> The Times, London, 30 October 1827

The weather was so fine, that I succumbed to the temptation of making a little excursion outside Brighton. I walked through an area of new buildings, which, before long, will be the most elegant part of the town, and climbed the slope which rises behind it to the north. Having walked for a short time, I noticed in the distance, between two hills, something which I could not make out very distinctly, but which seemed to be laid out in a very curious way. As I approached, by the look of the tattered tents as well as the swarthy skin and the sound of the outlandish songs being sung by the women and children, I realised it was a gypsy encampment, and which, from its arrangement, had all the appearance of a hamlet with the tent of the head man at its centre. I found that this extraordinary race, which I had already encountered as far away as the Russian desert, was no different here than there: I saw the same features, the same olive colour skin, the same clothes and probably the same vices. They are the last remnants of an ancient people whose origins are lost in the mists of time; they are never driven out, but neither are they tolerated or encouraged, and yet they persist everywhere and anywhere; for centuries they have travelled the many lands of the globe to which they have scattered and they have remained true to their ancestral roots; they wander endlessly from one nation to another, but their curious customs, language, castes and habits are in no way tempered or attenuate by their nomadic life. The successive countries which play host to these strange guests have all given them diverse names. In Hungary they are called Czigani, in Turkey Çingene, Zigeuner in Germany, Egyptians in Italy, Bohemians in France and Gypsies in England. Within their own group, they call themselves Pharoes. Their one and only trade consists of producing articles in metal; but I cannot imagine that they earn a living at this work in a country where the industry is so highly developed. To supplement their income, they have fallen back upon a quite other means of subsistence: they travel around the fairgrounds hawking animal remedies, telling country folk their fortune and exhibiting wild animals or curiosities. Some are lazy, others beggars or thieves; all they have acquired from the modern world is its tricks and its vices. I walked into the encampment, wishing to examine it in detail: amongst their carts glowed brushwood fires on which their meals were cooking, their horses were grazing on the heather surrounding the tents, a tame bear, freed from its chain, was resting beneath a tree. No sooner had I been spotted than I was deafened by a swarm of women and children entreating me for alms; and several young girls, some of whom were extraordinarily pretty, offered to tell me my fortune. One of them, who seemed to be no more than eighteen, I permitted to take my hand; while she was attempting to read my future in its lines, I could not help noticing her slim, lithe figure; beneath her swarthy skin, several of her features seemed a faithful replica of antique statuary; her large, dark, oriental-looking eyes expressed both reserve and sensuality at one and the same time.

I parted with a few coins in exchange for the happiness to come which she had predicted for me, as is the convention, and in a fit of gratitude, she decided to give me proof that happiness would be mine, by inducing me to admire the social graces of the bear which I had noticed when I had arrived. She went to fetch the animal, which followed her like a dog. Having called over a small boy of about seven or eight, she put him on the back of this novel steed which then started to gallop round us and leap like one of Franconi's horses,[199] all in meek obedience to its rider's voice. That was not all: when the child had dismounted, the girl made the bear stand on its hind legs and, having put a penny in one of its paws, we followed it to a tent where, in exchange for a coin, it received a glass of brandy, which it tossed down; the animal then gave every indication of wanting

199 *TN Antonio Franconi (1738–1836) is credited with being the founder of the French Circus in the early nineteenth century.*

to repeat the feat. When I had seen all there was to see, I walked away from the encampment, deep in admiration for Walter Scott, the great portraitist of nature, for having so often drawn his material from these nomadic people; for they are all that can be considered picturesque and elemental. I continued my walk, following round the plateau above Brighton, and returned to the Glocester Hotel from the direction opposite from that which I had set out in the morning. There, I had a piece of good fortune; one of those happy accidents of any journey which do more to create an intimacy than several months of intercourse in the polite society of a capital. M. D***y, whose acquaintance I had been pleased to make, and whom five years of living in Paris had so thoroughly assimilated to French life, had just arrived on the Dieppe packet and was kind enough to agree to dine with me, and so I was able to question him about Paris, as if I had been absent for twenty years and we had met in an oasis of a great desert. It is true that in Paris he moved in the same circles as myself and it is a great delight to be able to talk about those that we love. We conversed about the French *Poliorcetes*[200] as well as about his brother, the commendable and witty Chevalier S***t, whose excellent, robust qualities encourage people to seek him out as, in the past, they had sought Lafontaine; we talked of T***on, who never tires of showing Paris to visitors, and who, when the need arises, can speak up for the city so eloquently: E***nne, whose distinctive wit suits the stage just as well as the orators' rostrum; L***vre who, despite being a mere thirteen years old and still an adolescent to his core and in his imagination, outstrips many a young man of spirit and vivacity; A***to, the brilliant young grandson of that distinguished lady whose beauty is admired by everyone in Paris and who himself inspires affection in all those who know him. But we had to break off our tender reminiscences to talk a little of politics, for my companion held this to be his fifth element;[201] and, to do him justice, he is able to discuss rather than to argue, which is a quality all the more commendable for being uncommon.

We were agreeably distracted from the interesting topic of Europe by a troupe of itinerant musicians, who approached us playing their well-known tunes; amongst them we noticed five men who were singing, unaccompanied, a few English melodies called Glees. Whatever might be said about indigenous

200 *TN 'Poliorcetes' refers to a warrior renowned for capturing cities; in antiquity this was the name generally applied to Demetrius I (337–283BC). His French equivalent in 1827 and the man La Garde is referring to, was possibly Joseph, Viscount Rogniat (1776–1840).*

201 *TN After earth, fire, wind and water.*

English music, I can assert, without fear of contradiction, that the chords are characterised by precise harmonies reminiscent of those much admired songs heard in Switzerland and the Tyrol.

The hotel servants were talking amongst themselves about the appearance of a star and their excitement lead me to believe that a new planet had been discovered by a latter-day Herschel: I soon learned that they were referring to the charming Madame Vestris who, that very evening, was to perform in the theatre at Brighton.

Lucia Elizabeth Vestris (1797–1856) Contralto singer of light opera. She appeared at the Theatre Royal, Brighton and is referred to twice in the local newspaper:

The enchanting Vestris arrived at the New Stein Hotel, yesterday, from Worthing. She intends, we believe, to remain here a fortnight and we sincerely wish the salubrious air of Brighton may tend to her speedy recovery and also that she may appear on our Boards previously [*sic*] to her departure. Her sister is with her. BRIGHTON GAZETTE 11 Oct 1827

Madame Vestris has left the New Steine Hotel on Tuesday, in greatly improved health, to fulfil her engagement at Covent Garden. BRIGHTON GAZETTE 18 Oct 1827

Lucia Vestris is considered to be an early female transgender and cross-dressing artiste. When the Prince Hermann Pückler-Muskau saw her playing Don Juan at Drury Lane on 4 November 1827 he commented:

> 'Madame Vestris as Don Juan is the prettiest and most seductive young fellow you can imagine, and, it is easy to see, does not want practice.'

and on seeing her at the Haymarket Theatre he said of her:

> 'She is somewhat "passée" but still very fascinating on the stage. She is an excellent singer, and still better actor, and a great favourite of the English public ... Her great celebrity, however, rests on the beauty of her legs, which are become a standing article in the theatrical criticisms of the newspapers, and are often displayed by her in man's attire.' *November 1826*
>
> 'A TOUR IN ENGLAND, IRELAND AND FRANCE' 1831.
>
> Translator: Sarah Austin (1793–1867)

Image reproduced with the kind permission of the Lester S. Levy Collection of Sheet Music, Sheridan Libraries, John Hopkins University, Maryland.

I had hoped that M. D***y would accompany me to the performance, but he was, on that very day, setting off for London where he had important affairs to attend to. As he was taking his leave me, he urged me to make use of his apartment in the capital if I went there; I thanked him, but did not accept.

As soon as he had left me, I made my way to the theatre: Madame Vestris was singing in 'The Beggars' Opera' and in a comediette translated from French as 'The Invincibles'.[202] The auditorium was already almost completely full. It seems to me that Madame Vestris deserves the great enthusiasm which she has aroused: in both pieces, she played the role of a man with a grace and an ease which endows our sex with all the charm of hers. I will not expand on either the plays or the actors, preferring to give more details about both when I have been able to see and judge the theatres in London.

202 AN This same comedy was played in 1810 at the theatre in St. Petersburg: The Emperor Alexander was present in Madame Narishkin's box; he was so captivated by the military drill, commanded in Russian by Madame Philis, who played the role taken by Madame Vestris, that he could not stop applauding and the next day sent a very pretty diamond ring to the agile sergeant and twenty-five roubles pay to each of the soldiers in the feminine battalion.
TN The original title in French was: 'Les femmes soldats ou la forteresse mal défendue' ('The women soldiers or the ill-defended fortress'). The title of the comedy, written in 1809, might or might not have included a 'double entendre'. Tsar Alexander died in 1825, so must have seen Madame Vestris in her heyday.

Chapter VI

A morning walk – A traveller's reveries – Brighton's church and cemetery – The devastation of Brighton – Tattersall's grave – Charles II at Brighton – An incident in 1650 – Epitaphs – The German Spa – Clubs – A visit to the Royal Pavilion – Inside the Chinese palace – The sleeper awakes – The King at supper – The blacksmith and the miller from Sans-Souci – Worthless favourites *or* Brighton and Versailles.

Whilst remaining faithful to the aim I have set myself, I am far from forgetting that I am a Frenchman, and yet, at the present moment, being a punctilious chronicler, I will, for all that, continue to attribute to the laws, to the manners and to the customs of old England the praise she deserves.

In this country, the soldier is brave, the manufacturer tenacious, the statesman thoughtful and society in general hospitable and impartial. The more we are able to set forth the qualities of the English, the more we may pride ourselves on a rivalry which honours both parties. Yet, when we observe their lives in detail or *en masse*, when we observe their milieu, we find quite adequate reasons to remind ourselves, and with what pleasure, that we are the children of France.

The following day, I walked to *Church-street* and soon reached a flat part of the hill on which stands, you could almost say perches, the parish church of Brighton. I like to see a place of worship placed on high ground; it seems to become an intermediary between the sorrows of this life and hope for the next.

Looking down, on the one side across a vast stretch of land, and on the other a wide expanse of sea, I gazed at this elegant town spread out before me in all its variety. The weather was superb and, on the horizon, I could just make out the

The Parish Church of St. Nicholas, 1825
The view is towards the sea in the south. The Chain pier is just visible to the right of the Church. The bulky buildings to the left were the workhouse which had opened in 1822. Auguste makes no mention of the poorer sections of Brighton society.
Image reproduced courtesy of the Brighton Royal Pavilion, Museums and Libraries

lines of the Isle of Wight.[203] Through the hazy morning mists, Brighton looked like an enchanted city: everything in it is so neat, so ethereal that you tremble lest a puff of wind carry it off before setting it down on some cliff top in Normandy. Yet it was no færy but the whim of a king which created this most picturesque town on the confines of the sea.

Satisfied, or more correctly, delighted with this magnificent sight, I sat on one of the gravestones in the cemetery, and there, in this most egalitarian of all meadows, I gave myself to that melancholy which Montaigne calls 'solemn hedonism': I pondered the one inexplicable mystery, about which daily life teaches man next to nothing; I pondered the end of life, a thing of habitual indifference and intermittent terrors; in this spot, where all thoughts are cut short, I speculated about our uneasy desire which leads us constantly to roam foreign climes, to demand forever new horizons and new acquaintances that are so often severed as soon as they are formed. Why does man, whose anxieties gnaw at his future,

203 TN *It would be highly unlikely that La Garde would have been able to see the Isle of Wight. He was, most likely, looking at Chanctonbury Hill or, along the coast, at Worthing or Selsey Bill.*

wish to dull his awareness of the inevitable end by constant activity? In this life, absences are too short to warrant prolonged tears of grief; a pious heart must always count upon being reunited with those whom he has loved. And so my reverie took me back to thinking, and with what sorrow, of those loved ones from whom life had so long separated me.

At that very moment, I was distracted from my melancholy thoughts by Mr. Mackinnon, who had also wandered up onto the hill to breathe in the bracing air and to enjoy the impressive view.

'I did not expect to see you out so early in the morning,' I told him, 'and if such a pleasure had been promised me, my first choice of meeting place would have been somewhat more cheerful.'

'And yet this place,' he replied, 'is not without its attractions; the air you breathe is of the purest; you can immerse yourself in its atmosphere just as well as you can submerge yourself down there by stepping from the beach: and what is more, this is a place which reminds me of events which are not without historical interest.

'This parish church of Brighton, formerly Brighthelmstone, is dedicated to Saint Nicholas. Its architectural style and the techniques used to paint its stained glass windows are evidence of its antiquity which dates back several centuries. The more modern chapel you see here was added in the reign of Henry VII;[204] both buildings were damaged towards the middle of the sixteenth century during an attack made by the French on this coast. That was after the naval battle launched by Admiral Annebaut[205] against Lord Dudley de Lisle,[206] commander of the British fleet. Baron Paulin de la Garde,[207] commanding captain of the French galley boats, had been sent by the admiral to raid the Sussex coast: he sacked Brighton and the inhabitants took refuge in this church and were able to defend themselves for some while; when they were forced to surrender in large numbers, the majority of them were taken captive. You had no idea, my dear sir, that one day you would be warmly welcomed in a land where one of your ancestors had shown himself to be so hostile.'

---

204 *TN St. Nicholas' Church was to be extended again in 1853 and in 1892. La Garde would probably have great difficulty in recognising the modern church.*

205 *TN La Garde's spelling of names is not to be trusted. This is a reference to Claude d'Annebault (1495–1552) who, in 1545, lead attacks all along the British south coast between Newhaven and the Isle of Wight.*

206 *TN John Dudley (1501–53), created Viscount de Lisle and Lord Admiral in 1542. He seemed to be very much an armchair admiral as most of his time was spent in Parliament. He directed the Battle of the Solent in 1545, but it would appear that he did it from an office rather than from aboard a ship.*

207 *TN Paulin de la Garde was officially an officer of the French Navy; unofficially he is described as a pirate. He was present at the battle in the Solent during which the* Mary Rose *was sunk in 1545. His exact relationship to the author is not known.*

'Indeed, I am all the more grateful for that welcome. I have, in truth, read about this historical event in an account by Brantome:[208] he describes in detail the magnificent galley ship *La Réale*, built on the orders of Paulin de la Garde when he was commanded to go to London to ask, in the name of the Duke of Anjou (later Henri III) for the hand of Queen Mary.[209] I do not know why this marriage did not take place, but I do know that the baron's representations made not the least impression along the shores of the mighty Thames.'

'Do you see that tombstone close to the one on which you are sitting? The long, rhyming inscription carved onto the slab of black marble bears the date of 26th July 1674.[210] It is the monument to Nicholas Tattersall who, by his laudable devotion, rescued Charles II after his defeat at Worcester.'

'I know little of this episode in the adventurous life of your merry monarch; so this happened in Brighton, you say?'

'Remember that this town was no more than an insignificant village, inhabited for the most part by fishermen. Tattersall was the captain of a coaster in the coal trade. A certain Smith was landlord of a hostelry in West-street where to this day you can recognise the name of the inn by its sign: *The King Charles II*.[211] One foggy evening in the month of October 1651, a considerable crowd of men was

---

208 *TN Pierre de Bourdeille, seigneur de Brantôme 1540–1614, a French historian.*

209 *TN La Garde is rather shaky on his English history. In about 1570 The French king, Henry III was encouraged by his ambitious mother Catherine de Medici to ask for the hand, not of Mary I, but of Elizabeth I, Queen of England. Henry was roughly 19 years old; the queen was in her late 30s.*

210 AN Within this marble monument does lie
Approved faith, honour and loyalty;
In this cold clay be hath ta'en up is [*sic*] station,
That once preserved the church, the crown, the nation.
When Charles the great was nothing but a breath,
This valiant soul stepped between him and death.
Usurpers! threats, nor tyrant rebels frown:
Wich [*sic*] glorious act of his for church and state
Eight princes in one day did gratulate
Professing all in debt to him to be
As all the world are to his memory.
Since earth could not reward his worth here given
He now receives it from the king of heaven.
In the same chest one jewel more you have
The partner of his vertues [*sic*] and his grave,
Suzanna his wife died in 1672. Her son
Nicholas was buried with them in 1701.

TN The last four lines of this inscription do not appear in more convincing and apparently 'authentic' transcriptions of the epitaph. The last two lines seem to be pure doggerel. Perhaps Mr. Mackinnon had merely given La Garde the information and the author has taken them as part of the inscription.

211 *TN If La Garde had ventured down West Street in 1827 he would have spotted that the inn was called 'The King's Head' and not 'The King Charles II'.*

packed into the bar of the George Tavern[212] in West-street, warming themselves round a great coal fire. The conversation had turned to recent events:[213] the defeat of the royalist army by the parliamentary troops, the flight of the king and the arrangements that had been made for his capture.

'Everyone there, fishermen, soldiers, townspeople, were eagerly holding forth, depending on their opinions; their faint-heartedness or their greed leading, naturally, to the folly of cliques: some exhibited an intense desire to seize the king in order to earn the huge reward promised to anyone who handed him over; the thoughts of others ran more on the death penalty to be meted out to any individual who gave him refuge.

'Not a single voice was raised in defence of the fugitive, partly because the new regime was so well supported and partly because the fear instilled by the Puritan party stifled any feelings of loyalty or pity.

'Sitting alone beside a table on which stood a pot of beer, a lamp and a few pipes, a stranger, wrapped in a coat thrown on over his peasant attire, listened in silence: it was Charles! And indeed, throughout his flight, from the anxious time he had spent in the branches of an oak tree in the forest at Boscobel, where he had remained hidden for twenty-four hours, to his escape from Windham Castle[214] dressed as a woman, he had spent no more cruelly fearful moments than these.

'Smith, who had once happened to find himself at court, recognised the king despite his disguise.

'As a loyal monarchist, he trembled to think that a word or a gesture might betray his illustrious but unhappy guest; but Charles, inured to adversity by the danger of his situation, managed to master his emotions and the agonising apprehension which haunted him. As the evening wore on, the bar became empty. Smith was alone with the king. Two men then entered the inn: Colonel Gunter and Lord Wilmott,[215] both closely allied to the fortunes of the king. The two men had scoured the coast in vain, searching for a vessel; from the despair betrayed on their faces, the king had already seen that their efforts had been fruitless; and while they were still struggling

212 *TN La Garde seems to confuse matters regarding the name of the inn where this (apocryphal) event took place. Presumably the 'Charles II Inn' had been renamed the 'George Inn' in honour of any one of the four King Georges who had occupied the British throne by the time of writing in 1827.*

213 AN The Battle of Worcester, lost by King Charles II on 3 September 1651.

214 *TN La Garde is probably referring to the nights of 17–22 September 1651 when the fugitive Charles II spent the nights at Trent House near Sherborn in Dorset. This was the home of Colonel Francis Wyndham. There is no clear evidence that Charles disguised himself as a woman.*

215 *TN Colonel George Gunter, a Sussex man and Lord Henry Wilmot, 1st Earl of Rochester (1612–58).*

to conceal their unease and their fears, Charles, who had been a wandering fugitive for the past six weeks, was resigning himself to still continue roaming the same districts under yet more disguises. Smith, too, had understood this wordless scene and trembled at the thought of the dangers into which his king was about to plunge. He left the room and a few moments later returned, leading Tattersall by the hand.

'"You are the king," he said, turning to Charles, "and I am here to save you," then, turning to Tattersall, he said: "By entrusting you with this secret, I am proving my high regard for you; yesterday you asked me how soon I would allow you to marry my daughter Suzanna; your boat is lying at anchor: set sail, land our king on French soil and my daughter is yours."

'The following day, Charles took ship at five in the morning and, helped by a favourable wind, Tattersall was able to land him at Fecamp in Normandy within the day.

'When he returned, he married Suzanna, whose name you can see carved at the end of the inscription on the tomb before you.

'When the monarchy was restored in 1660, the good captain sailed his boat up the Thames and hove to, opposite Whitehall, in memory of his sovereign's lucky escape. Charles rewarded Smith and Tattersall for their loyalty by granting them each a pension of one hundred pounds which they could entail to their heirs.'

I copied the lines engraved upon the tomb.

In among the mass of headstones I noticed these other inscriptions which I found of interest. There was this on the tomb of Lady Ramsay's daughter:

O flower of flowers, wich [sic] *we shall see no more,*
No kind returning spring can thee restore[216]

And this by a young French girl to her mother:

She has returned to heaven from whence she came.[217]

This one, in Latin, was on the tomb of a young girl:

Exstincta amabitur.[218]

---

216 *TN La Garde writes both the English (with his inimitable spelling) and his own translation into French.*

217 *TN Given only in French, so presumably written on the headstone in French.*

218 *TN So sure is La Garde of his readers' erudition that he does not insult their intelligence by translating the Latin. Twenty-first-century readers will not be offended if offered the translations: Exstincta amabitur – She will be loved after her death;*

And I saw this most philosophical of epitaphs on the tomb of an archbishop:

Hic jacet pultis, cinis, et nikil[219]

Near the gate, on a simple stone bearing this year's date, I read these two simple words :

Michel Starginsky

As the illustrious author of *Martyrs* so beautifully put it: 'Who hath the oracle of his ashes, or whither they are to be scattered?'[220] Happy the man who has lived surrounded by his kin and who dies where he was born.

'I am sure that in this churchyard, neither the arrangement of the vaults nor the sculpture nor the inscriptions, the last vanities permitted to man, produce the same piously picturesque harmony as in the Père Lachaise Cemetery, which is unique of its kind,' Mr. Mackinnon went on. 'We ought already to have emulated it long ago in London; out of the twenty plans which have been put forward, not one has yet been adopted;

Kensal Green was the first 'landscaped' commercial cemetery to be built in London. It opened in 1833, its first client being Mrs. Margaret Gregory, wife of the editor of the Brighton Gazette. *Barnard Gregory (see pages 111 and 112) built St. Margaret's Chapel in St. Margaret's Place, Brighton, naming the chapel for his wife rather than for a favoured saint.*

---

but we still have much here which echoes your peaceful, shady groves in Paris: you can see that, in this apparently chaotic scene, the trees and the shrubs give shelter to the graves; the long, supple branches of the ivy wreath both trees and headstones; the cypresses and the slender poplars seem to waft to heaven the prayers of pious, loving hearts; this rustic setting lends the funereal vista a charm which links the reality of death to the reality of life and leads us to agree with one of our most famous authors: "*Come forth, and pass away. This is the*

---

219 TN *Hic jacet pultis, cinis, et nihil – Here lieth dust, ash, oblivion*
In 2008, as part of the 'Mapping the past' project in St. Nicholas' church yard, an inventory of inscriptions was made. Apart from that of Nicholas Tattersall, none of the above inscriptions was found.

220 *TN From 'Hydriotaphia' (1658) by Sir Thomas Brown*

great command of nature. Nothing remains, nothing is unchangeable but change."[221]

'So that we may dispel our gloomy mood,' Mr. Mackinnon went on, 'come with me, sir, to visit an establishment from which Brighton benefits greatly.

'It is a temple to health, containing within its narrow confines several of the numerous advantages with which nature has endowed many other lands: it is where artificial mineral waters are prepared, under the supervision of several eminent doctors.'

Following the line of the hills which rise above Brighton, we made our way to an extensive garden called *The German Spa*;[222] nothing seems to have been left to chance in making the place as agreeable as it is useful.

In an elegantly decorated room, many and varied ailments are offered relief by the fountains of Hygeia which dispense the curative waters of Bad Pyrmont, Spa, Carlsbad and Egra.[223]

'At present the season is too far advanced to be able to judge how useful this manufactory might be,' continued Mr. Mackinnon, 'for few people are taking the waters; but in summer, the place is bustling and, as happens everywhere else, the crowds flock in because the flock has already crowded in.'

'We have a similar establishment in Paris, *The Tivoli Gardens*;[224] these are considered to be of great convenience to those whose business prevents them from being long absent from the capital. Our best medical men have acknowledged that these manufactured waters have a chemical composition which can, without a doubt, rival natural waters; but what adds to the advantage of your *German Spa* is the change of scene and the suspension of all activity: this increases the efficacy of the cure as prescribed to those whose pleasures or whose labours have overtaxed them.'

'To the west of the town,' Mr. Mackinnon went on, 'there is a chalybeate spring[225] whose waters have been analysed by Doctor Henderson; like all the

---

221 *TN At this point, La Garde felt the need of a footnote to translate the English into French. Although he had assumed a knowledge of Latin amongst his readers, assuming a knowledge of English was a step too far. As the original of this quotation was generally ascribed to Heraclitus, La Garde is missing a good opportunity to show if he had any knowledge of ancient Greek.*

222 *TN The façade of this building remains. It is at the southern end of Queen's Park.*

223 *TN More usually known by its modern-day Czech name of Cheb but in Wallis's 1836 guidebook to Brighton, the name of this town is given as Eger.*

224 AN Doctor Boulland has just set up in Paris, under the name of *Néothermes*, one of the best equipped and most useful health establishments that a capital could hope to boast.
TN The main difference between the German Spa and the Tivoli Gardens was that the former produced an artificial mineral water, whereas the latter contained a natural spring. The spring in Paris is now buried beneath the Rue St. Lazare, between the Boulevard de Clichy and the Gare St. Lazare.

225 *TN St. Ann's Well in Hove.*

other waters of the kind, this particular one invigorates and fortifies. The spot where the spring rises is surrounded by trees; that there is so little foliage here on these bleak Downs, renders the effect all the more picturesque.[226] Unfortunately it is too late for me to suggest taking you there.'

We continued to discuss the various properties of the mineral waters which nature seems, everywhere, to offer to mankind as a powerful restorative for the abuses he inflicts upon his body: Mr. Mackinnon, who had visited nearly all the spas of Europe, described each of them to me, scientifically but without being in the least tedious; he entertained me with character sketches of some eccentrics whose foibles he pointedly ridiculed: he told me about illustrious people whom he had met and who, being ill or without their entourage, willingly cast aside the lens of decorum which magnified their peculiarities.

When we arrive on the Steyne he said to me: 'In the past, this open area was still a field covered in debris.[227] Now you see it transformed into elegant flowerbeds which afford delightful walks to the inhabitants of the surrounding houses. These embellishments are due to the benevolent concern of our king, George IV for the neighbours of his palace. To express their gratitude, the citizens of Brighton have commissioned a full-length statue of him from our renowned sculptor, Chantry [*sic*], and will place the effigy of our benefactor on the very site of his generous deed.'

'On your left you will see the house of Mrs. Fitzherbert; the house next to it is the club.

226 TN *The South Downs were denuded by centuries of sheep grazing. Later, the Victorians were to remedy the situation through their passion for planting trees, especially to embellish their burgeoning towns.*

227 TN *Mr. Mackinnon is being a trifle disingenuous: the Steine was the drying ground for the fishermen's nets and an essential part of their economy. The fishermen were removed to sanitise the area. It is now called the Old Steine.*

BRIGHTON CLUB. — This Club-house, which was formerly in Steyne-place, is now on the Old Steyne, was originally kept by Mr. Bedford. The present proprietor is Mr. Humphreys. The Club consists of two hundred subscribers, including Peers, Members of Parliament, and other gentlemen. The admission is by ballot, eleven members being present, and two black balls excluding. The regular stakes at whist are crown points, 3*s*. cards, Piquet, 5*s*. cards. All matters relative to the Club are managed by a committee of seven members. The annual subscription is three guineas, and for which the house is supplied with newspapers, magazines, reviews, &c. Beds may be had in the house; the charge is 3*s*. per night. Raggett's subscription house was discontinued prior to the establishment of this.

BRIGHTON GLEANER, February 1823

No doubt you know of this kind of establishment which has, of late, proliferated so extensively in London; apart from a few details, they are all very much one like the other: the *Alfred*, to which I belong, is one of the longest established in the capital. Its library is well stocked and select; its salons are tastefully and lavishly decorated and its members all highly distinguished gentlemen with regard to rank and ability. We are eager to welcome strangers and it would be a pleasure for me to sponsor you.[228] We have a similar establishment here in Brighton; this evening I will put your name down as a foreign visitor so that I may take you there as soon as you have a free moment. There you will make the acquaintance of several men who you will later meet at the *Alfred*.'

When I got back to the Glocester with Mr. Mackinnon, I found a most courteous reply from the Marquis of Conyngham along with an instruction to Mrs. White, the lady in charge at the Royal Pavilion, to allow me entry. I asked Mr. Mackinnon if he wished to accompany me on my visit. He had already seen the apartments several times; he was kind enough to say, however, that my company would be an added charm and agreed to act as my *cicerone*; we therefore made our way together to the palace.

228 AN It is a delightful duty for me to express my deepest gratitude to the gentlemen of the Committee of *The Alfred*. During my lengthy stay in London, they did not once neglect to renew, every quarter, their invitation to me to become an honorary member of their circle, and, for a foreigner, this mark of attention was all the more highly valued, for very many an Englishman of distinction has had to wait, impatiently, for a place to become free before he could be admitted. The kindness of the committee towards me was unfailing.

Sir Francis Chantrey (1841–81) sculpted the statue of George IV which originally stood in the north section of Old Steine Gardens where the War Memorial stands. The statue was unveiled in 1828, a very few months after La Garde's visit to Brighton. The statue has since been moved and now stands on a fairly secluded pavement south of the junction between Church Street and Marlborough Place. On 1 September 1827, the Brighton Herald *reported the arrival of the statue in the town:*

> During the week, workmen have been busily engaged in removing the rails, raising sheets, and other apparatus, necessary to raise the pedestal of His Majesty's statue, which arrived at Shoreham a few days ago, having been shipped at Plymouth. The ponderous masses constituting the pedestal, and which are composed of Devonshire granite, have since been brought to their destination, the Steyne, in carriages and are now nearly erected. The height of the pedestal is from 11 to 12 feet. The statue itself may now be expected in a short time.

Image reproduced courtesy of the Brighton Royal Pavilion, Museums and Libraries

If its exterior had impressed me as being quite outlandish, the fantastical taste of its internal decor astonished me even more.

The saloon, the banqueting room, the music room and the long gallery glitter in their golds and glowing colours; everything is upholstered in the most sumptuous fabrics; but the one thing, for a European royal residence, which excited my amazement was to see the way Chinese opulence and decoration had been painstakingly imitated. Nothing seems to have been omitted: the strange hues of the draperies, their ornate patterning and the shapes of the lacquer furniture made of cypress and laurel wood which give off their gentle fragrance; on curiously carved side tables made of precious woods stand a profusion of porcelain objects including vases of jasper and ivory; on the ceiling, dragons of gigantic proportions support enormous chandeliers shaped like the lotus flower, the symbol of perfection; on the walls of the long gallery, various paintings depict the natives of China dressed in the costume appropriate to their profession, from civil and military mandarins, ranked by the different species of animal embroidered on their silken robes, down to workmen dressed in simple nankeen tunics; from the common woman with her almond eyes and swollen lips to the stylish young lady with gold and jewelled clips in her hair, her face powdered with a thick layer of carmine and barely supported on tiny feet, the size of which often determines her value as a bride. In the smaller rooms are paintings which record the landscapes around Peking, as well as pagodas inscribed with sayings or mottoes by the most famous poets; everything, even the carpeting, is a faithful copy of an imperial residence in China.

In the music room Mr. Mackinnon pointed out the largest organ in the kingdom;[229] the delicacy of its tones,[230] their brightness and their range make this instrument superior to all others of its kind.

'This sort of instrument has, indeed, been perfected,' he added, 'since the days of the contraption made of bronze pipes and blacksmith's bellows in the eighth century which the Emperor Constantine Copronymus[231] sent to Pepin the

229 TN *This organ was built for the Royal Pavilion by Henry Lincoln in 1818. It was removed to its present home in the Ballroom of Buckingham Palace in 1855 where it was enlarged even further.*

230 TN *La Garde is possibly quoting from the 1826 inventory (which may have doubled as a tourist guidebook) of the Pavilion which describes the organ as being 'celebrated both for its great powers and its peculiar delicacy of tone'.*

231 TN *Constantine V of Byzantium (718–775) sent an organ to the Pepin, King of the Francs, in 757. Such an instrument was unknown in the West at that time.*

Short.[232] The organ you see here was built by Lincoln: its length, width and height are all of the same dimension. And now look at the fire surround; it is carved entirely in marble with its elegant statuary picked out in ormolu; and can you imagine those vast chandeliers laden with candles, casting their flashing shafts of light through a thousand coloured crystal drops, scattering a dazzling, sparkling film of pearls, rubies and emeralds into the immense mirrors, the largest ever cast until now; each and every shaft of light is reflected time and time again, thus creating a stunning, magical effect.'[233]

'I confess,' I said, 'that the attention to detail, the opulence of the furniture and the splendour of the whole do credit to the English manufactories just as much as they do to the artists who have so skilfully employed the products of their industry; and so it astonishes me all the more that any one of them would go so far afield to hunt out these bizarre designs, when they could have copied Greek or Roman masterpieces in their purest and most restrained forms.'

'The contrasts emphasize the beauty of the sum of the parts,' Mr. Mackinnon countered. 'What you call a pure style has often seemed to me merely monotonous, and perhaps my taste is bad enough to prefer all this *chinoiserie*.'

'Do you know, sir, what insane idea comes into my head when I look at the grandeur in this palace? I imagine a first-rate draper, leaving behind his wife and his shop counter in the rue St-Denis in Paris in order to go and glimpse the sea so that he can boast about it for the rest of his life as if it were a valiant deed. Having had him reach Dieppe, simple soul that he is with his Parisian lack of experience, I would like him to be invited aboard a steamer where the master would ply him with champagne, and, taking advantage of the agreeable moments of oblivion brought about by the wine, cast off from the shores of Normandy without our draper knowing it. Soon, along with his head, his stomach would be spinning from the effects of the swell and frequent falls would warn him that he did not quite have what we call "sea legs". At that point, he would fall into a deep,

232 AN There is no doubt a considerable difference between this first attempt at a mechanical instrument and the vast organ that has been built in the Ballroom at Birmingham: its case is between 45 feet high and 65 feet wide; the longest metal pipe is 5 feet 3 inches in circumference and 35 feet high; the largest wooden pipe measures internally more than 200 cubic feet. There are, in this full organ ten open octaves, and all the other elements are in proportion. Several sets of bellows are required to work such an instrument with its 60 keys and its five manuals. Overall, it fills a space of 380 feet and weighs 40 tons. *TN This footnote may well have been added after La Garde's visit to Brighton in 1827, but before publication of the book in 1834 as it seems he is referring here to the Hill organ built for Birmingham Town Hall in 1833.*

233 AN Before he became king, the Prince of Wales was not over scrupulous in paying his suppliers; no doubt it was his mirror dealer who wrote in large letters '*unpaid*' on one of the mirrors. Since then, the public has not been admitted to the Pavilion without a pass from the Lord Chamberlain.

all encompassing sleep, brought on by a drunken stupor, and even more so by seasickness; then I would like him to arrive in Brighton by night and, as the result of a whole succession of incidents, the reasons for which the unfolding saga would gradually elucidate, to be transported (still sleeping) into one of the saloons of the Pavilion where a myriad of lights, their reflections glittering in the mirrors, are rivalling the radiance of the brightest sun and where the perfumes of Asia are wafting up from golden incense burners. Having been gently laid on the downy cushions of a sumptuous sofa, he is woken by the gentle strains of that organ whose harmonious tones you have extolled to me. Left to his own devices, he goes from apartment to apartment. At last he reaches the banqueting room: an elegant supper, at which kingfisher nests and other Chinese delicacies are being served in profusion, is to complete this magical adventure. When, after some moments spent in gazing on these costly cabinets, on these excellent depictions of Chinese mythology and on the marvels from another hemisphere, marvels that are all new to him, when, I say, he has exhausted his admiration in this way, I would wish that an innocuous narcotic, mixed in one last sorbet, return him to his slumbers and that, having been transported back in the same steamship as that in which he came, he should find himself waking the following morning, hale and hearty, in the port of Dieppe. Do you believe that he would doubt for one moment that he had been to Peking and that he had visited the palace of the sacred Son of Heaven, of the one and only Ruler of All under Heaven, as the Emperor of China so modestly calls himself: and what is more, if he were still unsure, I would send him to a true believer, such as I met in Constantinople, who would not fail to explain to him how Mahomet, having been carried off by the angel Ithuriel, had time to roam the seven planets and the seven earths and to return to his own chamber, at the precise moment to prevent a vase filled with water falling to the floor, the vase having been knocked down by the angel's wing as he had whisked away the Prophet.'

'That is very much the story of the "Sleeper Awakened" from the *Thousand and one Nights* that you have adapted to suit the circumstances,' Mr. Mackinnon commented.

'True, but this evening I am going to suggest to Monsieur Morier that he further elaborate this idea; he could doubtless turn it into a charming episode for the novel he is writing about Hadji-Baba in London.'[234]

234 *TN Morier had already published* The Adventures of Hajji-Baba of Isphahan *in 1824. In 1828, he published* Hajji-Baba of Isphahan – in London.

'But why turn to fiction when you could tell of a glittering reality. Describe an evening spent by the king in his youth, by this prince who takes such pride in being called the foremost gentleman of his kingdom; show him into these saloons with their gilded panels, into this palace dedicated to pleasure, surrounded by his famous, witty friends, Fox, Sheridan, Thomas Moore and many others, for it was the very fact that he had chosen these men which proved the prince's fine judgement and good taste; look at them as they vie for the approbation of the ladies, those enchanting divinities of this temple, whose beauty did so much to enhance the brilliance of his court. A splendid banquet is spread; the guests take their seats to the strains of the most mellifluous harmonies,[235] the most exquisite dishes are served on solid gold platters, the wines, chilled on costly ice, sparkle in crystal goblets; everywhere there are garlands of flowers, baskets laden with fruit and fiery liquors. All around there is happiness, perfume, light, love; the air they breathe is an intoxicating philtre. If only the walls could speak, they would tell you that they have witnessed such enchanted scenes a thousand times, and that Mahomet could never have promised any more thrillingly sensual pleasures to the elect of his own paradise.'

I had no reply to this lyrical outburst, so much in harmony was it with my own impressions and feelings: to me it was the most suitable farewell to the bewitchment of this royal fairy tale.

Crossing the gardens which, laid out in perfect taste and, despite being in the very centre of the town, cover no less than seven acres, we made our way to the stable block. A circular interior is surrounded by sixty-two stalls; to the west is an immense riding school, two hundred feet long.

After having rewarded Mrs. White[236] we left. Mr. Mackinnon pointed out to me a sort of hut, occupied by a blacksmith, hard up against the palace walls: amidst these elegant buildings, it gave the impression of being a splash of mud on a costly fabric.

'You can see the power of our laws,' he said, 'and to what extent they are respected: the king has offered a considerable sum of money to the owner of this hovel to buy it: the obstinate blacksmith has demanded exorbitant amounts, no

235 AN The king's personal music was composed for wind instruments and can be considered as unique of its kind; each musician is a teacher of the first order and the band as a whole is perfect.

236 AN The least one could offer was a gold coin to the value of 25 francs.

The Royal Stables at Brighton
After seeing the exotic interior of the Pavilion itself, La Garde was, evidently, underwhelmed by the grandeur of John Nash's 1822 rebuilding of the magnificent domed stables. The circular building is now the Dome concert hall, the riding school has become the Studio Theatre in New Road.
Image reproduced courtesy of the Brighton Royal Pavilion, Museums and Libraries

doubt trusting, rather like the miller of Sans Souci, in the judges in London;[237] each party had right on their side, and, like the miller he has kept his bothy which, for some time yet, will continue to disfigure the approach to the palace.

237 TN *The miller who owned a windmill which blocked the view of Frederick II when he built Sans Souci Palace in Potsdam, countered the king's threat to expropriate him with a counter-threat to appeal to the judges in Berlin. The whole story was fabricated in 1787 by a French biographer of Frederick II. Frederick had, in fact, chosen to erect the windmill as a folly at the far end of a perspective.*

'Only one house, within the enclosure, of the range formerly called "Marlborough-row," is now standing, and which, though a let and nuisance to the design in process, His Majesty, from a most benevolent motive, has commanded should remain—that of supporting a small tenement, without the fence, which, in all probability, would fall, were the other to be removed, and speedily become as a heap of rubbish. Thrice the value, or more, we understand, has been proffered for the tenement in question, to take it down, and incorporate the few square feet of ground upon which it stands, with the palace gardens, but which has been refused, in the ungenerous expectation, it is said, of obtaining a still higher price for it. Though good sense and justifiable liberality cannot comply with the latter, the privilege, in all that appertains to the liberty and interest of the subject, is respected, and brilliantly exemplified, as above mentioned, in the sovereign's command.'

BRIGHTON GLEANER 1822

'Does that not remind you of the latest news from Berlin? The present head of the miller's family, having lost so much during the wars, found himself in financial straits; he has written to the king to remind him that his ancestor had refused to sell his mill to the mighty Frederick,[238] and to tell him that if His Majesty had inherited his ancestor's whim, Miller Frank would then regard the purchase of the mill as a great favour.

'The king immediately wrote him, in his own hand, a letter of which I have kept a copy which I can now show you:'

My Dear Neighbour,

I cannot consent to you selling your mill; it must remain your property as long as there is a member of your family living, for it belongs to the history of Prussia. I am, however, distressed to learn that you are financially embarrassed, and so am sending you six thousand reichsthaler to resolve the problem, in the hope that the amount will be adequate.

I remain your affectionate neighbour

Frederick William

238 *TN Frederick William III.*

Leaving Mr. Mackinnon, I hurried to dress for my outing to Kemp-town where Sir Robert and I were to dine at the home of the founder of this new town.

Whatever has been stated about the luxury and the opulence in England, twenty-five millions spent on a second residence seems exorbitant: our century,[239] being entirely practical, has none of these royal follies; we are no longer in an age in which Louis XIV abused nature at Versailles. When one thinks that such an immense sum of money has been used in building the Pavilion, and that with that amount all they have managed to create is something little short of bizarre, one would be tempted to censure such futile profligacy: the feeble outcome, compared to the exaggerated expense reminds us, with even more reason, of what used to be said of Versailles: 'It is merely a frivolous favourite.'[240]

239 TN *La Garde is perhaps too tactful to say: 'our country' i.e. France.*

240 TN *The Duc de Créquy had used these words to express the feelings of the Parisian population when Louis XIV abandoned his legitimate residence, the Louvre, for the frivolous mistress, Versailles.*

Chapter VII

An excursion to Kemptown – The young girl – A state dinner – Cooking at table – The town's developer – Return to Brighton – An excursion to the Devil's Dyke – Memories of Dresden – The last moments of General Moreau – Moreau's observation on Bonaparte – The whims of fortune *or* The unexpected legacy – The Abbé 'Thirty-thousand-men' – Fortune and misfortune.

Of all illusions, the most excusable is the hope of being spoken of after one no longer exists; such striving after fame is not as foolish as it might seem, for it can prompt the individual to undertake great things. It is this which leads to prodigious adventures in love and war, to the construction of grand monuments and to works of imagination, of wit and of science; thus, the pursuit of fame is a worthy aim, rightly open to any noble ambition.

In an elegant little *fly*, which was as fast as its name, I left the Glocester Hotel to drive to Kemp-town. This new town, just one mile outside Brighton, and the newest in Europe, gives the outsider the very clearest idea of how audacious English speculation has become.

Like most famous towns, Kemp-town bears the name of its founder. In France, as everywhere else, an individual might build one house, or even several: Mr. Kemp, who possesses immense wealth, one day conceived the idea of building an entire town and, to his very great credit, has carried it out. It is, in truth, high-minded enough to put your name to an undertaking which must necessarily encourage posterity to declare: *Te saxa loquuntur* (the stones speak your name).

Kemp Town, from the original text by Count de la Garde.
Many of these houses were no more than carcasses in 1827.
Image reproduced courtesy of the Brighton Royal Pavilion, Museums and Libraries

Kemp-town is built in the shape of an amphitheatre on a rising hill, and is both impressive and picturesque when seen in its entirety; its elegant porticos, reflected in the immense stretch of water which it overlooks, recall that noble image of Genoa the Superb. In the foreground, a vast circular garden has been laid out, the centre of which will be embellished with bubbling fountains as impressive as those in St. Peter's-square in Rome; and once the new throng of inhabitants has arrived and has breathed life into the rows of streets, the public buildings, the airy market places and all the spacious palazzi,[241] now in their final stages of construction, the founder may indeed rest assured that the magnificence of his colossal undertaking will be honoured by posterity which will preserve his deservedly famous name.

241 *TN Docwra Parry would beg to disagree: 'The great error was in calling it, or wishing it to be thought, a separate "town" from Brighton, to which distinction it has not the slightest claim. It has no earthly concomitant of a town: no steeple, market-house, shops, or inns. Had it been merely called Kemp Place, or Crescent, considered as a suburb to Brighton, and more closely allied to it, it would have been well; and no one could have disputed its claim to the character of a fine range of buildings.' Taken from* An Historical and Descriptive Account of the Coast of Sussex *by J. D. Parry, 1833, page 141.*

With my head full of these thoughts, I entered the town, which was, in its infant days, as nearly deserted as Pompeii after lying two thousand years in its tomb.

In a house,[242] which he might have chosen from amongst a thousand others, Mr. Kemp was holding a dinner for his family and his friends.

The steps and the hall were adorned with a phalanx of servants in sumptuous liveries who greeted me as I got out of my vehicle: my name, which I had given at the door, had already passed from mouth to mouth four times before reaching the drawing room.

Following the English custom, I was introduced to each of the guests and they in turn were introduced to me by name: this formality which, to tell the truth, somewhat overtaxes the memory, does allow you, from that point on, to converse with your neighbours at table; ten prior encounters would not have sanctioned such a liberty without this indispensable overture.[243]

A few moments later, Sir Robert and his daughter arrived. Dinner was announced; we gave our arm to the ladies and we went down to the dining-room. The table was set with a fine silver service; on a mahogany dresser was an abundance of silverware displayed shelf upon shelf, dominated by a serving dish of immense proportions on which were embossed the coat of arms of the Kemp family. I had not expected to find in England a custom which had so long been eradicated in France, but this has arisen from the English tradition of bequeathing the family silver to the next generation.

Amongst other elegant dishes, we were served turtle soup, which is, no doubt, fashionable merely because it is most expensive; I found the somewhat disagreeable taste reminded me of those soups made of sterlet (a fish found in the Volga costing anything from five hundred to fifteen hundred roubles) which are served at official diners in St. Petersburg.

The dinner, prepared by a French chef, was made up of a large number of dishes, all most carefully cooked; and yet, such is the power of habit, or perhaps

242 *TN Thomas Reed Kemp (1783–1844) occupied 23 Sussex Square for several years from 1827.*

243 AN General Montjardet, shortly before his death, quoted to me a most characteristic witticism on this subject. A lady of his acquaintance was reproaching Lord S*** for his ingratitude towards the general whom he now seemed to snub, after having received the most generous of assistance from him when his Lordship had been at the time no more than Monsieur D*** and living in Paris in a state not far from destitution. 'I do not understand,' replied the Earl of S***, 'what this Monsieur de Montjardet is complaining of; after all, I have never been introduced to him!' Montjardet took his revenge by writing, with that characteristic wit of his, a pamphlet entitled: *Biography of a English Peer of the Realm*; it reveals to the public the amorous adventures of this gentleman who is so punctilious with regard to introductions and it will encourage him, no doubt, to take more thoroughly to heart all treaties on gratitude and memory.

prejudice, that no one, other than the foreign guests and a few English travellers, touched any of the food which was not standard English fare: similarly, as we were enjoying an entrée, consisting of fowl, game and fish seasoned and prepared in the French style, the truly insular guests, the ones we might call the puritan natives, kept strictly to the roast beef and the boiled fish and vegetables. And yet, for these people, such stoicism entails, at one and the same time, the sort of effort from which they could easily free themselves, as well as a certain culinary *savoir faire* which is incompatible with their gravity, for in fact, once the fish and the vegetables have been removed from the water and placed on his plate, each guest is obliged, as it were, to concoct his own sauce; to this end, the diners are presented with a tray on which are arranged crystal phials containing everything they might need, such as chilli powder, Cayenne pepper, a wide variety of spices and even ready-mixed seasonings brought directly from the East Indies; in short, a veritable apothecary shop for the gourmet. It must, surely, be pointless to employ chefs from so far afield and to pay them so well if you are going to make your own sauces at table.

The champagne, which elsewhere is served only at the end of the meal to revive the mood, is drunk in England from the very beginning and vanishes with the dessert when it is replaced by *claret*: to me, the opposite would seem more natural. However, a great deal of it was served, and of a superior kind: as an exorbitant duty is imposed on the good as well as the indifferent, all the champagne imported into England is of the very best quality.

Unlike the usual English dinner, this one, although excellent, was short and the conversation lively and sustained, revealing much wit and geniality; we spoke of the new town and the plans for its improvement; there are already public baths, an hotel as well as a brewery and before long all the other comforts of modern life will come to enhance its elegance, just as soon as fashion permits the elite to live there.

With dessert we drank a toast to the success of the fledgling town and then my host added the words: 'and to all foreigners who set foot in it'. To this civility I replied that, having found myself a few years previously in St. Petersburg, at a public dinner given to celebrate the centenary of the founding of the city, it was my wish that a comparable ceremony should bring us all together, each year, to drink the health of Kemp's town and its growing prosperity, as in Tsar Peter's town.[244]

244 AN St. Petersburg was founded 120 years ago on marshland. Today it has 500 000 inhabitants.

A few moments later, the ladies left us to go up to the drawing-room.

'I hope,' I said to my neighbour, Mr. Marshal, 'that we will not spend many hours here drinking, for a table without ladies is a garden without flowers.'

'Alas, sir,' he replied, 'it is "the custom"! and, in England, once that word has been uttered, there is nothing more to be said or done; we cling to custom like a snail clings to its shell; and yet of late this lingering has been much curtailed.'

'I am pleased to hear it, for it must have considerably dulled your evenings. Those intimate chats, which start off so famously at dessert and which continue all the better in the drawing-room, are cut short by this long separation; and the serious subjects which are discussed, when the ladies are no longer with us, cannot fail to encourage that feeling which, in England, you call awkwardness and which a whole evening's pleasure will fail to dispel.'

After the ladies had withdrawn, the cloth was removed and the table, of magnificent mahogany, was festooned with drinking glasses; incomparable wines in crystal decanters of varying shapes quickly circulated on little silver four-wheeled chariots. In the past, and even today in some parts of society who cling to the old customs, the men drink for hours at a time, and often far into the night; our libations lasted no more than one hour, thanks to the changes which are influencing this aspect of English manners. As soon as coffee had been announced, we went up to the drawing-room

It was lit by an enormous chandelier, sparking with crystal pendants; the furnishings, the gold and silk curtains and the sumptuous carpets all heralded the brilliance and the grandeur which would soon reign supreme in Kemp-town. I noticed one felicitous innovation in this room, in that it was decorated with paintings by the greatest masters: until that evening, I had seen such pictures hung only in dining rooms. Several tables were laden with costly knick-knacks of ivory, gold and silver from England, China and the Indies. There was also a host of those little chronicles of pride and flattery which, given the name of *albums*, have appeared from Germany. Here it is the fashion to pile up as many of these extravagant trifles as possible, for they are, in a way, a barometer of the owner's fortunes.[245] We must forgive such vanity in a country where no other is displayed; in England, whether you are out walking or in a drawing-room, you will see neither insignia nor embroidery-encrusted uniforms. Their favourite bauble, for

245 *TN La Garde has pinpointed the move from true Regency simplicity and elegance towards 'Victorian' clutter.*

men must indeed have one, is to have the sum of twenty, thirty or fifty thousand pounds. Mr. Kemp wanted such a plaything; he built his town!

We started the evening with music. Miss Kemp played the piano, then the harp; she sang, in various languages, tastefully adjusting her style for each, songs by Rossini,[246] ballades by the Duchess of Saint-Leu[247] and that charming melody by Moore, *Come rest in this bosom.*

La Garde gives the full translation into French, but not the original English.

Come, rest in this bosom, my own stricken deer,
Though the herd have fled from thee, thy home is still here:
Here still is the smile that no cloud can o'ercast,
And the heart and the hand all thy own to the last.

Oh! what was love made for, if 'tis not the same
Through joy and through torments, through glory and shame!
I knew not, I ask not if guilt's in that heart,
I but know that I love thee, whatever thou art!

Thou hast call'd me thy angel, in moments of bliss, --
Still thy Angel I'll be, 'mid the horrors of this, --
Through the furnace, unshrinking, thy steps to pursue,
And shield thee, and save thee, or perish there too!

While she was singing, we admired a collection of landscapes and flowers which she had drawn and which indicated as much ability as it did application. All these talents, combined with the charms which nature had bestowed on her and of which she seemed to be unaware, may well confirm Fontenelle's quip, which I had the great pleasure of repeating to her: '*You have been taught everything, except the art of pleasing, and yet it is that which you know the best.*'

246 *TN Gioachino Rossini, aged 31 and at the height of his fame as a composer of operas, had visited Brighton and played at the Royal Pavilion in 1823.*

247 *TN Hortense Eugénie Cécile de Beauharnais, Duchess of Saint-Leu (1783–1837) was the daughter of Josephine de Beauharnais by her first husband. Hortense became step-daughter to Napoleon I when he married Josephine. Hortense was Queen of Holland from 1806 to 1810 through her marriage to a younger brother of Napoleon. She was the mother of Napoleon III. See Translator's Introduction.*

Later we danced quadrilles and waltzes; and during an interval, a young Spaniard, Signor Huerta, played the guitar admirably.

We are requested to state that the concert of the unrivalled performer of the guitar, Mr. P. Huerta, announced for Monday, has been postponed until the following day.

BRIGHTON HERALD, 17 November 1827

The concert eventually took place on 20th November and the program was as follows:

PART FIRST

RONDO – Beale – Piano .... Mr. Gibbon

OVERTURE – by Huerta – Guitar .... Mr. Huerta

AURORA QUE SAPETE – Flute .... Miss Clements

FANTASIA – by Huerta – Guitar .... Mr. Huerta

DE PICCERE BERDEGUER – Flute .... Miss Clements

GRAND SPANISH MARCH – by Huerta – Guitar .... Huerta

PART SECOND

THEMA – Piano – Gibbon .... Mr. Gibbon

OVERTURE – Guitar – Huerta ....Mr. Huerta

LE PETIT TAMBOUR – Flute – Lee .... Miss Clements

SPANISH BELAROS – Huerta .... Mr. Huerta

GOD SAVE THE KING – Douret – Flute .... Miss Clements

SPANISH FANDANGO – Huerta .... Mr. Huerta

Starts at 2pm. Tickets 7*s.* each and can be bought from Mr. Huerta at 26 Broad Street

Miss Marshal, who was seated near me told me of the subscription ball held every week at the Ship Hotel in Brighton, which emulates the highly fashionable one at Almack's in London.[248] The ball is under the direct patronage of three ladies whose consent must be sought before one can be admitted. The assembly room is very fine and one meets many fashionable people; it is the epitome of the London room. Miss Marshal persuaded me to take the necessary steps to gain admittance; I promised that I would do so.

During the evening, I approached the master of the house; a man to whom one could most fittingly apply Cowper's words:

'God made the country and man the towns.'[249]

He explained to me the various phases of his vast undertaking, as well as the obstacles which he had had to overcome to bring it to the stage at which I now saw it.

'It is a great pity,' I said to him with a smile, 'that we are no longer living in an age where fables spin their entrancing fictions, for I doubt whether Thebes was build to the strains of any more melodious tunes than those with which your esteemed daughter has delighted us this evening: she is a true rival to Amphion: her harp and her voice could have spared you the exorbitant bills from the architects and the masons!'[250]

'You will be able to judge what this town will, one day, be like from a general view which I have had engraved, based on my architect's drawings; I would be honoured to present it to you.'

'For me, sir, it will be a charming memento of my stay in Brighton; but in exchange, allow me to give you one of the drawings from my album; it is of a Turkish bath, typical of those built in Constantinople and which combine elegance with hygiene; such a bathing establishment would perhaps be an attraction for your town, and since a Chinese pavilion built in 1784 started one fashion in Brighton, why should not the construction of a bath rivalling Mohamed's adorn Kemp-town?' Mr. Kemp accepted my gift.

The dancing had long since ended; after a lavish supper, all the guests took their leave; I returned to my hotel, more than ever delighted, as much by the employment of my days as by the refinement of the English.

---

248 AN Each year, in London, the upper echelons of the aristocracy hire vast rooms to hold subscription meetings; but in order to be granted the favour of a ticket to these Almack's balls, you have to produce testimonials which are more demanding that those required to enter a noble order in Germany. – Foreigners need no more than the good will of their ambassadors.

249 *TN La Garde translates Cowper into French.*

250 *TN Legend has it that Amphion, when building Thebes with his twin brother, played so beautifully on the harp that the stones followed him to wherever Amphion wished to place them.*

Sake Dean Mahomed (1759–1851) was one of the first Bengali Muslim immigrants to the British Isles. At the age of 23 Sake Dean left his native Patna (and not Calcutta as La Garde suggests) in the company of his long-time protector, Captain Godfrey Baker. He settled in Ireland in 1784 where he met and married his Irish wife. Sake Dean and Jane lived in Ireland for some 25 years and at least two of their children were born there, but Mahomed expunged these years almost entirely from all his memoirs and writings.

Eventually, the couple left Ireland and had various business ventures: in 1809 they opened a 'Hindustanee Coffee house' (in reality the first Indian restaurant) in London. The venture was not unsuccessful, but drained the Mahomeds' finances to such an extent that the couple had to withdraw from it financially in 1812 when Sake Dean became bankrupt. On first coming to London, Mahomed had worked as an assistant in an establishment offering vapour baths.

In 1814 the couple moved to Brighton where they opened the far more successful 'shampooing' (head massage) baths in Brighton. The Brighton baths included 'The Indian Medicated Vapour Baths' which Auguste seems to have enjoyed.

Here, Mahomed appears in 'traditional' Hindustani costume. He may well have gone about his business in such garb, but he also chose to on several occasions to 'go native' and be portrayed in fashionable English clothes. Mahomed must have been about 60 years old when the portrait above was painted.

As with much else in High Society, the wits of the age were quick to put Mahomed's Baths to ridicule. Horace Smith, early in the 1830s, gave an account of Brighton in the satirical poem 'Clio Grub at Brighton':

In baths of all sorts Grub was pickled and stew'd,
And by Mahomet's critical hand was shampoo'd,
Who in rubbing and scrubbing such zeal did evince,
That the Turk has been black in the face ever since.
'Shampooing,' cried Grub, 'is of no real use,
Let me try what a long country-walk will produce;'

Image reproduced courtesy of the Brighton Royal Pavilion, Museums and Libraries

The Devil's Dyke looking towards the village of Poyning (1826)
Image reproduced courtesy of the Brighton Royal Pavilion, Museums and Libraries

In Brighton my time was divided between my musings and my enjoyment of the charms of its society; the following day, I was able to indulge both these pleasures during the course of a pretty country walk on which Sir Robert and his daughter suggested I should accompany them.

'We are going out six miles,' they told me, 'so that we can show you a spot called *Devil's Dyke*.' I took my seat in their barouche and in less than one hour we had arrived at the object of our excursion.

Having reached the summit of a high mountain entirely carpeted with an evergreen sward, one's gaze plunges down a deep precipice which, no doubt, owes its name *Devil's Dyke* to the terror it provokes.

'It is assumed,' Miss Wilson told me, 'that there used to be a Roman camp on this site; what makes this deduction credible is that when some men were digging in a neighbouring field a short while ago, they found an urn filled with coins and medallions bearing the effigy of various emperors from Antonius Pius to the Emperor Philip.'[251]

251 *TN Sicklemore:* 'About the year 1730, an urn was dug up in this neighbourhood, containing a thousand silver denarii, of different impressions, from Antonius Pius to Philip.'

Beyond the ravine, the landscape is truly bewitching; it is both pleasing and varied: there is a mass of hunting lodges, hamlets and elegant little thatched dwellings called *cottages* offering a thousand individual tableaux within the broader picture: but is it not always thus when nature has given us a beautiful view to which art has added its allure, either by rejuvenating its various attractions or by creating contrasts? You must see them to be able to judge; a description always falls short of conveying what one feels on catching sight of them.

'Each time I come here,' said Sir Robert, 'the shape of the hill reminds me of the one outside Dresden and on which General Moreau was struck down beside me.'

General Jean Marie Victor Moreau was fatally wounded at the Battle of Dresden on 27 August 1813 (see below).
General Moreau had, reputedly, been chatting to the Tsar Alexander of Russia at the moment he was struck by the bullet. Sir Robert must, therefore, have been moving in exalted circles. Tsar Alexander is on the left. It must be assumed that Sir Robert is one of the officers in red. The soldiers in blue are wearing the white cocard of Moreau's anti-Napoleonic Legion. In all the prints of the Battle of Dresden, the hill figures very prominently.
Mary Evans Picture Library

'Were you really so close to him, Sir Robert?'

'So close that his aide-de-camp, Colonel Rapatel and I caught him in our arms as he fell from his horse.'

'I have heard the account several times,' I told Sir Robert, 'but never from the lips of such an incontrovertible witness as yourself; and the story interests me all the more, for, despite the difference in our ages, auspicious circumstances had created an intimacy between General Moreau and myself of which, at the time, I was extremely proud: having hunted with him, occasionally on his estate at Gros-Bois, more often at Raincy, on Ouvrard's land, and having frequently met him in society, I became sincerely devoted to him. As with the rest of France, I deplored his reprehensible weakness which dragged him into an inexcusable plot[252] which not only deprived France of one of her most famous champions but led him to his death, slain by a French bullet.'

'When the two years of imprisonment to which he had been sentenced were commuted to exile in America,' Sir Robert told me, 'Moreau bought a country house below the Delaware Falls; it was whilst living in this retreat that he learned of the disasters at Moscow[253] and at once predicted the outcome. This news revived his resentment against Bonaparte; it was then that he received the first overtures from Emperor Alexander; this is what persuaded him to return to Europe.

'Indeed, in 1816 Mr. Parish, with whom Moreau had close ties in America, sent me all the letters relating to these negotiations, as well as those in which Moreau asked Parish for advice on such a delicate matter; I can assure you that, in his correspondence, Moreau expressed none but the most patriotic and least opportunist sentiments.

'He boarded ship, in secret, on 21st June 1813,' Sir Robert went on, 'accompanied by the secretary to the Russian Embassy. On 24th July he arrived in the port of Gothenburg. He spent three days there with his old brother-in-arms, the Prince of Sweden, and from there made his way to Prague where the sovereigns of the allied forces showered on him their marks of respect.'

'At that time,' I told Sir Robert, 'I was in Vienna with one of the men who, when Moreau was suffering his greatest adversity, showed him unsurpassed devotion;

252 *TN Moreau, once the head of Napoleon's forces, objected to the rising autocracy of Napoleon and so joined the Swedish and Russian cause in the last year or so of his life.*

253 *TN In 1812, the city commander ordered the deserted Moscow to be burned to the ground rather than let it fall into the hands of Napoleon Bonaparte's invading army. This was, in effect, the event which precipitated Napoleon's humiliating retreat from Russia.*

and certainly, had he been able to wait for this friend to reach Prague, his influence could perhaps have dissuaded Moreau from a line of conduct which will leave a perpetual stain on his memory,[254] for as soon as he had heard that Moreau had arrived, his friend had attempted to join him.'

'Dresden was attacked on 26th August. Moreau advanced on the city at the side of the Emperor Alexander and the King of Prussia; he rode along the column in the front line amidst bullets and cannon fire; the following day, the attacks started again; Moreau had just made a few remarks to the Emperor Alexander; as he moved forward to assess the movements of the enemy, a bullet shattered his right knee, went through his horse and shot away the calf of the other leg; it was at that moment that he fell into my arms, and, with the help of Colonel Rapatel, we laid him on the grass.

'Emperor Alexander ensured he received all the help it was in his power to give; a stretcher was made up from the Cossacks' pikes and he was carried into a nearby house where the Emperor's personal surgeon amputated his right leg; the general begged him to examine the other one and, on receiving the reply that it would be impossible to save it, Moreau calmly said:

'"Well then, get on with it, cut it off."

'The allied army being in retreat, he was carried to safety, on a curtained stretcher; he died in the early hours of 2nd of September.'

'Everything relating to a famous man is of interest,' I said to Sir Robert. 'I remember a ball, at the home of Madame Récamier, at which the hero of Hohenlinden[255] was, as ever, surrounded by strangers eager to make his acquaintance. I asked him if he had seen a new play called *Monsieur Musard* which had been recently staged at the theatre in the Rue de Louvois.

'"Indeed," Moreau replied, "it is one of those comedy of manners in which Picard[256] seems to have caught natural behaviour just as it is; nearly every one of the characters is more or less a daydreamer, and I myself must confess that, when I was at the wars, daydreaming made me miss at least twenty chances of reaping the benefits of a piece of good luck; in truth, I know of only one man who is exempt

254 AN Monsieur T***on was the head of one of the oldest banks in Paris. At General Moreau's trial, he did everything he could to save him. At the time, this dedication to friendship was considered a crime and punished by two years in exile; public regard, once it had forgotten the errors of the General, compensated the friend.

255 TN *In 1800, Moreau had not yet deserted Napoleon and was leading the French Revolutionary troops against the Austrians and the Bavarians. The battle of Hohenlinden was won by Moreau and his troops in December 1800.*

256 TN *Picard, actor-manager of the Théâtre Louvois in the early 1800s.*

from this failing, and that is Bonaparte: he is well aware that seizing the occasion is often the foremost talent of any hero".

'When, a few days later, I heard that Moreau had been arrested as an accomplice in the Pichegru[257] conspiracy, I was reminded of his pertinent comment, which no doubt he did not realise was to be a sort of prediction: but men can only hope in vain to halt the events of this world, for it is those events which bring with them the destiny which governs them and sweeps them along.'

As we returned from the Devil's Dyke, we talked of war.

'In this game that kings play,' Sir Robert said, 'it is the population at large which bears the brunt, their provinces are the stake and the men are the pawns.' Then we talked of the 1813 campaign, of the amazing revolution which it had brought about and of the Congress of Vienna, at which I had been present: this had been a drama worthy of Shakespeare, with scenes ranging from the appalling to the farcical, played out in the interval between the fall of Napoleon and the Battle of Waterloo. And so we covered, without noticing it, the six miles which brought us back to Brighton. The weather being a little cold, Miss Wilson stepped out of the barouche at her parents' house; Sir Robert and I had the coachman take us on to the promenade near the Chain Pier.

On our way we passed a carriage which was remarkable for its elegance amidst so many elegant carriages: in it sat a pretty young woman.

'There you have,' Sir Robert said, pointing her out to me, 'a most surprising example of the fickleness of fortune and the no less curious peculiarities of our national character.

'Mrs. Wakefield (such was the name of the lady) had a box at the Italian Opera[258] in London. It would seem that custom dictates that an English woman of distinction should attend regularly all the performances of this foreign spectacle. No less assiduous than the lady, an elderly gentleman would always sit in a stalls seat exactly opposite her box: no doubt attracted by some object quite other than the dancing and the music, he seemed to take little interest in what was taking place on stage and constantly fixed his gaze upon the charming person before him. The season came to an end; the following season again brought Mrs. Wakefield into her box and the gentleman with the lorgnette to his usual seat: so far, there was nothing further than a mark of admiration, paid with constant

257 *TN A conspiracy to return the French monarchy to power.*
258 *TN Royal Opera House, Covent Garden.*

and respectful discretion, to the lady's charms, thus giving credence, perhaps, to the adage which maintains that women yield more to the love they inspire than to the love they feel; but the fact that will surprise you most, as a Frenchman, is that he made not the slightest attempt to find out the name or the residence of the goddess of his dreams.

'Towards the end of last season, the seat in the stalls remained empty; it is to be supposed that Mrs. Wakefield may have felt some regrets at perceiving such constant devotion withdrawn.

'But then, having come to Brighton for the sea bathing season, she had completely forgotten such an unimportant event. One day a lawyer was announced at her lodgings; without further ado he asked her whether she was the lady who had occupied, during the two previous seasons, Box 11 in the second tier at the Italian Opera; he added that she must have noticed a gentleman of a certain age who had constantly gazed at her. On hearing this unexpected question, the lady imagined that the lawyer was none other than an envoy from the shy admirer; she assumed the stern, dignified mien of an English woman who believes herself to have been insulted; she rose from her chair to indicate to her visitor that the interview was at an end. The lawyer, perceiving that the lady had misinterpreted his intentions, hurriedly put her mind at ease in a very few words; he gave her to understand that the person he had just mentioned to her, one of the richest landowners in Jamaica, had died a few days previously and that according to a clause in his will, he had left the sum of sixty thousand pounds to a lady he had not named, but to whom he had merely referred as the occupant of Box 11 at the Italian Opera throughout the two previous seasons; and that, having asked for information and corroboration from the management of the theatre, he, the lawyer, had ascertained that the terms of the will could apply to her alone: he said that he was delighted to be able to tell her that the legacy was at her disposal at the offices of Mr. D***ond,[259] the London banker. Once she had assured herself that the deceased had no direct heirs, the lady had no lingering qualms about accepting a legacy which added an unexpected windfall to the considerable wealth which she already enjoyed.'

'Once upon a time, in Paris, Sir Robert, there was an *abbé* who was well known to all the regular political gossips in the Luxembourg Gardens and he was

259 *TN Probably a Mr. Drummond of Drummonds Bank, founded 1717 and now part of the Royal Bank of Scotland.*

called the *Abbé Thirty-Thousand-Men*: there, sitting beneath the tree of Cracow,[260] surrounded by a few local worthies of a pacific bent, this combative priest would make war, day after day, on the whole of Europe: aping Turenne or Vauban, he would take his cane and draw in the sand the military positions and fortifications he knew he could take; and all these erudite expositions would inevitably end with the words "Give me thirty thousand men … with thirty thousand men … all I need is thirty thousand men …" to the point where the name stuck. One of his kindly companions, who, like our *abbé*, had conquered provinces and won battles in the shade of the spreading chestnut tree, died, leaving a will containing a legacy of a considerable sum of money to the *Abbé Thirty-Thousand-Men*. The initial reaction of the heirs, who were not known to frequent the Luxembourg Gardens and who were not conversant with this bellicose language, was to laugh; but they very soon had to change their tune, when, with the support of some fifty other men who vouched for his services to the military and for his sobriquet, the *abbé*, duly reinforced with a favourable court ruling, came to request his legacy, which they could not shirk from giving him … Now, you must agree, Sir Robert, that my little anecdote is just as good as yours.'

These strange quirks of fortune led us to talk of the brilliant and equally curious chapters of Sir Robert's own military and political fate: it was an habitual pleasure with him to parade the pageant of his adventurous life which had been so filled with extraordinary events; he liked to dwell on the past and to recall all those intrepid deeds into which his lively, impetuous imagination had propelled him. At the age of twenty, for example, during the Flanders campaign, it had caused him to save the Emperor of Germany at the very moment when he was about to be captured by French hussars, an act of bravery which won him the Cross of the Order of Maria Theresa, which was, at that time, highly respected and greatly coveted; he also had a great need to be active, which took him in turn to Egypt, Russia, Brazil, Spain and Constantinople, as both soldier and diplomat, and then to France where he deprived the guillotine of the head of a victim[261] intimately involved in our internal political discord. But he was most rightfully proud of his career in parliament which had earned him both success and persecution but, which was, above all, distinguished by the spontaneous gesture which lead to the

260 *TN Several key places in Paris had a 'tree of Cracow' beneath which men would gather to exchange home and overseas political information (both real and imagined).*

261 *TN Antoine Lavalette (see pages 99 and 250)*

raising of a subscription of several thousand pounds in compensation for the loss of his commission and even of his half-pay, stripped from him as a consequence of the 'Queen Caroline Trial'.[262]

'Everything which is extraordinary appears to be grandiose,' he said to me, 'provided the result is crowned with success; but everything which is grandiose appears to be madness, if the result is the reverse.'

'And yet,' I replied, 'you will agree that a life passed in a cottage with the ones you love is often worth more than the fame acquired by having wandered the globe and conquered the world.'

262 TN *Caroline Amelia Elizabeth of Brunswick-Wolfenbüttel, Queen of the United Kingdom and of Hanover, wife of George IV, had died in 1821. She was detested by the King and popular with the people. At her funeral, the Household Cavalry was about to fire on a grieving but unruly crowd when Sir Robert intervened to prevent anyone in the crowd being injured. For this act of humanity, he was stripped of his commission. There was no 'trial' as such of the Queen, more a post-mortem tribulation.*

Chapter VIII

A grand-dame and the newspapers – The Duchess of St. A*** – The fate of an actress – Sir Francis Burdett – A lady patroness – An old acquaintance – The Congress of Vienna – The Prince de Ligne – A walk to the chalybeate spa – A day in the life of an English lady – The Brighton club – The gazettes – Gambling.

There is no degree in life which does not have its disadvantages, its difficulties or its dangers, and it is particularly rare for rapid promotion within society not to arouse spite, for spite always attempts to avenge good fortune by resorting to slander; it would appear that men take pleasure in the downfall, even that caused by those they despise, of any person which fate has raised above the multitude.

It was already too late to meet Lord Holland on his favourite walk, but as we were leaving the Chain Pier, Sir Robert was approached by a most elegantly dressed lady; the ermine trim on her velvet dress and the profusion of jewellery which adorned her, betrayed more wealth than taste.

'I have this very moment,' she said, 'received a letter from London giving me news from France; you will no doubt find it of interest.'

'As will my companion, who is French,' replied Sir Robert who then introduced me to the lady who, so I learned, was the Duchess of St. A***.

The news she gave us was of the death of Charles X, and although it seemed to be given in all good faith, it struck me as being a Stock Exchange rumour and was, indeed, refuted the following day: we discussed back and forth the likelihood of its being true and we walked on for some little time. From political news, we passed to other subjects: the duchess complained bitterly of the unseemly way in which certain newspapers took the liberty of writing about her, thus abusing a freedom which too often degenerated into licentiousness.

Harriot Mellon had been born in London, in 1777, to an impoverished Irish actress and an unknown father. With her mother and step-father, she toured the provincial theatres, finally becoming a feted comic actress. In Cheltenham, she met Sir Thomas Coutts of the banking family. She was 33; he was 75. After several years as his mistress, Harriot married Thomas thus inheriting a large part of his vast fortune when he died in 1822. By 1827, she had married the Duke of St. Albans, a man twenty-three years her junior. The marriage was a happy one.

Harriot was wealthy but rather vulgar in her behaviour. She was much lampooned by the press as the following extract from 'The Spirit of the Age' shows:

MOTHER MALONE'S FETE.*
(By the noble Author of " Boyle Farm.")

Old Highgate on Monday will witness a fete,
When her Grease of St. Alban's will blaze in high splendor,
Like a full blown red cabbage all goodly and great,
And 'Dukey dear,' acting as skip to attend her.
The feed will be fine,
Recherche the wine,
(And her Grease's Cognac for herself, quite divine)
And the Post upon Tuesday in delicate tone,
Will puff the grand party of 'Mother Malone.'

The Presentation of Dollalolla accompanied by the Mighty Thumb, 1828
In this lampoon, The duchess is being presented to King George IV. The title 'Dollalolla' is a cruel reference to her vast fortune. The Duke of St. Albans appears in his Ceremonial dress as the Great Falconer of England (see Chapter XI). It was the costume worn by the duke in 1821 at the coronation of George IV. Not everyone was impressed by the young duke:

And thou (however fools may talk)
Who knowest a hand-saw from a hawk,
As a Grand Falconer ought to do,
Receive our humble homage too.
'Twas a good business that you got her.
Spirit of the Age 1828

On the other hand, the duchess had a generous and honest spirit. She left her whole fortune to Thomas Coutts' only grand-daughter, Angela Burdett-Coutts.
The Duke and Duchess of St. Albans owned a large house at No. 1 Regency Square.
Image reproduced courtesy of the Billy Ireland Cartoon Library and Museum, Ohio State University

'I am so weary of being used as fodder for articles written by obscure journalists. They pry into my every movement merely to compensate for the lack of intelligence in their newspapers by relying on malicious gossip; only the other day, can you believe that they criticised me for going to church accompanied by two of my servants who carried my many prayer books; the fact is that some of these books were for the duke's devotions and the others for mine. What would these newspapers have said if, like the Duchess of N***, I had walked to church with my prayer books carried on a velvet cushion ahead of me? They are hot against me and censure everything I do, even the charitable donations I make. In truth, they are enough to turn me against doing any benevolent activity.'

'Oh, never! My Lady,' Sir Robert struck in. '"Do good deeds and let others prattle" is a saying to which all else must eventually give way; the satisfaction which one gains from doing good is to the soul what the perfume of flowers is to their gardener. Madam, a religious philosopher has said that you must do unto others all the good of which you are capable, expecting in return the opposite, or, as the Arab poet puts it: "When you eat, feed the dogs, even though they may bite you".'

I was too little conversant with the causes of these complaints to be able to take part in the conversation which was sustained by Sir Robert with the quick wittedness required to alleviate such grievances. He asked for news of her step-daughter's husband, Sir Francis Burdett.

'He left me yesterday,' she replied 'and was still very anxious about his wife's health; but he led me to hope that he would come and spend a few more days with me before the opening of Parliament.'

As we reached the gate which forms the entrance to the esplanade,[263] a servant arrived to tell the duchess that the duke had returned from the hunt, and this put an end to our interview; we handed her into a magnificent carriage to which were harnessed four horses decked out in most ornate trappings; on the leading horse was mounted a young postilion who wore, embroidered on the left sleeve of his splendid livery, the ducal coat of arms which included those of the English royal family. Before leaving, the duchess invited us to visit her often, both in Brighton and in London: a constant message of hospitality, which is becoming as familiar as it is agreeable to my ear.

---

263 See image page 128

I was impatient to know who my new acquaintance was, and begged Sir Robert to satisfy my curiosity and to give me some details about this lady who the newspapers so distressed with their bad manners.

'As you heard when I introduced you to her,' he told me, 'that is the Duchess of St. A***; and I can give you the details about her past which Prince Pückler-Muskau[264] assures me he got from the lady herself: her story reveals the intriguing caprices of fate! When barely out of her cradle, she was abandoned in a hovel on the edge of a wood, and later cared for by gypsies whom she left whilst still a very young girl. Like the witty Barber of Seville, she might well have said: "Brought up in their ways, I soon tired of them etc". Later, chance brought her into contact with a band of itinerant actors; her graceful, seductive figure, her natural acting style and her cheerful character quickly earned her the reputation which attracted the manager of the Drury Lane theatre to engage her to play minor roles; her talent soon promoted her to playing major ones. Another whim of "His Majesty, Luck", as the great Emperor Frederick would say, caused her to be jostled, rather roughly, by the rich banker C*** as he was walking in Piccadilly; after introducing himself, he asked the lady to accept his apologies.

'The following day, Miss M*** (as she was called before her marriage) was playing in her own benefit performance; by way of reparation, Mr. C*** sent a written request for a box; the booking enclosed a bank note for twenty-five pounds sterling. The idyll, which had started at first sight, blossomed at a first meeting and the affection eventually became a legacy of over two million pounds, that being the amount which the banker bestowed on the amiable actress to whom he had given his heart and his hand.

'One natural consequence of these gifts of good fortune which protect the lady has been the appearance of the ducal coronet which now adorns her brow, for she has just recently[265] married the Duke of St. A***, Grand Falconer of England: a union which places her in the first rank of the nobility. One point worthy of notice is that the duke is descended from the famous actress Nell Gwynne, the

---

264 *TN Prince Hermann Ludwig Heinrich von Pückler-Muskau (1785–1871) Soldier, traveller and landscape artist, the Prince was fascinated with English country houses and, above all, their parks. His letters tracing his various visits to England in the years from 1826 to 1829 reveal that he spent three days in Brighton in late November 1827. In the letters, translated by Sarah Austin, he included a few lines on the Duchess of St. Albans. He stayed in the York Hotel, as did the Esterhazy family. It may well have been during that November that he met his old friend La Garde. See Chapter VI.*

265 *TN 16 June 1827*

mistress of Charles II; it is to her charms that the duke owes his title, so to a certain extent one can say that he has not betrayed his noble origins. That reminds me of another example of a rapid rise within society; it is part of English history of which I am sure you are aware.

'During the reign of Charles I, a young country girl, who had come to London to go into service, found work with a rich brewer: her beauty caught her master's attentions and he married her. Having been widowed and with her affairs in disarray, she was recommended to Mr. Hyde, who later became Lord Chancellor Clarendon; tempted by the lady's immense wealth, Mr. Hyde proposed marriage, the lady accepted and from that marriage was born the famous Miss Hyde who married the Duke of York, the man who was to become King James II, when he succeeded his brother Charles II. Miss Hyde was the mother of Mary[266] and Anne, both of whom became queens of England.'

I quoted to Sir Robert two lines from Ariosto:

'Fu il vincer sempre mai mirabile causa
Vincasi o per fortuna o per ingenio[267]

and went on:

'Similar examples of unions with actresses are rare in France; we have maintained our prejudices against the delightful art of the stage and neither time, nor the levelling effect of the revolution have been able to overcome them.'[268]

'Prejudices which went as far,' Sir Robert continued, 'as making you refuse to bury your great actors in consecrated ground; Garrick has his tomb in Westminster Abbey, alongside those of our kings. In England, sir, you will find that beauty and talent gain in brilliance from the adulation or the marriages which assimilate them into our most respectable families: only a few days ago a nobleman of the highest rank and in possession of an immense fortune, embellished his declaration of love to a beautiful young singer, Miss St***, with a blank cheque which she could complete with any amount she wished. "Duchess or nothing" wrote the young lady on the sheet of paper before returning it; here we have the struggle between virtue, love and pride: love, perhaps, will triumph.'

266 TN *The Dutchman William reigned with his wife Mary from 1689. They were succeeded by Anne who reigned from 1702 until 1714*

267 AN To be victorious, was ever glorious, Be we by fortune or by wit victorious.

268 TN *La Garde is a little out of date. The Revolution saw the end of systematic excommunication of actors and actresses. However, until that time, the religious rights of the profession had been rigorously curtailed: 'Think of Le Kain, excommunicated – dying without the sacrament – refused the burial of the Church, and flung into the common sewer ... whilst the body of Garrick was attended by British peers to Westminster Abbey'.* The Retrospective Review, *1824.*

'And yet, Sir Robert, prejudice prevails universally; have we not ourselves found oppressive customs in the various countries that we have travelled together, and even in this free land, where the human spirit seems to be so far ahead of its time; would you allow a Roman Catholic to become a legislator, a general or a magistrate in the land of his birth, in the land which he has made richer by his industry and which he has adorned with his works or defended with his life blood? Our customs, our laws, our ideas and our feelings are all imperfect, as we are ourselves: man sees, far off, those fanciful regions where perfection is to be found; he talks of them, but an insuperable power prevents him from reaching them; and as for the races we wish to enlighten, they are no more than overgrown children who wail when we bathe them clean.'

'Ah!' exclaimed Sir Robert, 'even the sun has its blemishes! And, I have no doubt, those we have will soon disappear from our laws, and despite one of your great speakers having said: "There are paths where one may not leave the rut for fear of falling from the cliff", as long as we have a Parliament in England, and orators who have the courage to make their voices heard, the joint causes of reason and justice will triumph sooner or later over ignorance and prejudice.[269]

'The lady who has just left us complains, with justification, of the unseemly attacks of which she is victim; her slightest movements are scrutinised, her every word is analysed, and she seems to be followed so that the every last detail of her private life can be criticised; caricature (that form of assassination which too often goes unpunished) pursues her in all its forms, it wearies her as it does her husband, with its barbed ridicule; and yet it is her name which one constantly sees heading the majority of charitable works and of worthy donations. Since she has been mistress of this large fortune, no one begs her in vain for her pity or her help and it can reasonable be said of her "that she is rich for the unfortunate". And what is more, even had she only the merit of using her immense wealth to come to the rescue of a great name in its moment of difficulty, the aristocracy should be grateful to her. To my mind, it is time to put a stop to this tasteless mockery; after all, what does it show? Envy, which like a burning coal blackens everything which is cannot consume.'

269 AN Not long after, this law was repealed, thus allowing all subjects, whatever their religious beliefs, to benefit from the same rights and the same advantages. *TN The Roman Catholic Relief Act of 1791 had already allowed Roman Catholics to enter the professions. The Catholic Emancipation Act of 1831 removed the final legal barriers to Roman Catholics taking a full and free part in English public life.*

'Your opinions seem all the more just,' I replied, 'for, by adopting the principal of refusing to attack innocent vanity and of respecting inoffensive pride, it is more useful to praise Lady St. A*** for the good which she does, were it merely to persuade her to persevere.'

'I understand you wish to attend an Almack's ball,' Sir Robert went on. 'Nothing is easier; before we go to Lord Southwell's, where we are expected for dinner, I will introduce you to Mrs. Herbert, one of the lady patronesses. She will put your name on the list and you will merely have to collect your ticket from the Ship Hotel tomorrow morning.'

LADY PATRONESSES' BALLS

THESE BALLS will commence at Shuckard's, OLD SHIP HOTEL, on Wednesday 7th November next, and which will continue on each succeeding Wednesday until further notice.

The Lady Patronesses request that all applications to them for tickets be made two or three days previous to the periods specified, as no tickets can be issued on the day of the Ball unless to persons who arrive too late at Brighton to attend to these regulations.

The dancing will begin precisely at HALF PAST NINE, and the doors close at TEN.

BRIGHTON HERALD, 27 October 1827

As we walked, I asked whether it was Sir Francis Burdett, whom the duchess had mentioned, who was the orator who had earned such a tremendous reputation by his speaking skills.

'The very same,' he replied. 'He entered Parliament sponsored by[270] the Duke of Newcastle, first for the small town of Boroughbridge, then for Middlesex and finally for Westminster. From the very beginnings of his parliamentary career, he was a member of the association dedicated to the success of the reform movement, and having not once deviated from his principles, merits the title, by which he was often called, of defender of the people.[271] He married one of the daughters of Lady St. Albans' first husband, hence the family's connection with her.'

270 *TN Sir Francis Burdett (1770–1844) seems have bought his seat for Boroughbridge (Yorkshire) from the agent of the Duke of Northumberland in 1796. Despite this rather unorthodox (to the twenty-first-century mind) way of entering Parliament, Burdett was a great reformer and instrumental in gaining rights for Roman Catholics.*

271 *TN Sir Francis was more popularly known as 'Old Glory.*

We found Mrs. Herbert surrounded by her daughters who were both beautiful and interesting, as are nearly all Englishwomen, praise which is easy to apply universally and which is well deserved.

In London, a lady patroness is an authority: she is appealed to and courted by the multitude of those who long to have a ticket, for she is the person who has in her gift the highly desirable seal of approval which appears to bestow the cachet of elegance and good taste. I have heard several examples of a rebuff which has been unimaginably severe: Baroness R***, despite the enormous reputation for wealth which attaches to her name, had the greatest difficulty in obtaining admission and it needed as much in the way of diplomacy, negotiation and conferences to determine whether she was to go to the Almack's ball, as if it had been a matter of fixing the interest or the credit of an empire; the price of the ticket is, however, a mere seven shillings (about eight francs).

Although the ball in Brighton attempts to rival its equivalent in London, the lady patronesses here have not yet reached that level of rigorous investigation. My name was put down with no difficulty, and once we had achieved our goal, we made our way to Lord Southwell's; the extremely kind welcome I had always received was as warm as ever, and I find I have something new to admire at each new visit. As always, I expressed to this delightful family the great pleasure I felt at being in Brighton and that they were, in a way, one of the main reasons for that pleasure:

'My stay here,' I added, 'will be one of the most agreeable episodes in my memoirs of my life.'

'Do you generally write them down?' asked Lady Southwell.

'Yes, My Lady, you can return to memoirs at a later date and have all the pleasure of hearing the voice of a former acquaintance.'

'And will you publish them?'

'Perhaps, My Lady; publishing a book is like sending a letter to known and unknown friends that one has throughout the world: and if I succeed in conveying the many and varied sensations given me by both the generous welcome and by the people to whom I am indebted for it, maybe my readers will stop reading and come to see and admire for themselves.'[272]

---

272 *TN In early 1828 the literary magazine* Athenaeum *published in English, eight weekly instalments of: 'Eight Days at Brighton by a Foreigner of Distinction'. This distinguished foreigner can be none other than Auguste de la Garde. Given that La Garde does not claim to be a very fluent English speaker, his text must have been translated for him. The* Athenaeum *text gives the main lines of La Garde's stay in Brighton, but does not go into as much detail as the 1834 French text. Many of the author's most revealing comments about Brighton are missing.*

At table there was a lady whose face I seemed to recall; but given the many long years since I had left Vienna and the fact that time had wrought so slight an alteration on her features, I did not dare to assume that my memory was exact; when, as we were going up to the drawing room, I was told that the lady was indeed Mrs. Concannon, and that her husband had been a Member of Parliament, my pleasure at seeing her again sent me rushing to her. If it is true, as many wags claim, that a woman's most inviolate secret is her age, it is delightful to be able to tell a lady who you have not seen for many years that, in our eyes, she has barely changed: there is no flattery in saying that Mrs. Concannon inspired this genuine compliment, and her friends joined me in assuring her of a fact that she was not tempted to dispute.

Mrs. Sarah Anne Concannon married Lucius Concannon in 1770 and thereafter moved in aristocratic circles. Eventually she was in effect exiled to Paris for her excessive gambling, as mentioned in the Morning Herald *in 1802:*

> December 18: "The visitors to Mrs. Concannon's petits soupers, at Paris, are not attracted by billets previously circulated, but by cards, afterwards dealt out, in an elegant and scientific manner; not to mince the matter, they are the rendezvous of deep play: and the only questionable point about the matter is, whether the Irish, or the French, will prove victors at the close of so desperate a winter's campaign.

Lucius Concannon M.P. (1764–1823) seems to have been no better than his wife, having shared her exile and helped run illicit gaming rooms (and, reputedly, a brothel) on the Continent. Somehow, Lucius later managed to procure a seat in Parliament, first representing a 'pocket' borough (i.e. one under the complete control of the local landowner) and then a 'rotten' borough (i.e. seats bought rather than won in elections).

Whilst, in an impromptu concert, several distinguished artists held the guests' attention, Mrs. Concannon and I withdrew to a side room where we were able to talk at length about our shared reminiscences.

She enquired eagerly after our friend M. Jules G***.

'He has been in Bucharest, madam, for the last two years, ever since I last saw him. Time and events, whilst they have parted us, have done nothing to lessen our mutual affection: I hear from him regularly, and my thoughts are the magnetic needle which tend constantly in his direction, for he is a lifelong friend.'

'Then I congratulate you, sir, for you can say, as did Ecclesiastes: "A faithful friend is a sturdy shelter; he that has found one has found a treasure".'

This quotation will not seem unusual on the lips of an English lady whose constant study is the holy scriptures.

She told me that, following the death of her husband, she had settled in Brighton[273] and in a very few words, told me the story of what had become of her since we had last met; it all seemed so recent to me, and so recently passed, that I truly felt, especially as I looked at her, that I was continuing a conversation with her that had been interrupted only the previous day, and yet, our last meeting had taken place … fifteen years previously!

Our reminiscences brought us back to that extraordinary time, or rather that extraordinary spectacle, which the Congress of Vienna had produced in 1814 but of which I have heard no detailed account elsewhere. We had been present at the magnificent fêtes, balls, banquets and parades, we had taken part in the endless entertainments in the presence of the crowned heads of Europe and her most illustrious public figures, who had joined in with the most wonderful light heartedness, despite the very recent end to twenty years of war and amidst the most complicated of negotiations. Within a very short time, we had talked over the galaxy of European dignitaries that the Congress had gathered in one place. Many amongst them seemed to have appeared for no reason other than to cast one dying ray of light upon this unique scene. This melancholy feeling brought us to the painful memory of the death of my illustrious friend, the Prince de Ligne,[274] who had breathed his last in my arms.

During her stay in Vienna, Mrs. Concannon had had the honour, as I had had myself, of being admitted into the inner circle of this astonishing man, old in years and yet still so young at over eighty summers. She had been close enough to him

273 AN Mr. Concannon, who had spent a considerable fortune in entertaining his friends, died at Boulogne-sur-mer, in a state bordering poverty. Unsolicited, these same friends set up a subscription fund for his widow. Mr. Adair took on the management of this fund and from the interest, they were able to give Mrs. Concannon an annuity of five hundred pounds sterling for life. This story would make a good paragraph in any Ciceronean treatise on friendship. There is nothing uncommon about such subscription funds. When the reckless Mr. Fox lost his whole fortune at the gaming table, the members of White's club met and, within a few days, paid over to him a considerable sum which earned the statesman, in all his unfortunate profligacy, an income of three thousand pounds sterling. *TN On 3 February 1823 a certain Lucius Concannon was buried at St. Marylebone in London. Place of death is not recorded.*

274 AN Died in Vienna on 13 December 1814

to be able to admire his sharp mind and his inexhaustible charm which flowed over in constant quips which others rushed to note and to quote; we recalled that he exercised his innocently satirical wit primarily on that most strange direction which the Congress had taken, for pleasure seemed to be the only business of any importance; whether we had been there to participate or to observe, we had all taken part in the general intoxication and we agreed that this uninterrupted succession of fetes, festivities and balls justified the prince's evocative pun: 'The Congress is not working. It is dancing.'

Our memories came thick and fast; the men, the events, everything which was of note, or which followed in the wake of this memorable gathering was rapidly recalled as we spoke. Seeing the importance Mrs. Concannon attached to this period, I confided to her that I had made a collection of sketches of the immense spectacle and that I intended to publish them at the earliest opportunity:[275]

'You will allow me, madam, to present you with a copy as soon as they are published, in memory of the pleasant moments which our meeting has given me and which I cherish.'

She agreed, and we took our leave of each other, in the hope that we would soon meet again.

The following day, at two o'clock, the time of day set aside for paying calls, I was ushered in to Baroness Dimsdale's house just as the lady was about to take her carriage to visit, as she told me, the chalybeate spring[276] which Mr. MacKinnon had mentioned to me; she suggested I accompany her. Being curious to discover a part of the area surrounding Brighton which I still did not know, I eagerly accepted; we set off on the Worthing road, and soon arrived. Although this spring does not have the curative powers attributed to the famous spa at Tunbridge Wells, doctors still recommend it as an excellent tonic. It generally serves as a meeting place or promenade, for it is the only spot close to Brighton where trees have been able to grow; and they are most welcome: their greenery, whilst being less abundant than in certain other parts of England, forms an oasis in the middle of the completely denuded hills surrounding it. They shade an elegant cottage in which lives the custodian of the spring, and, on fine summer days, many strollers crowd together beneath the leafy coppices in preference

275 AN The author of this present volume will soon publish the tableaux of Viennese society at the time of the 1815 Congress, which until today has only been examined from a political point of view. *TN La Garde published* The Journal of a Nobleman, being a Narrative of his Residence at Vienna during the Congress *in about 1833.*

276 *TN St. Ann's Well, Hove.*

to the pier and the esplanade, despite the fact that the latter are constantly cooled by sea breezes. During our return drive to Brighton, we talked of how English ladies occupied themselves. I had noticed that each hour of their day was given over to habits which practically never varied and to which custom bade them almost always adhere. According to what the baroness told me, in addition to my own observations, I believe the following picture is not inaccurate:

An Englishwoman gets up early; I can say nothing of this first scene of the day: in England, a lady's bedroom is a mysterious sanctum to which no one is admitted; by nine o'clock her toilette is complete: she will normally be wearing a clean and elegant morning dress which demands no less care and time than when she puts on her best finery.

The morning is spent in making music, reading, drawing or overseeing her children's education, which will be in the capable hands of a governess.

At one o'clock she will be 'at home': this is a custom which has the advantage that the caller can be certain that he will not disturb her by his visit, for he is expected; then lunch[277] is served, this is a light meal taken between morning tea and dinner; it is made up of cold meats, cakes and preserves; any visitor is invited to stay to eat; it is also at this hour that most children take their dinner.

Two o'clock is the time set aside for taking the air: the horses are harnessed, but before going on her ride, an English lady will visit the shops; there she will spend an hour, sometime more, choosing fabrics, jewellery, and those curious knick-knacks which are to be found in profusion on mantle shelves and drawing-room tables; and such is the force of habit that even here, where she is staying for such a short time, she rigorously obeys the rules, and so shopkeepers have opened up, in Brighton, emporia full of luxury items which are no less extravagant than those to be had in London.

At four o'clock, you can see her in state in her barouche following the line of carriages which parades along the sea front from Kemp-town to the last house in the King's-road. It is on this delightful promenade that people meet and decide upon which gatherings they will attend in the evening. Before she returns home, she will call at houses in various parts of the town where she will leave her card: in England these cards are dispensed in prodigious quantities and are remarkable for the fact of being three times the size of the ones fashionable in France.

277 *TN* 'The word *lunch* is adopted in that 'glass of fashion', Almack's, and *luncheon* is avoided as unsuitable to the polished society there exhibited.' H. D. Best in 'A Personal and Literary Memoir', 1829.

The Linen Drapers 1827
Mary Evans Picture Library

Once home, she makes her second toilette, this time for dinner. If she is to receive guests, the evening will be spent in conversation, making music and taking tea. This is followed by her third toilette, for the ball. If she has no guests, she takes the opportunity of repairing the fatigues of the previous evening by wisely adopting the Spanish and Italian fashion of retiring to take a indispensable *siesta* for a few hours, for although summer in Brighton is a period of rest for fashionable folk, the balls and the soirées still continue into the early hours as they do in London.

At nine o'clock she is dressed and be-jewelled for the ball: she sallies out into the same circle of pleasures which she enjoyed the previous day and into which the following day will plunge her, like clock-work.

Baroness Dimsdale invited me to stay for dinner; the only guests outside the family were Mr. MacKinnon and myself. After coffee had been served, the baroness left us. Mr. MacKinnon stated his intention of spending the rest of the evening at his club; I was very curious to learn about one of these establishments, which originated in England, and to compare it with those I had visited on the Continent, I therefore accepted his suggestion that I accompany him.

Our *cercles* in Paris are only too similar to the equivalent sort of gatherings in England for me to need to describe them; you can find the same level of opulence in the furnishings, in the service and in the servants; even the social class of the members is more or less comparable; there is talking, but very little and it is rarely loud or with people that one does not know. Visits to Brighton are normally very brief and this accounts for the fact that it is very difficult to achieve any level of intimacy. However, you need only be a member of a London club to find acceptance in a Brighton club without having to submit to any further election.

I did note one habit, which might well seem to be trivial but which, in my opinion, is characteristic of the independence an Englishman will display wherever he goes, and it is this: he greets no one on entering, he does not even take off his hat until he sees fit. I pointed this out to Mr. Mackinnon.

'It is the same in both houses of Parliament,' he told me, 'moreover, you must have noticed that if a lady acknowledges a gentleman when out walking, the latter replies with a mere nod of the head.'

In the club, there was a table laden with newspapers and periodicals.

'In this club we are far from having a complete collection of all the newspapers which are published in Great Britain, that is, all these clarions which the lowly require in order to be heard by the great. Since the time of Elizabeth I, when the first newspapers were attempted, this type of activity has grown to such an extent that nowadays we have roughly four hundred publications, as many of them daily as weekly; this brings the number of copies distributed annually across the three kingdoms to thirty-two million.

The three kingdoms La Garde mentions were England, Scotland and Ireland. The population of Great Britain in 1821 was 21,000,000; each person in the land would therefore have the equivalent of 1.5 copies of a daily or weekly newspaper available to him or her per year. At the beginning of the twenty-first century, the population stood at approximately 60,000,000. Some 12 million newspapers circulate daily (including Sundays); add to this about 41 million copies of weekly or monthly publications. This gives a total circulation of approximately 6500 million copies. The British citizen has available over 100 copies of newspapers or magazines per year. La Garde was impressed by the figures he quotes. A modern reader is not.

Brighton, for example, which did not have a single newspaper twenty years ago, now has three,[278] despite the fact that the town is practically on London's doorstep.'

We walked through several rooms in the club in which there were tables set up exclusively for whist, piquet and other games called games of negotiation as opposed to games of chance, the latter being strictly prohibited: each member has a winnings or losses account opened for him, the balance of which is not settled before the end of each month. The members were playing for high stakes and the wagers seemed to me to be excessive, which indeed proves man's need for powerful emotions.

278 *TN The* Brighton Herald *(1806), The* Brighton Gazette *(1825), The* Brighton Guardian *(1827);*

Chapter IX

A soirée with Lady S*** – The anniversary of the Gunpowder Plot – Mohamed's Baths – Colonel Fa*** – Young English ladies' conversation – Princess Esterhazy – The Duke of Devonshire – Prince Koslowsky – Napoleon's niece – Mr. Brummel *or* A King's friendship – The orphan in the prison – Reunited with her child.

For many years, England appears to have been the home of science and philosophy, at a time when they were practically unknown to the rest of Europe. If France can boast of having given birth to Descartes, who was the first to carry the torch of doubt into the night which beset the world, our neighbours rightly claimed that their illustrious compatriots, Newton, Locke and so many others, perceived and fixed upon ideas which the French philosopher did no more than glimpse; and so they claim for themselves the title of 'founders'.

Nowadays, Germany and France are friendly rivals. Having at last been called upon by their national character and the nature of their institutions to take part in these philosophical enquiries, which they had so long disdained, they now declare that this is a title which they will not surrender to the English. But it is my opinion that, at present, our two continental countries have nothing to compare to what I may call a most singular phenomenon: that of a woman who enquires into the metaphysical sciences to such depth and who reaches a level of genius which it is given to so few men to achieve; such an achievement I have just witnessed.

Amongst the people I had met at Lady Southwell's lodgings was Lady Mary S***: this lady enjoys a well deserved reputation in England; she had invited me to spend the evening at her home: I found there were few guests and this afforded me the unexpected pleasure of an intimate gathering. We discussed deep philosophical questions, to which Lady Mary seems, in large, to have devoted herself. I confess that the topic was completely new to me; indeed, I was reminded of something the Prince de Ligne had once said to me, namely that: 'silence was also a form of wit'. Being entirely without the latter, I had to rely on the former and limit my participation to that of attentive listener; a role which I found interesting and informative, especially when Lady Mary was speaking. I will not add my appreciation to that which her works have already won her; she brings profound wisdom and a singular felicity of style to the most complex questions; far from shirking difficulties, she seeks them out, overcomes them and even the most demanding of intellects agree unanimously that her writings hold a place in the first rank of those philosophical works which this century has produced.

Lady Mary Shepherd (1777–1847) published at least two treaties on metaphysics: An Essay on the Relation of Cause and Effect *(1824) and, very recently, as far as La Garde is concerned,* Essays on the Perception of an External Universe *(1827). She was staying at 20 Lower Rock Gardens. Like the Duchess of St. Albans, she did not escape the notice of those with a sharp tongue:*

> "Joseph dined yesterday with that crazy metaphysician Lady Mary Sheppard, who swore to me that she read and mastered Mr. Locke's profound treatise at eight years old. The best of it is that Joseph will not admit that she is insane, as she gives him fricandeau."[279]
>
> Correspondence of Mr. Joseph Jekyll to his sister-in-law Lady Gertrude Sloane Stanley, dated 7 October 1826

Occasionally this learned conversation was interrupted by a sweet voice and sounds which were as pure as the maiden who produced them: Lady Mary's daughter could be heard lightly running her elegant hands over the keys of her fortepiano; the attention we had been paying to the profound thoughts of the mother was momentarily suspended by the charm which her daughter lent to her playing; this was as brilliant as it was natural and merited Monsieur de Montlosier's delightful saying: 'Music is the idiom of the sensitive soul, as words are the expression of the scholarly soul.' Indeed, our soul never speaks so loudly as when it is awakened by music; it is like the nightingale who never sings better than when it hears its own echo rebound.

279 *TN A form of roast meat.*

After performing one of Cramer's most highly regarded pieces, she sang, to her own accompaniment, a ballade by Moore: *Farewell, but whenever you welcome the hour.*

La Garde gives the full translation into French. Here is the original from Moore's 1821 collection called 'Irish Melodies'.

I.

Farewell!—*but, whenever you welcome the hour,*
That awakens the night-song of mirth in your bower,
Then think of the friend, who once welcom'd it too,
And forgot his own griefs to be happy with you.
His griefs may return—not a hope may remain
Of the few, that have brighten'd his path-way of pain—
But he ne'er will forget the short vision, that threw
Its enchantment around him, while ling'ring with you!

II.

And still on that evening, when pleasure fills up
To the highest top sparkle each heart and each cup,
Where'er my path lies, be it gloomy or bright,
My soul, happy friends! shall be with you that night;
Shall join in your revels, your sports, and your wiles,
And return to me, beaming all o'er with your smiles!—
Too blest, if it tells me that, 'mid the gay cheer,
Some kind voice had murmur'd, 'I wish he were here!'

III.

Let Fate do her worst, there are relics of joy,
Bright dreams of the past, which she cannot destroy;
Which come, in the night-time of sorrow and care,
And bring back the features that joy us'd to wear.
Long, long be my heart with such memories fill'd !
Like the vase, in which roses have once been distill'd—
You may break, you may ruin the vase, if you will,
But the scent of the roses will hang round it still.

These Irish airs which Moore composed according to the dictates of his heart, were very much the fashion of the time; they could be found on every piano and were repeated every day by the prettiest lips. Being nearly all written in the minor key, they seem to take their inspiration from that form of melancholy which prompted Monsieur de Chateaubriand to say: 'In every land, man's indigenous melody is one of sadness, even when it expresses happiness; our heart is a flawed instrument, a lyre stripped of many strings. In the infancy of any race, when art is still in its imperfect state, it allows man to retain his own vernacular music, his own inherent melodies; it seems that he can express his joy only in tones redolent of suffering.'

At her mother's request, Miss S*** agreed to sing a piece of sacred music (*Oh Lord, the maker of all things!*) composed in 1528 by King Henry VIII of England before he had severed his kingdom from the Roman communion.

'I had no idea that the executioner of so many women could have been so sensitive to music,' I exclaimed.

'He played the English flute as well as his daughter played the spinet,' Miss S*** told me. 'You have only to look at the *Virginal Book* composed for the queen by the best musicians in the kingdom to see that.'

Lady S*** then asked me whether the strange ceremony taking place that morning had surprised me: and indeed, in various parts of the town I had come across numerous groups of children carrying, shoulder high, straw effigies dressed in very strange clothes; these children had been taking their effigy from house to house, singing ancient hymns as they went; each occupant was quick to give them a few coins. I had absolutely no intimation as to the origins of these extraordinary festivities, but seeing the delight of the youngsters, the excitement of the onlookers and the general air of satisfaction made it clear that this was a celebration. I had refrained from enquiring about the origins of this ritual, which undoubtedly recalled some important event or some ancient practice.

Lady S*** informed me that such festivities took place every year on the fourth[280] of November in memory of the uncovering of the Gunpowder plot, attributed to the papists and the aim of which was to blow up the whole of Parliament in one fell swoop. The effigy, which they burn, represents Guy Fawkes,

---

280 *TN Guy Fawkes was discovered and arrested beneath the Houses of Parliament on November 4th 1605 as he was preparing his assassination attempt on the king, James I. It was James himself who, sometime later in the seventeenth century, designated November 5th as the date to celebrate the 'joyful day of deliverance'.*

the instigator of this heinous plot, and not one town, not one village will ever fail to celebrate this memorable anniversary.

I expressed my desire to Lady S*** to learn more about this event which, although part of English history, was so little known to me. Young R***, nephew to Lady S***, then gave me the following explanation:

'The English Catholics had expected patronage from James I, a patronage which the monarch did not grant them; they resolved to take their revenge by massacring the king, his family and all the peers of the realm in one single attack.

'Percy and Catesburg,[281] two men who belonged to the best families in England, having placed themselves at the head of the conspirators, rented a house which gave access to the cellars beneath Westminster Hall. There they carefully placed thirty-six barrels of gunpowder in order to set the Hall ablaze on the day when the king was to come to address Parliament; never had a conspiracy been carried out so simply, with such daring and in greater secrecy.

'When the moment arrived, Percy, a religious fanatic, ready to sacrifice his king and all the public figures of the kingdom, failed to resist the call of friendship which pleaded with him to spare Monteagle, his childhood friend and one of the peers who was to sit in Parliament; he sent his friend an anonymous letter couched in these terms: "*If you love life, do not attend the opening of Parliament, for God and men have concurred to punish these corrupt times; the danger will be over in as short a time as it takes you to burn this note.*"[282]

'This warning caused the plot to abort. Monteagle was frightened by this confidential note and could not guess its motive which no clue, no hint would reveal to him. He informed King James who, struck by the ending of the letter: "*the danger will be over in as short a time as it takes you to burn this note*" and believing it to refer to a fire or a bomb, guessed the intentions of the plotters and, on the very night before the day on which Parliament was to meet, he had the cellars beneath the Hall searched; at one of the outer doors, a horse was found, ready saddled.

281 *TN La Garde's spelling of* Catesby.

282 *TN According to the Gunpowder Plot Society, the text of Thomas Percy's letter is as follows:*
My lord out of the love i beare to some of youere frends i have a caer of youer preseruacion therfor i would advyse yowe as yowe tender youer lyf to devys some excuse to shift of youer attendance at this parleament for god and man hath concurred to punishe the wickednes of this tyme and think not slightlye of this advertisment but retyre youre self into youre contri wheare yowe may expect the event in safti for thowghe theare be no appearance of anni stir yet i saye they shall receyve a terrible blowe this parleament and yet they shall not seie who hurts them this cowncel is not to be contemned because it may do yowe good and can do yowe no harme for the dangere is passed as soon as yowe have burnt the letter and i hope god will give yowe the grace to mak good use of it to whose holy proteccion i comend yowe.

'Guy Fawkes was there, armed with a lit taper, and in the cellar were thirty-six barrels of gunpowder.

'Once he had been arrested, he admitted everything and named his accomplices, who were caught, tortured and executed.

'It is to commemorate that hideous plot that every year we hold this ceremony and during the night, on all the hills overlooking the town, effigies of Fawkes will be burnt amidst cheering by the people and fireworks which they let off in celebration.'

> The 5th November, and the Gunpowder Plot passed off on Monday, with much less noise and bustle than has been usual at such celebrations here for years past. The libraries, and shops generally, were closed soon after sun set, and but few carriages were to be seen in the public streets. The southern enclosure of the Steyne was the chief scene selected for the fiery display, and there, hand-grenades, serpents, squibs and crackers constituted the principal of the hissing and sparkling missiles. No accident occurred, and, by ten o'clock, tranquillity in all parts seemed to prevail. The Police and Watchmen were all on duty, as spectators, merely, for in no instance, that we have heard of, was the exercise of their functions required.
>
> Lewes, Brighthelmstone and Sussex Advertiser, 12 November 1827

Lady Mary criticised this lingering barbarity which, by keeping alive an unjust aversion to Roman Catholics, was not one of the least obstacles to the efforts being made daily to lead the nation towards more benign attitudes in matters of religious tolerance.

Before the evening ended, Lady Mary did me the honour of presenting me with a copy of her book entitled 'The Perception of an External Universe'.

'I gratefully accept, madam, but I must confess that I will understand only what you will have the goodness to explain to me: whether in my capacity as a military man or as a traveller, I have spent my life in camp or on the road, surroundings in which I would have sought in vain the answers to such profound questions; but I am a malleable schoolboy when my teacher, such as yourself, holds the secret of making it a pleasure for me learn to my lessons.'

When she heard this, Lady Mary was kind enough to translate for me a few extracts from her book, and, amongst others, the one in which she deals with the extent to which one should believe in miracles; to this she could most certainly have added the miracle of a woman devoting the finest days of her life to gathering and deducing the proof of such inexplicable truths; had France not been able to claim for her own the Marquise de Châtelet, the first to introduce to her compatriots the sublime secrets of Newton's philosophy, it would be tempting to believe that England alone is capable of producing women able to delve into a science which seems so little suited to them.

Once the evening was over and had put an end to our delightful talk, I tried, as soon as I was at leisure, to discover anew in her book all those delights I had found in her conversation, but in vain.

Despite the lateness of the season, several people were still venturing into the Ocean's almost constantly rumbling waves; I had very little inclination to emulate them and preferred the Indian baths which had been established in Brighton by Mohamed, so the following day I set out for that establishment with the intention of comparing it with the ones I had frequented in Constantinople and in Moscow.

Here in Brighton, the bather is enclosed in a tent made of flannel which is quickly filled by a cloud of fragrant steam; then two arms belonging to an invisible body find their way into the tent and subject the bather's limbs to a succession of alternately gentle and vigorous manipulations which are known as *shampooing* and which impart to the body both strength and pliancy. In Moscow, the proceedings are less constrained; when the bather is stretched on his marble couch and covered with a thick layer of soapy foam, young slave girls of between twelve and fifteen years of age, wearing nothing but a simple apron, perform, and far more seductively, the function of *shampooer.*

In Constantinople, the bath is taken in a vast marble hall where one strolls through a constant haze of steam: as soon as one's blood has become as hot as it can, its agitation is quelled by a cascade of icy water. This proves to be as bracing as the delightful sensation is instantaneous.

In the baths at Brighton can be found the same refinement as in all the similar establishments in England: Mohamed, who was born in Calcutta, had made a particular study of the art of the bather, and is so attentive as to details that their beneficial effects seem to be immediate.

After resting a short while, I made my way to the esplanade to breathe in the invigorating sea air and to enjoy the pleasant conversation of the luminaries of this modern Portico.[283] There I found Lord and Lady Holland, His Lordship on his pony, Her Ladyship in an open, hand-drawn barouche, much like a handcart but carefully designed to place her in a position from which she was able to take part in the conversation. The presence of these two people, due to the powers of attraction which they both exert, had soon gathered around them the majority of their friends: this open-air club immediately acquired a very real interest from the importance of the topics under discussion. Lord Holland brought to such gatherings a freedom of expression which turned the statesman and parliamentary orator into a simple, easy-going man who repaid the adulation he was afforded with friendship; discussions took place without acrimony, positions were held without prejudice; these chance exchanges could well have served as an epitome of good taste and political debate; it is an art, according to Fox, which is acquired less by study than by the observation of people and events. We continued our discussion of the situation in Greece and of the influence that country's regeneration would have on the political balance in Europe; as the name of Colonel Fabvier[284] had just been mentioned, I was asked if I knew him; I replied that I often used to meet him in Paris before he had gone to Lyon as chief of staff to the Duke of Raguse; I had lost sight of him and since then, unwarranted persecution had dragged him into a form of opposition which had proved disastrous to him: a pamphlet, which he had had published at the time and in which he tore aside the veil which had been thrown over the causes of the insurrection in Lyon, had excited much resentment against the author; the events during the war in Spain resulted in his being exiled from his own country. He finally retired to London and took up his investigations into the application of chemistry to the arts, thinking all the while that he would return to Persia where he had once held a post in the French embassy and where he had left behind him a reputation as a brilliant artillery officer. Whilst he was in London, his homesickness and his uncertainty as to his future led him into a fit

283 TN *In third-century BC Athens, the philosophy of stoicism was developed by a group of philosophers. Their meeting place was the Portico of the Agora.*

284 TN *An incorrect spelling. La Garde is referring to Charles Nicolas Le Febvre (1782–1855), a liberal-minded soldier who, in 1817 had been suspended from his military duties in France and in 1820 had been charged with conspiracy relating to a popular insurrection in Lyon. There was insufficient evidence against him and he was released. In 1823, he had joined the anti-monarchist movement in Spain before taking up the cause of Greek independence of which he became an important leader. La Garde was not to know that within three years, Le Febvre was to become the military governor of Paris and that for the last ten years of his life he would be a French peer and member of the National Assembly.*

of despondency which seemed incurable, either by time or by providence; it was therefore with as much surprise as delight that, a few months after, I learnt from the newspapers of his arrival in Greece and of his most recent exploits which were, once again, to cover his career in glory. And so, little causes produce great effects: a single pamphlet gave Greece a valiant protector, thus possibly changing the face of the East.

I was summing up, in a very few words, the colonel's life when I was interrupted by the arrival of two young ladies who joined Lady Holland; the graceful bearing and the maidenly roses in their cheeks which were beginning to replace the pale hues of childhood, prompted that form of interest which early youth so readily attracts: these were the daughters of Lord Granville, the British ambassador in Paris.

Lady Holland quizzed them about their studies: the thoroughness and the clarity of their answers astonished me; indeed this was often the effect wrought on me by my conversations with the English girls I had met up to that time. These girls display a variety and a breadth of knowledge, a soundness of taste as well as an indefinable gravity and thoughtfulness in their speech such as I had met with nowhere else.

This result is due, I think, to the good, sound reading which is available to them in a vast number of periodical publications: in France it is only in the last few years that we have begun to have this sort of periodical in which articles appear on different questions relating to the arts, the sciences and literature, all subjects being treated in depth. In England, the most distinguished intellects do not scorn spending time on a host of weekly journals; not only must these journals evoke an interest in every very possible subject, but they must also be aware that an Englishwoman is obliged to spend her Sunday reading, as music, gambling, dancing and all other amusements are forbidden; she may resort solely to her studies.

The weather being fine, the fashionable strollers flooded onto the resilient pier; so bold in its structure is it that one cannot cease to marvel at its audacity.

Sir Robert drew my attention to Princess Paul Esterhazy, wife of the Austrian ambassador. I had seen this lady in Vienna, at the time of the Congress: some of her features brought to mind those touching expressions so often seen on the face of her aunt, the late queen of Prussia; her figure is elegant, her demeanour is natural and the charm of her intellect excuses her aloofness.

Princess Paul Esterhazy (1794–1874) was born Princess Maria Theresia von Turn und Taxis. She had married Prince Paul in 1812, not long before he became Austrian ambassador to the Court of St. James. The couple had three children by 1827. The family often spent time at the Royal Albion Hotel in Brighton.

> Brighton may be now said to be the abode of the Russian, Portuguese, and Austrian ambassadors. The families of the two former reside here, and the Portuguese ambassador, who is now in town, is expected to return in a day or two. Prince Esterhazy has been on a shooting excursion for a few days with the Duke of Wellington, and other noblemen, at the seat of Sir John Shalley, at Maresfield, about twenty miles distant, but is expected to return to the York hotel this day.
>
> The Times, 1 February 1827

'But,' I said to Sir Robert, 'this pier is indeed a cosmopolitan pageant; I feel as if I have been transported to the banks of the Neva when I see that Russian nobleman who, by the opulence of his furs and the cut of his pelisse, I would take to be a Muscovite boyar.'

'That Russian nobleman,' Sir Robert replied with a laugh, 'is the Duke of Devonshire;[285] and yet your misapprehension is forgivable, for the duke has recently returned from Moscow, to which city he had gone in order to represent our king

285 TN *William George Spencer Cavendish, 6th Duke of Devonshire (1790–1858). The 'Bachelor Duke' was Lord Chamberlain of the (Royal) Household in 1827. Over his lifetime, he embellished the gardens at Chatsworth House to the designs of the young Joseph Paxton. He died in another of his eight stately homes: Hardwick Hall in Derbyshire.*

at the coronation of the new Tsar; he has no doubt returned with that sable coat.'

We made our way over to him and he met us with a courtesy very much in keeping with his countenance and his manners. As he was introducing me, Sir Robert told him of my error; the duke used this as a pretext to tell us about Moscow, about the festivities and a whole host of details, interesting to me for the memories they aroused in me.

The two people who came to join us could not have reminded me more vividly of Mother Russia; one was Prince Kozlowsky, formerly the Tsar's ambassador to Turin and whom I had known very well at St. Petersburg, and especially at Vienna at the time of the Congress of Vienna.

'The prince,' Sir Robert told me, 'is considered to be the most witty man of our age, an age which is not, let it be said, lacking in wit; he is one of that small band of foreigners which English society has admitted most enthusiastically to its ranks; a decision which has been justified, moreover, by his wide ranging erudition and above all, his conversation, which is full of information, passion and eloquence, and which would be perfect were his monologues not so frequently to exclude dialogue.

'The other is Monsieur La***ky,[286] attaché to the Prince de Lieven; going under the self-effacing name of Polonius, this young man has published poetry in French which would not be disowned by your own two poets, Casimir Delavigne and Lamartine.'

'I delight in encountering illustrious people and names,' I told Sir Robert. 'The Duke of Devonshire has long been famous for his admirable patronage of the arts and it was no doubt his mother's[287] elegant verse which our poet Delille translated; on the other hand it can be said of Prince Kozlowsky that he is the worthy successor of the man sent, as a model of wit and Russian courtesy, to Voltaire at Ferny.'

'But since you are attracted to names with an historical resonance, that is added reason to meet this pretty compatriot of yours who is coming towards us on the arm of Sir Sidney Smith; she is the daughter of Lucien Bonaparte and is married to Mr. W***, an Irish gentleman. He saw her in Rome and stole her heart by promising to escort her to her uncle on St. Helena; the marriage took place, but

---

286 *TN Xavier Labensky (1790–1855) was a Polish diplomat who first served his country in St. Petersburg and then joined the Russian consulate in London.*

287 *TN Georgiana Spencer, later Duchess of Devonshire (1757–1806). The notoriously profligate duchess wrote her poem 'The Passage of the Gothard Pass' on leaving Switzerland to set off through Revolutionary France in 1893. The poem was, however, much embellished by her in later years. The poem was translated into French in 1802.*

the journey never did, for news of the emperor's death arrived just a few days after the wedding; the rest is a fragment of history which she tells most amusingly: I will leave her to tell you her own tale, for you will no doubt be introduced to her.'

Laetitia Christine Bonaparte (1804–71) was niece to Napoleon I and daughter of Lucien Bonaparte; aged just 17 she married Sir Thomas Wise in 1821. She left him in 1828. She had two sons by Sir Thomas (Napoleon Alfred and William Charles) followed by three more children, possibly by different fathers. Napoleon III, her cousin, paid her an annuity and banished her from France, on the grounds that she was an embarrassment to the imperial family of the time.

The mere name of this lady would have sufficed to awaken in me a lively interest, even had there been no reason to admire her beauty which allied both French elegance and Italian vivacity.

'Do you see that young woman surrounded by all those pretty children?' Sir Robert asked me. 'That is Lady Uxbridge,[288] whose father has just been appointed as Lord-Lieutenant of Ireland, or "Viceroy" as you would say in French. You will no doubt see her this evening with her husband at the Almack's ball, for I trust that you have not forgotten to send for your ticket. Unlike the London fashion, here in Brighton the ball starts early; that does not prevent it from continuing most possibly until daybreak. I intend to accompany my daughter. If a family dinner holds no fears for you, may I invite you to share ours, after which we can set off together for the ball?'

I accepted Sir Robert's invitation and left him to go to change my morning coat for my evening finery.

On returning to my hotel, although it was only early in November, I was surprised to find that my room was icy cold; but here the practice is quite the opposite of that in France, for in England, as soon as the guest has left his room in the morning, it is customary to open all the doors and windows, whatever the weather: it is claimed that renewing the air is vital for one's health, the result of which is that draughts are created in every nook and cranny. To my mind, this

288 *TN Eleanor, Lady Uxbridge (c1799–1828) This young woman was the daughter-in-law of Henry Paget, 1st Marquis of Anglesey. Henry Paget was appointed Lord-Lieutenant of Ireland in late February 1828, some two months after La Garde had left Brighton. The author is clearly conflating two events: meeting Lady Uxbridge in Brighton and hearing of the appointment during his later stay in London. Eleanor was to die some seven months after meeting La Garde, leaving three small children, the youngest being only seven years old.*

peculiar behaviour is the cause of the many rheumatic complaints from which the English suffer; but here, as everywhere else, despite the experience being a costly one, it is good form to take little notice of it.

At Sir Robert's I met Mr. Brummel,[289] his two daughters and an agreeable young man, Mr. Lambton, brother of Lord Durham and distant relative of Lord Grey.

Mr. Brummel is the brother of a man who, for fifteen years, until 1810, was held to be the archetype of what is called in England 'the dandy'.

The story of his life, from that point of view, was perhaps one of the most curious of our century: being known by the sobriquet 'Beau' Brummel and taken by the fashionable world as the arbiter of fashion, he was accepted by the Prince Regent into his intimate circle; but one tactless remark, which George IV never forgave, lost him, forever, the favour of his august patron.

At a dinner in the Brighton Pavilion, when the high spirits of the banquet seemed to authorise a certain familiarity, the wine ran dry. At that precise moment, the Prince Regent happened to be standing next to the fireplace; Mr. Brummel quipped: '*George, ring for the servant*', a phrase which has been repeated time and time again throughout England. The prince did indeed ring, and when the servant appeared, he said to him: 'Bring Mr. Brummel's carriage'. The latter understood and withdrew; the prince never again set eyes on him.[290]

During dinner, I was struck by the remarkable similarity between one of Mr. Brummel's daughters and Countess Rosalie Rczewouska, a lady I had had the good fortune to meet in Warsaw; I commented upon this to Sir Robert, who had also known the Countess.

'May I enquire about the lady,' Mr. Brummel then asked, 'who my daughter so reminds you of? I assume from her name that she is Russian.'

'No, sir, she is Polish,' I told him, 'and one of the most distinguished women in her country, as much by her noble rank as by the astonishing story of which she is the heroine and which, in a century which is so prolific in extraordinary events, seems to trump the most touching fiction to be found in a novel.'

These few words were enough to awaken Miss Brummel's curiosity and I was not slow to satisfy it.

---

289 *TN William Brummell, elder brother of the more famous Beau Brummell, would have been in his late fifties in 1827.*

290 AN A few months before his death, the King finally pardoned Mr. Brummel who was subsequently appointed English Consul in Le Havre. *TN Most accounts agree that Brummell's offensive words were: 'Alvanley, who is your fat friend'; a remark aimed at the Prince Regent for having snubbed the 'Beau' at a banquet he, Brummell, and Alvanley had hosted some weeks previously.*

'During the Terror which inundated France with guillotines and tears, Princess Fanny Lubomirska, who was as famous for her noble birth as for her beauty, lived in Paris. As her sole occupation was that of raising her only daughter Rosalie, who was five years old at the time, she believed that, in France, she was protected by the sacred laws of the rights of man; but she was denounced to the revolutionary committee as a conspirator against the Republic and sent before the murderous tribunal; she was indicted, charged and condemned to death all within the space of a few days; such was the fate of the too trusting foreigner.

'Despite being separated from all her own servants during her imprisonment in the Conciergerie, she had been allowed to keep her daughter with her; on the day the unfortunate mother was dragged to the block, she entrusted Rosalie to the care of her companions in misfortune; but these ladies, who soon suffered the same fate as the princess, bequeathed Rosalie to other women prisoners until the poor child, after being adopted and passed from victim to victim, was taken in by the prison laundress, a Madame Bertot. This worthy woman, moved by the girl's plight, added this sixth child to the five to whom she was already mother and so became guardian angel to the orphan in the dungeon.

'Despite being raised in conditions so very different from the ones which fate had intended for her, already Rosalie allied the finest qualities of the heart to the most felicitous gifts of nature; her readiness to help her benefactress in her work, and her eagerness to please, combined with her affectionate manner, led her adoptive mother to make no distinction between the young orphan and her other children.

'The Terror was over, and the list of victims, which had been published throughout Europe, had acquainted the princess's friends with the knowledge that, in a land said to be free, an illustrious Polish noblewoman had paid for her imprudent confidence with her head.

'When he learned the dreadful news, Count Rczewousky,[291] the Countess's brother, hurried to Paris. With the help of the authorities, he set about tirelessly tracing the daughter of his wretched sister; for several weeks he tried every manner of enquiry, but in vain; promises, descriptions, public notices, nothing was overlooked: the poor laundress read neither the newspapers nor the announcement of the promised reward; the jailer in the Conciergerie, the only person who could

291 TN *The masculine form of Rczewouska.*

have furnished any information about the orphan, was dead and, already, his post had been taken by others; nothing, so it would appear, seemed destined to put the count on the track of the darling child; everything led him to the fearful conclusion that poverty and neglect had hastened the end of the orphan's life. Yet Providence seems to have exhausted its trials for Rosalie and now permitted more favourable circumstances: the laundress of the Conciergerie also served in the Hotel Grange-Batelière,[292] the place where the count had taken lodgings on arriving in Paris.

'One morning, as Rosalie, accompanied by her adoptive mother, was returning laundry to the hotel, the count caught sight of her as she crossed the courtyard; struck by her beauty, he thought he could discern in the girl's features some resemblance to those of his sister.

'"What is your name, my pretty one?" he asked the child.

'"Rosalie, sir," she replied.

'"Rosalie! you say, my little maid ... Is this child yours, my good woman?" asked the count, turning to Bertot's wife.

'"Yes, sir, she is my very own, for I have cared for her these last three years; but when I say she is mine, I was not the one who gave birth to her, for she is the daughter of a poor prisoner and she has neither mother nor father; but, you see, sir, for me, misfortune is like bird lime, I cannot resist its cries."

'"You say she was the daughter of a prisoner?"

'"And a very great lady, what's more, sir, who was guillotined with so many in Robespierre's time."[293]

'From that instant, the count no longer had any doubts but that this was his niece: to convince himself completely, he spoke to her in Polish. Hearing that accent which reminded her of the sweet impressions of her childhood, Rosalie's tears started to flow and she threw herself into the arms of the count, saying:

'"Oh sir, I can understand you, I can understand you! Please say it again. That was how my mother would speak to me."

'Overjoyed, the count pressed Rosalie to his heart, shedding the sweetest of tears over her.

---

292 TN *This hotel was well known in the early nineteenth century and was in the Rue Pinon. The street name disappeared, as did the street itself, under the rebuilding work of Haussmann in the 1860s. It would have been in what is now the 8th arrondissement, off the Rue d'Artois, just south of the Boulevard Haussmann.*

293 TN *Maximilien François Marie Isidore de Robespierre (1758–94) A dominant figure in the extremist Jacobin movement and instrumental in the death of King Louis XVI and the Terror, Robespierre eventually came to be seen as too despotic. He was arrested on 27 July 1794 and guillotined on the 28th.*

'"Rosalie, oh my Rosalie, I have found you," he told her. "You are my niece, the daughter of my beloved sister."

'Then, turning to the good Madame Bertot, who had been rendered dazed and speechless, he said, as he returned the girl to her arms:

'"My dear woman, you will always be her mother, you will never leave her: since the abandoned orphan has been a part of your family, your family will never cease to be a part of hers; and that, from now on, is how we will share her with you."

'As he spoke, he gave the laundress a purse filled with gold and made her undertake to take lodgings that very day, with all her children, at the Hotel Grange-Batelière.

'Soon after, he left Paris to return to Poland and good Madame Bertot followed, with her Rosalie.

'The children of the laundress were most conscientiously brought up under the watchful eye of the count; the boys entered the university at Wilna and thereafter joined the Polish army where they became aides-de-camp to Prince Poniatowski; the girls were given handsome dowries and were married to Polish gentlemen.

'As for the beautiful Countess Rosalie, the orphan of the prisons, who you so greatly resemble, miss, she married her cousin, Count Rczewousky and, at the time when she told me her touching story, during the Congress of Vienna, wealth and happiness had spread their golden veil over her fate; her benefactress, the estimable Madame Bertot, still lived nearby, and the countess had never ceased to love her like a mother and to call her "my salvation".'

'That is an anecdote,' said Miss Wilson, 'which history will perhaps overlook, but which deserves to be engraved upon the heart of every woman.'

'Yes,' agreed Mr. Lambton, 'such deeds should be known and published, so that public esteem may reward feats which are, alas, only too rare; I may add that a single example of devotion, which one might call a happy accident, often suffices to allow a man to pass into posterity.'

'The story of Lavalette no doubt proves that,' added Sir Robert. 'Some men work their whole life to imprint their name onto the future and yet have far less success than did Lavalette upon being arrested by the Assize Court, from which, happily, he managed to escape;[294] but there is, in truth, a most singular analogy

294 *TN With the aid of Sir Robert Wilson. See page 99.*

between the polish orphan's adventure and this tale of Montaigu's heir: For several years a disconsolate mother, Lady Montaigu,[295] having exhausted every enquiry in an attempt to find her child, who had been lost by a careless servant, found herself face to face with a young sweep who had come down the chimney and into her ladyship's bedroom. Through the soot which covered him, she believed, having that discernment which only a mother possesses, that she could make out the distinctive mark that her son bore on his face; she examined the boy, questioned him and, by this quirk of fate, the lost child was returned to his rightful inheritance and to the arms of his illustrious family.

'To celebrate this miraculous rebirth, each year, in their town house, the Montaigus give a feast to the Guild of Chimneysweeps of London; the servants hand round the dishes wearing their grand livery and her ladyship in person does the honours of this banquet for the poor children whose work and poverty had been shared by her son.'[296]

Soon after, the ladies left us for short time to add a few adornments to their ball gowns; but as nature had already taken care of the greater part of their toilette, they soon returned downstairs and we set off for Ship-street, which was at no distance from the house Sir Robert had taken.

---

295 TN *La Garde's spelling of Montague.*

296 TN *The Montagues gave the chimney sweeps a feast on 1 May in their house in Portland Square, London from the early 1780s until well into the following century. There is no indication that the story of the lost son is true, but much to illustrate that the Montagues were very charitable aristocrats, concerned with the hardships of working people.*

Chapter X

Madame de Staël's quip – Almack's Ball – English ladies – A review of society – Contrasts – An heiress – Mr. Thelusson's will – Dancing in England – A lover fined – Young ladies and the law – Supper – The sham Shakespeare.

Madame de Staël's admiration for English government is generally acknowledged: in her work *Considerations on the French Revolution,* the celebrated lady's swan song, her high regard is everywhere evident, often to the point of extravagant enthusiasm. But it does not seem that she extended her appreciation to English social customs: in particular, the large number of assemblies were not at all to her taste; she considered them to be chores, tiresome gatherings which were more wearying to the body than to the mind: 'Everyone is elbow to elbow,' she says, 'as if one were in the crush bar at the theatre. You have to exert yourself prodigiously to cross a drawing room and are nearly suffocated.'

Lurking in this unwarranted quip may perhaps be detected the secret motive which occasioned it: 'The crowd is so great,' Madame de Staël continues, 'that not even beauty has room to be seen.' This somewhat bitter remark allows us to glimpse that, for her, these drawing-rooms were too cramped, not only for beauty, as everyone knows, but for her to deploy her superior mind. One is reminded of the ease with which she transformed conversation into a, doubtless admirable, monologue, but which erred in that it constantly obliged everyone in the group to take up the role of benign listener, thus firmly prohibiting them from becoming participants. However, in England, there is a multitude of such gatherings and they do not easily lend themselves to such conduct: *inde iræ!*[297]

---

297 TN *Inde iræ*: *'Hence the resentment'. Here, la Garde is perhaps too tactful to write 'Hence her resentment' referring to Madame de Staël.*

I would counter this self-regarding remark by a famous lady with my own simple observations: in England, I have been to a great many gatherings; at them I have found sufficient space to admire freely the beauty of several women; I have not been so crushed or squeezed that I could not enjoy the conversation of many others; and lastly, I have been able, making no exertion whatsoever, to extricate myself, safe and sound, without having run the slightest risk of being suffocated.

It was nine o'clock when we left for the Ship Hotel.[298] Unlike the London fashion which does not allow you to arrive at the ball until after midnight has struck, the rooms were already full. The fashionable world believes that, in Brighton, it may a little relax the customs which, in all other places, bind it with a law both rigorous and absolute. A little thought would, however, have sufficed to ban from England such a callous use of the night time which the ardent temperatures of Italy barely excuse. In Florence and in Naples, one lives, and one can live, at night; in London, one should live only by day. In Venice, I have seen performances which started at midnight; that I can understand, for the cool, perfumed air of the morning counters any fatigue; beneath the misty skies of England, on the contrary, the vapours of the night become damper and colder with the dawn; they clutch at the vitals, which, having lost all power to resist, are overtaxed by them. It is in such conditions that the young girl, sparkling with jewels, leaves the ball, where her soul has just blossomed with so much happiness; intoxicated with the festivities, the compliments and the pleasures she is, upon the instant, frozen to the marrow, thus she pays the price, through much suffering and often even death, of a senseless ritual. She perishes because it is not permitted that a polite assembly begin before midnight or end before seven o'clock in the morning: it is fashion which kills her.

Although the ball was given in an hotel, or more properly, a tavern, I was dazzled, on entering, by the profusion of lights, by the opulence of the dresses and the brilliance of the hangings. All the women were sumptuously dressed and radiant with diamonds and other precious stones. Their dress did not display, it is

---

298 *TN Now known as The Old Ship Hotel. The* London Times *reported on 15 November 1827:*

The Almack's Ball, last night, had, as was anticipated, a very full and brilliant attendance. The rooms have been newly fitted up and decorated, at an expense of nearly £900, under the direction of Mr. Crace, the artist by whom the gilding and ornaments of the Pavilion here, and of the Castle at Windsor, have been executed. Their appearance is magnificent.

The Old Ship Hotel
Image reproduced courtesy of the Brighton Royal Pavilion, Museums and Libraries

true, that exquisite refinement which our Parisian ladies exemplify to perfection, but English ladies excel by their very own particular type of beauty: they have a fresh complexion,[299] delicate skin, a chaste profile and wear a maidenly expression which recalls those enchanting compositions by Raphaël and Correggio: it would be a truly faultless combination, were they to add to it, in so far as their outfits are concerned, that indefinable *certo non so che.*[300]

Leaving Sir Robert and his family, I wandered through the various rooms. As good luck would have it, it was not long before I chanced upon my old friend, Mrs. Concannon, who most kindly agreed to be my guide. Once we had examined the various knots of people, we went to sit on a sort of dais which ran round the main room and from where we could study the whole gay scene spread before our eyes.

With her wealth of memories, Mrs. Concannon combined in her conversation both interest and variety. Her observations were concise; within a very few moments she had characterised the various individuals who passed by us in this lively parade.

---

299 AN This proves the truth of Voltaire's quip to Mr. Sherlok who had asked him his opinion of the fare in England: 'Very fresh and very white' replied the philosopher of Ferney, playing on our two French words *chère* (fare) and *chair* (flesh / fair sex).

300 *TN The English prefer the French phrase 'un certain je ne sais quoi'. In plain English 'a certain something'.*

'Do you see,' she said to me, 'that lady and that young man who are coming towards us: what a contrast there is in the way they look! The lady is morose and out of sorts, she seems to carry the burden of many troubles; the gentleman is lively and bright: in him you can see reflected all the joy of happiness and a carefree life; the lady has possessions, the gentleman, merely hopes: that is the secret of their two lives.

'The lady, Miss W***, commands a fortune amounting to some two million pounds;

Sophia Elizabeth Wykeham (1790–1870) In the early 1820s Miss Wykeham had been courted by the Duke of Clarence, the third son of George III. Although extremely rich, Miss Wykeham was also considered to be somewhat eccentric. A marriage between the pair was therefore forbidden by both the Prince Regent, the duke's older brother, and the Government. The duke never lost his affection for the lady and upon becoming King William IV in 1830, he made her a peeress. For very many years Miss Wykeham, who never married, rented a furnished house for the fashionable season at 65 Regency Square.

---

she could be happy, but a pernicious idea is ruining her life; being convinced that the proposals she receives are occasioned by her wealth alone, she has rejected them all, even the one which would have placed her on the very steps of the throne. Now she is isolated and beginning to think that wealth does not always guarantee happiness; this figment of the imagination, which we entertain during the long years of our childhood, has credence only when we share it; too often, to wish to be loved for one's self is to pursue a chimera.

The other person is Mr. Charles Thelusson;[301] you are no doubt aware of his forebear's will, in which the dying man stipulated that his considerable fortune be invested in such a way that the accumulated interest might be left to the male child of the fourth generation upon that boy reaching his majority; the will requires that, in the absence of a male heir, the moneys be used to cancel the English national debt. This outrageous clause, which has disinherited four successive generations, has given rise to an Act of Parliament to prevent such a thing occurring ever again.[302]

301 TN *Charles Thellusson (1797–1856).*
302 TN *The Accumulation Act of 1800.*

Mr. Charles Thelusson is the father of the child destined to benefit, one day, from a fortune so vast that the imagination can hardly grasp its magnitude.[303] In but twelve years time the great question of whether this boy will be richer than any king in Europe will have been resolved. He need do more than live!!!'

'It would seem to me, madam, that a novelist with a modicum of imagination and basing himself on these impending events would easily sketch the plot and all the intrigue of a novella. It would lend itself to the strangest of incidents and could be called "*Thelusson reaches his majority*":[304] the author would have his hero submit to all sorts of nonsensical or solemn situations brought about by the disposal of such a colossal fortune: he would use it either charitably to bring about all manner of improvements, even extending to the moral faculties of objects of his charity, as did the philanthropist Owen in his Lanark establishment,

---

Robert Owen (1771–1858) The new, philanthropic ideas of Robert Owen were already taking hold in Brighton as shown by the item in the Brighton Herald *on 20 October 1827:*

> We are informed that a society, called the Brighton Co-operative Society, has been formed in the town, the ultimate object of which is, the establishment of a community on Mr. Owen's plan, setting aside emigration. We have not heard of the intended site.

According to Timothy Carder's Encyclopaedia of Brighton, *the Co-Operative Society opened its shop, the first of its kind in Britain, on 1 January 1828 at 31 West Street.*

---

or he would be swept into a delirium of ambition, using his millions as so many levers to arouse passions, corrupt the masses and accede to the power supreme; whether it be to good or evil that he finally succumbs, the possibilities are infinite. Let him be successful in winning glory, love, ambition, fame, let his life encompass all things, but let not fulfilment blunt all his cravings and lead him to despondency and discontent. Why should that surprise? Fortune's favours are like those of love,

303 *TN In 1859, Charles' son, Charles Sabine Auguste Thellusson (1822–85), along with his relative Lord Rendelsham, eventually inherited the 'accumulated' sums of money left by their great-great-great grandfather. However, there had been so much legal dispute about the precise meaning of the original will that each man inherited very little more than the original sum of money left by their forbear at his death.*

304 *TN La Garde is being most prescient. It is believed that the legal wrangling associated with the Thellusson fortune inspired Charles Dickens to create the fictional case of Jarndyce v. Jarndyce. Dickens called his novel* Bleak House *(1853).*

one can rarely pass from illusion to reality without losing something in the process. The outcome of our true pleasures is the *aurea medicritas*;[305] there is no pleasure for man once he has exceeded this golden mean. I recall that when Count Potocki died at Tulczyn, the children from his first marriage inherited his enormous wealth. Two of them, who were students at the University of Leipzig, had during their father's lifetime, received no more than a few ducats a week in pin money. Once they were masters of their inheritance, their first extravagance was to buy an entire perfumer's shop in Odessa simply to enjoy the delights of hurling every item of stock out of the window; and then their eldest brother, Count Schesney,[306] lost three million florins playing faro with his bailiffs on his Tulczyn estate; shortly thereafter, his friend, M. de Fontenay, who had always stood by him, was obliged to borrow one hundred gold louis to bury him at Aachen, where the count had died. Alas! human nature! ...'

The dances, from which there had been a brief interval, started again: a few young officers in uniform appeared, wearing their sword at their side. I confessed my surprise to Mrs. Concannon.

'It is a chivalrous gesture, but in poor taste,' she told me. 'The good sense of the public will soon prove to it be a mistaken one.'[307]

If, no matter in which land you find yourself, it is enjoyable to dance for pleasure at a ball, it can be said to be an indispensible accomplishment in England. As one may speak only to those to whom you have been introduced, and in general one is introduced to a lady only in order that one may dance with her, a stranger runs the risk of being never able to approach any lady if he does not first undergo this crucial preliminary. Mrs. Concannon, having told me of this custom, offered to introduce me to those ladies with whom I wished to dance; as dancing these days is no more than an elegant promenade around the room, I accepted her present offer in order to avail myself of it later.

'Who,' I asked her, 'are those ladies in the quadrille just near us?'

'Miss Ricards,[308] Miss Stewarts, Miss Sartorys and Miss Smith; the latter is

---

305 *TN The Golden Mean – the desirable middle way between two extremes.*

306 *TN La Garde's simplified form of Szczesny*

307 *TN The correspondent of the* London Times *must have been at the same ball, for he reported on 20th November 1827:* The gay circle at Almack's were not a little scandalised at the ball last week, by the appearance of no less than four officers of the 52nd wearing *their swords*, and actually dancing with them. How they contrived to get through the mazes of the quadrille without coming in contact with their fair partners, remains a mystery: but their exalted brethren of the cavalry regiment stationed here (the 7th Hussars) have indulged in many a jest at their expense.

308 *TN La Garde seems to be struggling with names such as Richards and Stewart.*

the niece of Mrs. Fitzherbert. The young lady, having been born in England and brought up in France, combines the most pleasing qualities of the two countries.

Marianne Smythe (birth date unknown – 1859). In 1817 Mrs. Fitzherbert became surrogate mother to the young Marianne. The young girl was probably an illegitimate daughter of Maria Fitzherbert's brother, Jack Smythe. Most theories that she was the legitimate daughter from the secret marriage between Mrs. Fitzherbert and the Prince Regent have now been discounted as being highly unlikely. Marianne married Edward Jerningham in June 1828.

She is brimming with talent and good education; in both her bearing and her dress you can observe the social graces we associate with your female compatriots and with which she has returned to us.'

Indeed, I had picked her out from among her companions: they were all beautiful, alive with youth and health, but, no doubt from native intuition, I found Miss Smith had something of the Frenchwoman about her which immediately attracted favourable attention. Her complexion was pale, but her pallor was dazzling, her long black lashes framed her fine blue eyes and gave her features a kindly, melancholy look. In short, the calm expression of benevolence on her face was equal to the elegance of her bearing.

The quadrille was followed by a waltz; a young man whose lively, agreeable face spoke of the qualities of his heart, was partner to Baroness Dimsdale.

As he passed near us, Mrs. Concannon said to me: 'There you see a prime example of our elegant young men. A somewhat scandalous trial has made no little contribution to his becoming fashionable. Being the adored lover of the wife of one of the richest bankers in London, he was one day caught unawares by the jealous husband, whose indignation exploded in damaging publicity: the transgressions, however, continued unabated, and, as compensation for this *criminal conversation,*[309] young Mr. W*** found himself subjected to a fine of several thousand pounds. He would have had to pay it or lose his freedom, had his beautiful accomplice not come to his rescue by paying the whole amount. Chastened by those inconveniences which accompany such adventures, he sought out a calmer and more natural form of happiness and found it in his marriage to that charming lady who you can see next to Countess Cowper.

309 *TN La Garde uses, in English, this coy English phrase which referred to adultery.*

'As for the rich and anxious heiress, Miss W***, you can see that she has resolved to become a little more philanthropic, for she is waltzing with one of our military veterans, Baron S***, who has thirty years' service to his credit; but really, what he is undertaking now demands as much gallantry as a good twenty campaigns, unless the saying is still true that there is no incense which turns a lady's head more than the one which does not burn for her.'

Whilst the refreshments were circulating, Mrs. Concannon took the opportunity to introduce me to Miss Smith, to whom I immediately offered my arm until the next quadrille began. If I had been delighted by the many charms which others so admired in her, I was all the more enchanted when we had spent a few moments in conversation! Having but rarely the need to defend themselves against seduction, young English ladies bring to their intercourse with men a naivety and a freedom which a foreigner must struggle to comprehend. Once the next dance had ended, Miss Smith again took my arm and we strolled through the ballroom for a considerable time; on escorting her back to her friends, I took a seat next to Mrs. Fitzherbert.

The kindly look which shone on the lady's face, with its regular, still noble features, inspired real admiration. Her conversation was as captivating as it was varied. Her exalted position had enabled her to know and to judge everything that had had any influence or reputation at the English court.

The dances had come to an end some moments previously and now the crowd was hurrying into the room where we were sitting; everything was set out for drinking tea. A host of elegant little tables had been set up and on them were placed, on one side toast or buttered bread, and on the other *muffings*, a sort of unleavened cake, piled up on Japanese porcelain dishes. The artificial need for tea, that innocent stimulant, which our English neighbours have created for themselves, costs England very dear, since the East India Company sells tea to the English to the value of more than three million pounds every year. The Customs and Excise returns show that, within the three kingdoms, thirty-one million pounds in weight is consumed. The rest of Europe in its entirety uses no more than twenty-two million. But what can reason do when confronted with fashion and custom which demand that, in this country, the Chinese leaf is preferred to the mocha bean? And so this taste, which has become a basic necessity, is now so widespread that there is not the poorest hovel in which it is not taken twice a day, not an artisan's family who would not rather give up its dinner than its dish of tea.

Groups of like-minded guests soon clustered around the elegant tables. I noticed that, taking little account of their elders, the young people rapidly, almost instinctively, broke into sociable pairs which parted only when the strains of the next dance were heard. I had already observed that the young men, at the end of a quadrille or a waltz, instead of escorting their charming partners to their mothers or their chaperones, protracted such a delightful intimacy by strolling about with the young lady, not merely in the ballroom, but through the neighbouring rooms and often even into the garden, thus sampling that most pleasant harmony which has so accurately been called 'the couple'; and yet to me this way of going on seemed so different from our own, that I took the liberty of expressing my surprise to Mrs. Fitzherbert.

'Many other customs which are peculiar to us will perhaps surprise you more,' she replied, 'especially if you wish to compare them to those in your own country: although we have been close neighbours and good neighbours for many years, we differ fundamentally in our habits and even in our manners; I do not doubt that you find the contrast striking. Our young girls, it is true, have far more freedom than in France, and that might seem all the more surprising to you, given that they come into society at a much later age and that, until such time as they do, they leave the schoolroom but rarely and are never seen in our drawing rooms until the day they are presented at court. You will perhaps think, for that very reason, that the danger to them is all the greater, placed as they are between the pitfall of their inexperience and the intoxication of freedom; and yet it is far from being the case; in England their salvation rests with two authorities against which one appeals in vain: public opinion and the law. A young girl has nothing to fear from seduction; her naïve confidence is never abused by those impertinences, couched in honeyed phrases, which you call 'declarations': the man who talks to her of love, marries her, a fact which is confirmed by everyday events. Public opinion will exclude from polite society any man who tries to seduce a young girl; if, in addition, the merest *billet doux*, written in his hand, is produced whilst he still refuses to marry the girl, this exhibit, construed as breach of promise, is enough to render him liable to pay damages: if he persists in his crime, an occurrence which is, fortunately, rare, he is taken to court, disgraced and ruined by the heavy fines imposed upon him. You will agree, sir, that such curbs are of great assistance to morality.'

I listened with delight to these invaluable details, for the age of the speaker[310] guaranteed their accuracy; but every pleasure must come to an end; Mrs. Fitzherbert's departure with her charming niece brought about that of my enjoyment in listening to her. I escorted the ladies to their carriage, and, having asked for and received permission to call on them at home, I returned to indulge in all the varied entertainments that the evening had to offer.

The guests were dancing a *reel*, a sort of Scottish dance which is noteworthy for its elegant figures and which demands extraordinary agility to be successfully performed. I confess there is somewhat of a contradiction between our neighbours' stiffness and this dance which is gayer and more lively than a Neapolitan tarantella; but taken all in all, beauty is often revealed by contrasts; the young girls' faces, normally so wholesome and so pale, turned suddenly bright vermillion, lending added sparkle to their charms.

At midnight, Sir Robert and his family retired; but thanks to my friends, both new and old, I had been introduced to the dancing, talkative notables in the rooms. In order to counteract what is commonly maintained about the supposed reserve of the English, all I need say is that, the same evening, more than ten invitations to balls or to dinners for the following days were extended to me, and by people I barely knew; indeed, at one o'clock I was a guest in the Ship Hotel at an elegantly elaborate supper given by Mr. Thelusson for his friends. And yet it was the first time that I had met the gentleman; I could not have refused his pressing invitations and I later had every reason to congratulate myself on having believed in his sincerity.

The meal began with a an abundance of oysters and other sea foods, dishes which are, apparently, a prerequisite of any English supper; then we drank copious quantities of champagne, considered by our neighbours to be an essential luxury; this gave rise to a thousand pleasant exchanges; there was no end to the compliments heaped upon France, and they were so well-intentioned that I needed fear no embarrassment in hearing such frank praise.

Amongst the guests, there was a man whom others were calling Shakespeare. I was so taken aback that for several minutes, I supposed myself to be mistaken; but as the same name was repeated several times and without the least affectation, there could be no doubt that I was in the presence of some descendent of the

310 *TN Maria Fitzherbert was 71 years old in 1827.*

English Aeschylus. One thing, however, confused me, whilst yet arousing my curiosity and that was the fact that they were calling the man both Shakespeare and Ireland in turn. I became completely lost in my conjectures and therefore all the more impatient to learn the truth.

It is considered good manners, in English society, for the master of the house to introduce his guests to each other. This custom has the advantage that you know from the outset the rank, by and large, of the people with whom you are mixing; nevertheless, it has the disadvantage for the foreigner that he cannot immediately classify the various names and hesitates to make any enquiry on the matter. After some wavering, I was bold enough to ask my neighbour if the person in question was, indeed, called Shakespeare and if he was related to the poet who was England's crowning glory.

He told me that the man's name was Ireland, that 'Shakespeare' had been added following a curious adventure in his youth and that Shakespeare was, correctly speaking, what we would call a *sobriquet* in French.

That the name of Shakespeare, this hallowed name, should be given as a nick-name was impossible for me to believe; I was only too aware of how the English worshiped the Bard to the point of fanaticism; I knew that they did not admire merely the style but the sublime beauty which flowed from his astonishing genius; I knew that he is not only one of their national heroes but that he is a god whose name cannot be uttered with too great a respect, that there is an undying fervour which one can compare only to the frenzy which seized everyone on the day when Voltaire, in his eightieth year, died in Paris, laden with laurel wreathes and amidst unprecedented acclamation. Full of these feelings, I intimated to Mr. Ireland,[311] a man of most agreeable humour, that I would like to hear from his own lips, the story of the events which had earned him the nick-name of Shakespeare; he readily agreed to satisfy my request: and this is, more or less, what I have retained of the story.

Mr. Ireland's father, a lawyer of some distinction, owned, in Hertfordshire, a country estate next to the vast estates of Lord A***. Several times, His Lordship had had recourse to the talents of the lawyer and neighbourly relations had quickly replaced the business footing on which they had stood. Mr. Ireland, the lawyer, had just the one son, a student at Oxford who spent all his vacations at

311 *TN William Henry Ireland (1775–1835)*

his father's house; having been received at Lord A***'s castle, the young man there met His Lordship's niece, Miss Arabella who possessed, conjoined to the most perfect beauty, a large fortune. I will not attempt to portray the lady; I will say only that when I first saw her, twenty years after the period of which I speak, she still justified the efforts which Mr. Ireland made to win her.

When he had left the University, the younger Mr. Ireland spent ever more time at the castle; soon he noticed that Miss Arabella's heart was not insensitive to the ardour which he felt for her; but there were so many obstacles to overcome! How could it be reasonably believed that he, fresh from a seat of learning, having no name and no position in the world, could hope to claim the hand of such a beautiful and rich heiress? Yet he was not discouraged, and love lent him ingenuity. His fate depended on Lord A*** who alone, as guardian and uncle of his beloved, could give her hand in marriage. Before all else, young Mr. Ireland had to court His Lordship's goodwill by adopting his tastes: he would emulate him when he hunted the fox, when he went to the races at Duncaster or Newmarket, when he spent long hours at table after dinner; all this alone would have advanced the young man but little towards his passionately desired goal. His Lordship, like any good English gentleman, loved hunting, racing and claret; but these were not his Achilles' heel: fortunately, two other passions gave the lover a stronger hold over him: the first, that of manuscripts and the second, a keen and unbounded admiration for Shakespeare. Thus, his study was decorated with the most interesting original documents: the work of statesmen, writers, artists, indeed anyone who had contributed to the glory of England in their different way had found their place in this vast collection, some in the form of voluminous hand-written tomes, others by a scribbled note or a signature. But despite his library containing the rarest and the most magnificent collection of his favourite author's works, despite having collected, at great expense, an infinite number of portraits and busts of the Bard, one single thing made this valuable assortment imperfect as far as he was concerned: he had never succeeded in obtaining the signature of the great poet whom he revered. Young Ireland often witnessed his disappointment and thought he could see a way by which he could overcome an obstacle which had at first seemed insurmountable; perseverance and love did the rest. The young man set off for London where he shut himself away in the British Museum and there, by constantly pouring over Shakespeare's original manuscripts, he managed to familiarise himself with, and indeed to copy perfectly, the handwriting and the signature which he had before him: Buffon rightly said: 'Patience is genius.' Once Ireland believed he had mastered his copying to a point where it would deceive even the most experienced eye, he acquired some antique parchment and, taking as the text of his forgery a real event in the life of the poet, he fabricated a mortgage deed for the sum of thirty pounds, written and signed entirely in Shakespeare's own hand. This deed had apparently been written at the time when Shakespeare, risking prosecution by Sir Thomas Lucy in whose park he had been arrested several times for poaching, had left the county of Warwick to come and try his luck in the London theatre.

Being both excited and anxious regarding the probable success of his forgery, Ireland hurried to Lord A***'s castle to offer this unique item to His Lordship. He had been given the task, so he explained, of cataloguing an old library and had found the document behind some boxes where it had been left along with other, trifling papers; he had asked to be given it and had come to make His Lordship a gift of it, with his compliments.

So delighted was Lord A*** with the acquisition of this treasure that he immediately invited all the literary men he knew to examine it. They compared it, they poured over it, they discussed it and the result of their inspection was that, in their opinion, the document was indisputably authentic. This was Mr. Ireland's first great success; emboldened by this judgement, he had conceived an even more audacious project which, if he could carry it off, would not leave him without the hope of realising his dearest wish. By dint of reading and of studying Shakespearean manuscripts, he not only absorbed the beauty which he found in them, but he even dared to conceive that it would not be impossible for him to imitate, not just the handwriting but the style, the manner and indeed the real *humour* of the great master. Full of this bold idea, he went to Stratford and there sought for inspiration and enlightenment from the places which had witnessed the birth of so many sublime thoughts. There, in the house where Shakespeare was born, and where he had lived, in the very room which had seen so much inspiration flow and from which Ireland barely ventured, other than to walk the banks of the Avon along the path leading from the illustrious man's birthplace to the church containing his tomb, the young man composed a complete tragedy in a very few months, managing to reproduce, with remarkable success, the great man's flashes of genius, his beautiful lines, even his flaws, in short, everything which so fundamentally makes up the originality of the creator of Hamlet and of

Othello. But this was not all: by sorting through the store rooms of book sellers and antiquarians or anywhere where he hoped to find old manuscripts, and by dint of research and some financial outlay, he procured a considerable quantity of blank sheets of paper, all produced at the time Shakespeare was alive, such as are found at the beginning of any volume. On these dusty sheets, and using an ink to which he carefully gave an appearance of antiquity, he copied his tragedy, with admirable tenacity, all the time imitating Shakespeare's hand, and not forgetting the deletions and marginal notes one sees, albeit rarely as everyone knows, in the Bard's manuscripts.

His Lordship's delight knew no bounds when young Ireland brought him this new treasure. The nobleman, who had for so long despaired of owning one page, one single word in Shakespeare's hand; who had, in his despondency, thought even of abandoning his collection; was now the one who was the owner of an unknown, unpublished tragedy! his reputation was made and this addition to his collection made it the foremost in the land. The news of the appearance of this manuscript produced an extraordinary sensation: a bookseller offered three thousand pounds for it. Mr. Ireland refused. The literary world, anyone with any pretentions to the world of art or of criticism was in turmoil. Soon a whole host of essays, articles, treatises, brochures and pamphlets erupted; everyone took a stand, for or against, everyone believed himself to be involved in the debate. His Lordship did not take the least active role; for him, defending the authenticity of the manuscript was defending the honour of his collection as a whole. One solitary mystery blighted his certainty – but failed to shake his faith: he had never been able to persuade Mr. Ireland to reveal the source of this priceless treasure. The young man retreated into obstinate silence, replying merely that the manuscript in question had been found amongst papers which had, at one time, belonged to Lord Southampton, who, in Shakespeare's time, had been famous for his friendship with the unfortunate Earl of Essex and that the play, having been commissioned by Queen Elizabeth, had only ever been performed in her private apartments, as was stated in the preface, and finally, that the play had been given to him, as payment in kind for important services rendered, by a person who had little interest in such rarities and whose name he had given his word never to divulge.

Soon, thanks to the importance acquired by this literary and national controversy, Mr. Ireland became a man *à la mode*. To his handsome appearance and his exceptional wit, was added a talent to declaim his tragedy with a perfection that John Kemble[312] would have envied him; and since His Lordship, owner of the manuscript, refused, as one can well imagine, to loan it out to be read, one had to obtain from Mr. Ireland the signal favour of hearing him recite it. He gained admittance to the most exalted circles, he was even sought after by the Prince of Wales who honoured him with particular attentions and took him into his inner circle.

Amongst the sceptics and the opponents of this literary phenomenon was the celebrated Sheridan;[313] whilst doing justice to the undoubted merit of Mr. Ireland's work, his experienced eye gave him an inkling that there were some passages which betrayed a style other than Shakespeare's. One day, in one of the numerous London clubs, he virulently attacked the authenticity of the document in His Lordship's presence. To all Sheridan's criticisms, to all the proofs which he was able to muster and put forward in his double capacity as a powerful orator and a playwright, His Lordship merely replied:

'I wish to God that this work were not authentic! England would reap the glory of having a second Shakespeare!'

However, his belief, which until that moment had been so strong, was unable to counter such a savage attack. Hardly had he left the club than he was assailed by a thousand contradictory thoughts and a doubt which left him little repose. During this time, young Ireland was confessing to Miss Arabella all the anxiety caused him by her uncle's attitude towards them; at that very moment, His Lordship returned and, being most agitated by his recent conversation, repeated it in detail. He ended by exclaiming: 'No sacrifice would be too great to remove this uncertainty from my mind; you alone, Ireland, you alone can end it; if you will condescend to speak, you may put what price you wish upon your words and I will pledge to pay it.'

'There is a price, My Lord,' the young man replied, 'to which is attached the future of my whole life; it is at the centre of my thoughts, the motive for my every deed, it is the only price which would tear my secret from me.'

'Speak,' exclaimed His Lordship, 'if it is within my power, you shall have it.'

At these words, the young man fell at his feet, emboldened by the hope that these solemn promises had aroused in him:

312 *TN John Phillip Kemble (1757–1823) actor manager associated with both the Theatre Royal, Drury Lane and the Theatre Royal, Covent Garden.*

313 *TN Richard Brinsley Sheridan (1751–1816), playwright, poet, theatre owner, M.P., friend of the Prince of Wales.*

'I love your niece,' he told him, 'and I believe that my love is returned; in order to win her, I have had to leave the straight and narrow path: I have made the attempt; and my audacity is perhaps inexcusable. You may be the judge, My Lord: I am the author of the tragedy believed to be by Shakespeare.'

'You, Ireland? You! But what proof can you give me?'

'An irrefutable one, My Lord. Let Your Lordship choose a theme and I will straight away compose, as you watch, a piece which will be in no way inferior, I hope, to the ones which love has already inspired in me.'

The offer being accepted, His Lordship chose the title *Vortigern and Rowena* from an event in an account of the Saxon conquest. The promised text was finished within a few weeks; and to make the task the more decisive, Mr. Ireland presented his tragedy to Sheridan, who, at the time, was the owner of the Drury Lane theatre. Mr. Sheridan was delighted when he had read it and entrusted the leading roles to John Kemble and Kemble's own sister, Mrs. Siddons. When performed, the play was an astounding success and proved that it was in no way inferior to its predecessors.

His Lordship generously forgave a deception which had duped the whole of England as much as he had been:[314] but he had given his word of honour and, as an honourable man, he kept it. Having married Miss Arabella and become the master of a great fortune, Mr. Ireland, with no regrets, abandoned the writing of Shakespearean plays; but it was only on the death of His Lordship, who had demanded absolute secrecy, that he revealed the ingenious subterfuge to which he owed his happiness. Although the warmth of this literary quarrel had become muted, the furore had been so great that Mr. Ireland had been given the nick-name Shakespeare, and it had stuck, as had the illustrious position in society which it had earned him.

---

314 AN Mr. Ireland also claimed to have found, along with Shakespeare's papers, a lock of the great poet's hair; these he shared with his most ardent admirers. The latter, proud of their treasure, had the hair mounted in rings and bracelets, abandoning, with great regret, their sweet illusions only when it was no long possible to believe in them. He had conceived this idea, he told us, during a visit to Stratford, when he had seen with what veneration people had kept trinkets made from the wood of a mulberry tree that Shakespeare had planted in his garden. When the tree was cut down, the town bought it from the owner and had several small items, such as boxes, caskets, snuffboxes and fans etc, carved from it; these they gave to distinguished persons whom they wished to honour. Also made from this mulberry wood is the box in which the town had sent to Garrick a scroll giving him the freedom of Stratford, in recognition of the actor's homage to the great poet in the erection of the monument which Garrick had placed in the vicinity of Hampton (*House, Richmond-upon-Thames*) and the play he had written entitled *Jubilee* which he had written in the Bard's honour.

It is possible that William Ireland was a compulsive hoaxer. Not only did he fabricate counterfeit documents, he seems to have fabricated most of the story he told La Garde:

- *Samuel Ireland, William's father, was a publisher and engraver, not a lawyer;*
- *Samuel and William lived in London, not Hertfordshire;*
- *Samuel went to work in a law firm at the age of 16; he was never an undergraduate at Oxford;*
- *It is known that, throughout his life, William lied about his age;*
- *There is no known connection between the Irelands and any Lord A***;*
- *William Ireland forged manuscripts to please his father, a Shakespeare aficionado;*
- 'Vortigern and Rowena' *was booed off the stage at its one performance in 1796;*
- *William admitted his forgeries to his father in 1796, at the tender age of 21;*
- *After 1796, William spent his life in straightened circumstances, often to the point of penury;*
- *William did not marry Lady Arabella, he married Miss Alice Crudge.*

Often, in this life, we owe our successes to such bravura; any man whose talents are unknown will live in obscurity, for he has no pedestal, as our most witty of critics, Jules Janin,[315] has said; others shine only because of their reputation, for reputation is the bell which rings at the slightest movement, but whose sound often dies the moment it has rung.

It was nearly three o'clock in the morning when our party broke up; several of my new friends escorted me on a somewhat lengthy tour of the town by the brilliant light of the blazing gas lamps which, literally speaking, rivalled the

315 TN *Jules Janin (1804–74) Janin was known, when a very young man, as a talented author, but it was not until 1830 that he became a drama critic. It is highly likely that la Garde added this comment, or even wrote this chapter, several years after his visit to Brighton.*

daylight. What was most remarkable was the number of people we met who were still abroad, on foot, on horseback or in their carriage; where had they come from? where were they going? It was all a mystery to me. In any case, I doubt whether Versailles, in its earlier glory, had ever, at such an hour, been the scene of so much activity.

Chapter XI

Tea – A boat race – Betting – England and the House of Orleans – Falconry – A luncheon with the Duchess of St. A*** – The Saxon hunter – Exercises – A director of the East India Company – A family concert – A ball for a stranger.

In Brighton, almost everyone takes breakfast at the same hour; this is a most commendable habit: nine o'clock is the time most usually chosen. However, what will seem perhaps a little surprising to the ladies in Paris is that, before an English lady goes down to the salon where tea is prepared, she has already completed her toilette. You will see no hair-papers hidden beneath an Indian wrap; the lady's hair will have been tastefully and elegantly arranged; not one single ribbon will be out of place; not one single waist will be without its corset or concealed beneath a voluminous wrap; each element of her dress will be in its place, pinned, laced and tidy like a Quaker's gown.

Seated at the head of the table, surrounded by all the items requisite to her important function, the mother of the family painstakingly prepares the indispensable infusion; she will invariably repeat this indulgent routine one hour after dinner has been taken. She butters bread, rinses cups two or three times in the large bowl at the centre of the table,[316] knows and measures out the right quantity of leaf, both green and black, mixes them together, judges accurately the time needed for the tea to infuse, adds sugar, brown or white, to each cup before pouring the tea into the cup and finally adding cream or milk according to the taste of each guest: this whole operation, which may seem so simple in itself, is

---

316 TN *In the early nineteenth century, tea was made at the table. An urn of boiling water was placed in the middle of the table. The teapot was always warmed before use by 'rinsing' it with hot water. It is possible that the same applied to the cups. Superfluous water was tipped into a large bowl designed for the purpose.*

a sort of state ceremonial for the mother, the sister or the eldest daughter of any English family. You can see that she bestows upon her task the significance of a vital duty and the tender care of a labour of love.

Such early morning habits have become a necessity in a country where time is a resource eked out in minutes; the English are not miserly with their money, but they are with their time: one might even say that their enunciation is designed to make least use of it; the English swallow their letters and hiss their words, for the language consists for the most part of monosyllabic utterances; two words are often rolled into one thus creating a sort of spoken shorthand which supports Voltaire's saying: 'The English afford themselves two hours a day more than us by gobbling down what they say.' All this seems to be the result of their incredible energy in commerce, in industry and in trade, the whole is perfectly summed up in that forceful but nigh on untranslatable word, *business.* In England, *business* is what *destiny* was for the Ancients; it can be described as 'inevitable activity'.

Owing to these inbred practices, ten o'clock had hardly struck before I received a visit from my new acquaintances. Every single one of them, with affectionate kindness, repeated the invitations which they had extended to me the previous day. This was the very manner in which, when I had arrived at Bucharest in Dacia[317] some while previously, the most notable Boyars had greeted me and, without in the least knowing who I was, put their homes and their hospitality at my disposal; this Dacia, so rarely visited, is one of the very few countries in Europe where such noble and touching customs are still practised. The Prince de Ligne, whom I am so fond of quoting, rightly quipped: 'My only criticism is that, everywhere, nations are becoming *unbarbaric* a good deal too much and a good deal too soon'. Hospitality, that fine quality common to the early centuries of our era, must have been the prerogative of those simple, bucolic times of the golden age; as far as our overseas cousins are concerned, the progress of civilisation has not allowed them to claim it entirely as their own; they are generous, they are charitable, but hospitable with reservations.

Amongst the unofficial visitors was Sir John Lil***, whose acquaintance I was delighted to make. This young officer, who had distinguished himself during the Peninsular War, had returned with a bullet in his knee which occasionally reminded him only too intensely of his glorious exploits. He came one morning to invite me to accompany him onto the beach to watch a spectacle new to me: a race

317 *TN Roughly equivalent to modern day Romania.*

between sailing *yachts*. In Venice, I had seen gondoliers standing in the prow of their craft, rowing with one oar and skimming swiftly and skilfully over the Rialto in an attempt outdo one other, just as a Dutchman's skates glide over the canals at Harlem; I had also seen jousts between boats armed with several oarsmen battling to win the prize for speed; but here, everything depended on skill and nautical science. Such sport struck me as most interesting and I readily accepted his offer.

When we reached the shore, the esplanade and the long pier were already crowded with onlookers and enthusiasts, the majority taking an interest in the success of each contender in proportion to the amount of money that they had wagered on him. There were seven participants ready to take up the challenge in the watery arena; the elegantly dressed sailors were already hoisting their sails and waiting anxiously for the signal to free them to the winds. The aim was to cover a circuit of two miles in length marked out by fishing boats at anchor; the winner would be the first man to return to the starting point.

A cannon shot rang out: at the signal, the seven competitors sped off. Sometimes flying along with sails unfurled, sometimes sailing close to the wind with amazing agility, they had soon put to good use all the resources and all the skills of old sea dogs. Blown along with the speed of arrows, the *yachts*, responding to the guiding hand of their pilot, criss-crossed each other, heaved clear, shot ahead and, in their ætherial ballet, resembled nothing more than those birds we could see wheeling in the airs above our heads; on land, the display was no less remarkable; hope and anxiety in turn showed on the faces of the gamblers, their prospects varying with the chances of success; some appeared calm and confident, fully trusting in the boat upon which they had pinned their hopes, others were composed and patient and yet others could barely control their anxiety, alternately pacing up and down the beach or encouraging a competitor with voice or gesture, but which the sailor was too far-off to interpret. At last, after an heroic struggle, valiantly fought, general acclamation decreed *Water Witch* to be the victor. The sailors who had taken part in this triumphal feat landed amidst universal applause and the captain stepped forward to collect his prize from the judges: a handsome silver cup donated by the Royal Navigation Society of London.[318]

As soon as the race had ended, the crowd of on-lookers broke up into small groups of men; amongst these, my new friends and I went to sit on a bench on the

---

318 *TN La Garde means possibly* The Royal Yacht Squadron *which had been founded in a tavern in St. James, London in 1815. The Squadron became* Royal *in 1817 when the Prince Regent began to take an interest in the sport.*

pier where several musicians were adding their reasonably tuneful sounds to the sonorous murmur of the waves of the English Channel.

A similar event was recorded by the Brighton Gazette *on 12 November 1827:*

> On Tuesday afternoon, a second sailing match took place between the *Spring* and the *British Fair*. The day was extremely favourable, the wind westerly, with a good breeze, and the sea rather ruffled. The match was for £40, and the distance 10 miles, viz: to beat to the windward five, and to run five miles; two boats having been stationed to point out the line of demarcation; the one opposite the Marine-parade, a short distance from the shore, and the other off Bexhill abreast of Beachy, bearing south-west of Hastings. The *British Fair* and the *Spring*, at the firing of a pistol, weighed anchor, with their jib-foresails, mainsails and mizensails set, sailed round the boat to the eastward, and stood to sea, the former taking the lead. In coming about, at a quarter past one, the *British Fair* speedily weathered the boat station off Bexhill, to accomplish which, the *Spring* was obliged to make another short tack, and consequently lost some little time; both boats now ran rapidly before the wind towards the destined goal, at which the *British Fair* arrived about five minutes before her competitor, and was declared the victor. Roper, the commander of the successful boat, was welcomed to the shore, to the loud huzzas of the surrounding spectators, who conducted him to the Cutter Inn, where potent libations were drank to his health and future success. Palmam qui meruit ferat.[318]
>
> BRIGHTON GAZETTE, 12 November 1827

The conversation, which gradually drew in each one of us, turned to the of the visit of the Duke of Chartres[320] to England, to where his father had just brought him with the intention of introducing him to the king; the king would thus become intimate with all three generations of the Orleans family. My friends talked much about the enthusiasm which the young prince's easy-going qualities had aroused and of the flattering reception he had received wherever he had been.

---

319 *TN 'Let he who has earned it bear the reward'.*

320 *TN Prince Ferdinand-Philippe-Louis-Charles-Henri de Bourbon, Duke of Chartres (1810–42) son of Louis-Philippe, Duke of Orleans who, in 1830, was to become Louis-Philippe, King of the French – he was never styled either the 'King of France' or the 'French King'. The Orleans family was the younger branch of the French royal house of Bourbon.*

Prince Koslowski, that Russian nobleman whose wit and knowledge are as sound as they are varied, was one of our party. He explained, in reference to the prince's visit, the connections existing between England and the Orleans family, and as the subject interested me most particularly, this is what I remember of the main points of the story:

'The name of Orleans,' Prince Koslowski told us, 'originates in two famous marriages between England and France. The first was in the reign of Charles II when the English king, an extravagant hedonist, sold his friendship to Louis XIV by joining forces with him to defeat Holland.

'The plenipotentiary, whose credit and skill had set the seal on this injudicious union, had been hurriedly sent to France by the English; this was none other than the charming Henriette,[321] Duchess of Orleans, the wife of Monsieur, brother to Louis XIV.

'Being the only person to be in possession, together with Turenne and Louvois, of the secret which concerned the peace within Europe, she reaped the great credit of single-handedly concluding the negotiations which placed the British fleet at the service of France.[322] It is impossible to give an account of *Madame's* achievement at this time, of the celebrations which accompanied it, of the extravagant festivities which were given for her not far from these shores, without recalling at the same time the mortal blow which struck her down when she returned. One may even say that her sudden and tragic end excited a universal wave of regret and sympathy throughout Europe. The youth and the beauty of the Duchess of Orleans, along with her wit and her grace had captivated the hearts of everyone; she was a worthy subject for Bossuet's genius[323] and perhaps this great priest was never more eloquent that when he delivered the simple, moving words: "Madame was gentle unto death."

'However, this alliance, sealed amid so much mystery, did not last long. A second union, between the French Regent[324] and George I had a happier fate:

---

321 *TN Henriette-Anne (1644–70) was the youngest daughter of Charles I, and so sister to Charles II. 'Monsieur' (Philippe, Duke of Orleans) was Henriette's first cousin. As wife of 'Monsieur', Henriette's official title was simply 'Madame'.*

322 *TN Henriette is credited with preparing much of the groundwork for the Treaty of Dover (1670); she was not involved in the final drafting of its terms. However, La Garde incorrectly states that Henriette was sent from England to France. It was the Louis XIV (her brother-in-law), who sent her to England.*

323 *TN Jacques-Bénigne Bossuet, Bishop of Meaux, is best known for his funeral orations. They included that on the death of Queen Henrietta Maria, wife of Charles I in September 1669, and then nine months later, in June 1670, that of her daughter, the 26 year old Henriette-Anne.*

324 *TN Louis XVI had become king in 1715 at the age of five. His great-uncle, Philippe, Duke of Orleans, acted as Regent until 1723.*

barely had five years passed than England, having united with Holland and the Holy Roman Empire,[325] managed to shake the great Louis' throne; but then, following hard upon the vicissitudes of war came the no less perilous intrigues of diplomacy: Cardinal Alberoni had dreamed of overthrowing Europe; in France it would have been done by removing the Duke of Orleans as Regent; with the help of Peter the Great and Charles XII, both of whom were astonished at seeing themselves allies, the Cardinal had plotted to bring down the English constitution, drive out King George and restore the Pretender. The alliance between France and England immediately extinguished the Cardinal's vast projects and made it clear that these two countries, openly united, could defy the rest of Europe.'[326]

The prince then reminded us of the great sympathy which the father of the present Duke of Orleans[327] had aroused when, having fallen out of favour, he had left the court and travelled to England. At that time, the French revolution was looming: it was a period when we were far from foreseeing the excesses which have since tarnished it. In whatever way one judges the Duke of Orleans, he was then regarded as the representative and the leader of that rational portion of the French nation which wished to introduce English institutions and customs into French government and society: this explains the welcome he received in England.

As for the interest now aroused by the presence of the Duke of Orleans and his son, there is in it nothing which should surprise. The English have come to appreciate what is noble in his character, his courage and his resignation in exile, his enlightened taste for the fine arts, his wide and varied education and his ancestral values which act both as precept and example. Neither do the English forget with what admirable hospitality their distinguished countrymen have been received by the duke in his magnificent homes at the Palais-royal and at Neuilly. In the present duke they see, thanks to the solid, virile education he has

325 TN *Ruled over by the Habsburg Emperor, Charles VI.*

326 TN *The treaties La Garde is referring are probably the Treaty of Utrecht of 1713 and its ratification, the Triple Alliance of 1717 (signed by Great Britain, France and the Netherlands). The second is the Quadruple Alliance of 1718 (signed by the original three powers but also by the Holy Roman Empire).*

327 TN *The Duke of Orleans in 1827 was Louis Philippe de Bourbon (see footnote 320 above). His father had been Louis-Philippe-Joseph and was styled Philippe Égalité. He was guillotined in 1793, the same year as his distant cousin, Louis XVI.*

received, the image of a prince worthy of his father and equal to his century.[328]

This interesting outline gave rise to political conjecture and insights on the present state of Europe: I would have delighted in taking part, but the day was well advanced; it was with regret that I had to remind myself of an appointment at my hotel, and so we went our separate ways.

Two days previously I had received an invitation to a form of spectacle which one sees rarely described outside the pages of mediaeval chronicles, and which is a mine of images and customs quarried by our modern novelists; I refer to hawking.[329] Everyone of importance in Brighton had been invited. The Duke of St. A***, in his capacity as Grand Falconer of England, wished to bestow upon his duchess the insignia and the prerogatives of his rank. The constant, envious curiosity which dogged her wherever she went must also have attracted a great number of onlookers, who were no doubt eager to see how she would fulfil this important duty. It was commonly agreed that, on this occasion, the newly-weds had proved themselves to be as generous as when they gave garden parties at their villa, Holly Lodge[330] or lavish balls in their mansion in Piccadilly,[331] for

---

328 AN Since I made this rapid sketch, a storm has destroyed what a storm revealed, but this political upheaval was soon followed by calm and the sympathetic relationship which already existed between the two countries has grown and been strengthened by the many memories of previous association. A recent marriage has just extended and spread the tender shoots of a closer union between our two peoples and, although such alliances are not always a positive guarantee of eternal peace for the two nations, they appear, at least, to be the most probable.
The Duke of Orleans (who, today, is a Prince of the Blood) had been able to convince himself of these facts during his previous visit to England, where he had been received with great enthusiasm, less, perhaps, for his personal qualities than as a representative of a principle adopted by the two great nations and as a guarantee of political sympathy: for what is the desire of all nations who see clearly their true interests? Repose after so much commotion, happiness paid for by so many sacrifices and freedom, protected and upheld by the law.

329 AN The art of falconry has been honoured since time immemorial, as much in Europe as in Asia, although nowadays it is no longer practised other than by a few Tartar tribes and at the court of certain Indian princes. From Asia, it spread to Europe. In AD 506, the Council of Agde was compelled to forbid men of the Church from participating too enthusiastically in the sport. In the twelfth century, the art of falconry had reached its zenith and all the monarchs of Europe vied to display the most finery as they hunted; but one can well believe that they were all surpassed by the magnificence of the Khan of the Tartars, as Marco Polo has shown. The kings who hunted the most energetically were Frederick the Great, Edward the Confessor and the Emperors Frederick I, Frederick II and Charlemagne, indeed the first three of these wrote treaties on the subject. In the reign of Edward III, the killing of a falcon was considered a crime punishable by death, and Henry VII punished the theft of an egg by one year's imprisonment if the thief was caught on his land. Elizabeth reduced the sentence to three months, provided that the criminal deposit an indemnity for seven years. It was during the reign of James I that Sir Thomas Monson paid 1,000 pounds sterling (26,000 francs) for a pair of these birds, so passionate was his love of hawking. The invention of gunpowder brought about the end of this tradition and today it has been practically abandoned in Europe. In Great Britain, however, there are 5 or 6 hawk-houses and a Grand Falconer who receives a stipend of 1,372 pounds sterling (3,300 francs).

330 *TN Holly Lodge in Highgate had been leased to the duchess in 1809, when she was still a single woman of 33 and at the height of her fame as an actress. The Lodge never belonged to either of her husbands. The estate owned by the duchess (and bequeathed to her first husband's grand-daughter, Angela Coutts-Burdett) is now a select estate of private houses, many with spectacular views over London.*

331 *TN On the corner of Piccadilly and Stratton Street.*

when wealth commands and taste obeys, bewitching results are not difficult to achieve.

The place designated for the meeting was a stretch of heath land, dotted with heather about three miles from Brighton on the Hastings road.[332]

The path leading to the spot was thronged with hunters wearing their distinctive dress and accompanied by a crowd of ladies on horseback wearing the obligatory hunting habit; their delightful hats, despite the veils, did not entirely conceal their delicate features which glowed with the pleasure to come and the briskness of the ride.

Nearly every horse in the cavalcade was a thoroughbred; some so costly, as I was told, that their prices ranged from six thousand up to fifty thousand francs. Then came a long line of all manner of carriages, most drawn by four horses; on the continent it is rare to find a equipage in which everything is handsome, but here in England such minute attention is paid to each lavish detail that the whole is always perfect.

At midday, when everyone had gathered, the Grand Falconer moved forward on his horse, accompanied by his servants dressed in their fine green livery; following them came the falconers carrying on their wrists the securely hooded birds; their magnificent brown plumage showed they were feral females, for it is significant that, in the world of falcons, the female is larger, stronger and bolder than the male. Being experts in the art of falconry, the hunters let loose a quarry, murmuring encouragement to their birds whilst awaiting the duchess's orders.

At her signal, the birds' hoods were removed; at first they seemed stunned by the light which suddenly dazzled them; but soon they were soaring into the air, rising, hovering majestically in the sky, before spotting their prey and suddenly swooping down on it, swift as arrows, seizing the fluttering pigeon, the quivering partridge or the golden feathered pheasant; finally, obedient to their masters' signal, they returned with their kill and, triumphant but dutiful, came to rest on the courtier's gloved hand. To evade the talons of a homing falcon, one pigeon flew amidst the carriages and into the arms of two pretty ladies who gave it refuge in their phaeton, thus saving its life. Two of the falcons, however, of the breed known

---

332 *TN There was a cliff top road in the 1820s leading to Rottingdean. The hawking could have taken place on the high land immediately before reaching Rottingdean from Brighton. However, the event more likely took place on the Brighton to Lewes Road. This might have placed the hawking ground on the Stanmer estate belonging to the Pelham family.*

as peregrine falcons[333] and who were less familiar with this form of hunting, or who preferred the pleasures of freedom to their pandered slavery, continued on their way, flying north, doubtless back to their native lands, despite the signals and the whistles of their masters. When they saw what was happening, large numbers of hunters and spectators set off in pursuit of the fugitives; shouts mingled with bugle blasts; the air rang with a thousand different cries; but soon, despite the deafening clamour, the two stubborn hawks had doubled their speed and disappeared from sight; they had flown, taking their magnificent silver bells, the best that Milan can produce, to some fortunate hunter in the Highlands of Scotland.

This minor set-back apart, the hunt was most amusing; all the guests seemed completely satisfied. This was no less true of the luncheon which had been set out in a vast marquee in the heart of the heath: several tables had been arranged to seat over one hundred guests. The most dainty dishes, the most exquisite wines and an abundance of the most exotic fruits made up this incongruous entertainment where, in a measure of excessive refinement, the servants wore white gloves. One minute the hunters' horns had been trumpeting out their joyful fanfare, and the next a band of musicians inside the tent regaled us with elegant sonatas. As was the custom, the guests did not forget to include the Grand Falconer and his hospitable duchess in the many toasts they proposed; the last of these was to the hope of seeing hawking re-established, for it had been the prerogative of the nobility for many centuries and one to which the aristocracy of this country is extremely attached.

Our beautiful hostess, a novice duchess still,[334] did the honours of her banquet with all the self assurance of long habit and her meeting, as an equal, with the representatives of the very best families proved with what ease clever women can rise effortlessly to their new position.

Chance had seated me next to a young Saxon, Baron G***,[335] of whom I had already heard as being one of the notable foreigners to be found in Brighton and who was often compared to that elegant Frenchman, Count Charles de Mornay, whose personal advantages and whose illustrious and time-honoured name recommended him.

---

333 TN *In the early years of the twenty-first century, peregrine falcons are still a familiar sight in central Brighton as they nest on the tallest building in the city, Sussex Heights. The translator has recently been introduced, whilst in a country lane near Lewes, to a hunting falcon as it sat impassively on its trainer's wrist.*

334 TN *Harriot Mellon may have been a 'novice duchess', but at the age of 54, and having been married in her youth to one of the richest men in England, it might be assumed that she could handle the festivities with aplomb.*

335 TN *Possibly Baron Heinrich Adolf von Gablenz (1862–43). Heinrich Adolf could not be described as young by 1827. However, his son Ludwig was only 13 in 1827 and too young to have had the experiences described by Gablenz.*

*The Baron G*** must have been quite a dandy as Charles de Mornay, aged only 23 in 1827, was one of the best known dandies in Europe. In 1841 Marguerite Gardiner, Countess of Blessington wrote:*

> 'Count Charles de Mornay was presented to me to-day. Having heard of him only as:
>
> *"The glass of fashion and the mould of form,*
> *The observed of all observers,"*
>
> I was agreeably surprised to find him one of the most witty, well-informed, and agreeable young men I have ever seen. Gay without levity, well-read without pedantry, and good-looking without vanity. Of how few young men of fashion could this be said! But I am persuaded that Count Charles de Mornay is made to be something better than a mere man of fashion.'

At first, our conversation was all of hunting, and I was surprised to hear with what expertise he talked of this art. I complimented him on his lively knowledge, assuredly an excellent passport into English society.

'Please do not be surprised,' he said, 'I was a hunter from the first moment I could cling to a saddle: King Frederick-Augustus,[336] who was passionate about everything pertaining to this royal pastime, hunted regularly, twice a week, preferably wearing the uniform of Grand Falconer of his country.

'Whilst still a child I entered his service as his personal pageboy and the king's affection for my father, who, during the recent campaigns had commanded part of the Saxon army, transferred to me. He was delighted that I so quickly came to share his taste for his favourite passion. He constantly singled me out to accompany him, and thus, throughout my childhood, acting as beater to flush out stags or roe deer, confronting wild boar or running after wolves were, for me, activities far preferable to studying and they remained my passion, even after I had taken up my military career.[337]

---

336 *TN Frederick Augustus Joseph Maria Anton Johann Nepomuk Aloys Xavier (1750–1827), King of Saxony.*

337 AN In an edition of *The New Sporting Magazine* in 1831, Baron G*** has published an article on boar hunting in Saxony which shows a great deal of talent in the writing. *TN This 1831 edition contains a letter from a certain 'Nim South'. The letter refers to* '… my old friend Baron Gablenz, who shows us that his is as good a hand across a sheet of paper, as he is across the country. The Baron and I are old croneys, and many a good days sport we have enjoyed together in Sussex, and many a pleasant evening we have passed together at Brighton, in the Albion Hotel and elsewhere.'

'Now, as you most certainly know, the land around Dresden, and especially the area we call Swiss Saxony, is more thickly wooded and more mountainous than the great hunting estates of England: greatly accustomed as I was to the difficulties and obstacle in Saxony, I would never hesitate to enter, with some expectation of winning, any one of those competitions which, here in England, are called *steeple chases* and which demand no more of the prospective winner than a determination to risk one or two of his limbs.'

From the subject of hunting we turned to accounts of our travels and compared the various countries we had both visited; thanks to our mutual experiences, we were soon on intimate terms. Having only recently returned from Russia, where he had accompanied the Saxon envoy, whose duty it was to pay the King's respects to Emperor Nicholas on his accession to the throne, Baron G*** seemed to be still enchanted by the consideration he had been shown; but to me it was no surprise that he had known success in such a military court where a fledgling captain who could talk of tactics, manoeuvres, equipment and the like must have been a figure of no little interest, for although the young baron was highly knowledgeable in the science of the hunt, it seemed to me that everything relating to the art of war was no less familiar to him.

Recalling our nomadic days, we flitted from Naples to St. Petersburg and from Madrid to Stockholm. The range of parallels to be drawn between societies and customs which were so far apart and so different was vast: the baron's sound observations confirmed what I had often heard – to be precise, that the Germans do not pass judgement in haste; they look around them with that composure which is so characteristic of them and with that rational coolness which gives their conclusions weight and impartiality: it was for this reason that Madame de Staël rightly called Germany 'the land of reason'.

When the luncheon was over, the duchess ordered the tables to be removed and all the guests readied themselves to dance, for what is remarkable in a country so apparently indolent is the decided taste for all forms of exercise, even the most strenuous. And so we see the English at their sport: fox hunting or shooting for part of the year, sending the dust flying at New Market on spirited racehorses, driving for all they are worth behind four horses harnessed to a light carriage, rowing or sailing boats on the Thames, exercising themselves at *cricket* or occasionally at the murderous sport of *pugilism*: these are the beloved passions of the young fashionables: as for dancing, no sooner has the season put an end to

The York Hotel, at the south end of the Old Steine, was later known as the Royal York Hotel. The building functioned as a hotel from 1819 almost continuously until 1929. From 1929 until 2008, it was owned by Brighton Corporation. It housed the education offices and, for a number of years, the Registry Office. In 2008, the building again became a hotel, under the name of Radisson Blu Hotel and reverted to The Royal York Hotel in 2013. In 2015, it became part of the Youth Hostel Association group.
Image reproduced courtesy of the Brighton Royal Pavilion, Museums and Libraries

the London balls, no sooner has the last bar of the last quadrille or the last gallop faded away than they start dancing in every spa resort, for in this country the ladies have managed to replace the tedious hours at table of a few years previously with this graceful exercise. After I had waltzed with three or four ladies, the baron suggested that I send my horses to the stable and that he would escort me back to my hotel in his barouche. I gladly accepted this chance to acquaint myself better with this delightful young man; he invited me to a fancy dress ball which was to be given that same evening at the York Hotel where he was staying.

Having been in the town for several weeks and being overwhelmed by the courtesy and the wide-ranging consideration that he had been shown, the baron wished to show his appreciation.

'If you want to convince me,' he said, 'that you wish to prolong our new acquaintance as much as I wish it, you will accept my rather belated invitation and this evening we will plan a way to meet another time, for tomorrow I am to leave Brighton.'

I accepted with pleasure; the baron left me at my hotel where I had just the time to change before going to visit Mr. Ed***,[338] one of the directors of the East India Company, who had invited me to dine at his home when I had met him a few days previously at the Baron Dimsdale's. We sat down to dinner at seven o'clock, and once again, spread before us was opulence and refinement worthy of one of the four-and-twenty merchants, those provisional rulers of the British Indies, rulers of a colossal empire which goes by the modest name of the *United Company of Merchants of England Trading to the East Indies.*

Mr. Ed*** was so easy-going in his person and in his manners, amidst all the immense wealth which surrounded him, that I entertained myself by casting him in the role of the representative of that all-powerful colossus we call 'trade'. Seeing in him what an orator had once said of the whole English race, I found myself thinking with surprise about this *de facto sovereignty* which commands fleets and armies, which coins its own money and which, from the counting houses of the City, governs the cities of Bengal, Madras and Bombay: a population of more than one hundred million souls.

The territorial possessions of the Company date back no further than 1698. That was the year in which it acquired three little villages on the banks of the Ganges; it undertook to pay the nabob an annual sum of 1,195 rupees. And that was the basis of the power which, within less than one hundred years, was to overrun the immense Mogul empire, and was to replace the three villages with the gigantic city of Calcutta and its 600,000 inhabitants.

The revenue of the Company comes, in the main, from the taxes imposed on land and on market sales, from levies on transport and stamp duty, and above all, from the monopoly which it has on salt, opium, tobacco etc.

The income from land tax exceeds one hundred and fifty-four million pounds and the various monopolies produce a profit estimated at seventy-five million. Trade is also an immense source of wealth; for example, the tea which the company imports into England realises an annual surplus of at least thirty

338 *TN Neil Benjamin Edmonstone (1764–1841) served the East India Company for 34 years in India where he became extremely powerful. As a servant of the Company, he was appointed to the post of Chief Secretary to the Indian Government (under British control) and later became a member of the Company's supreme council. On his retirement to England, he was elected to the Company's Court of Directors which numbered just twenty-four men. They managed the Company on behalf of the 1,976 members of the Court of Proprietors.*

Tea harvesting in Assam 1830
Image courtesy of the Wellcome Trust Collection

million pounds.[339]

The part of India directly controlled by the company is divided into three presidencies or governments, namely:

Bengal (capital, Calcutta) inhabited by 58,000,000 inhabitants
Madras (Madras) 16,000,000 inhabitants
Bombay (Bombay) 11,000,000 inhabitants

But the Company also has its vassal states and these amount to some forty million individuals subject to its rule. Thus, there are one hundred and thirty-five million

339 AN There is perhaps no other commodity on earth which is subject to such a great proliferation of taxes as the leaf of the tea plant. Firstly, it makes a profit for the small farmer who grows it; secondly there is the blender who prepares it for market; then it is taxed five or six times along its route to Canton; when it reaches there, apart from the enormous profits for the merchants and the Imperial duty levied on it, each district officer taxes it in a more or less arbitrary manner. Finally it is shipped to England and a substantial freight charge is paid on it: once it has arrived at its destination, independently of the liberal profit which it has earned for the Company, the Exchequer imposes a one hundred per cent tax relative to its value; then there is the profit to be made by the brokers, the wholesalers and finally the vast range of profit made by each and every retailer.

human beings groaning beneath the yoke of a few hundred merchants who live three thousand leagues away and who rule by proxy.

These kings of India live, almost to a man, in London; take a walk through the City and you will meet one at each turn; there are one thousand, nine hundred and seventy-six of them. Between them, they have set up a Court of Proprietors in which each man has the right to vote to elect the directors and decide upon the dividend; the Court of Directors is made up of twenty-four members, elected for two years, at the end of which period two-fifths of the members are replaced: this is where the power of the Company lies. The Crown, as sovereign power, has reserved the right to supervise the enterprise, which it does through a Board of Control of which all ministers are members as of right. This Board examines, approves or disapproved decisions made by the Court of Directors; it is the Board which, in particular, decides on any matters concerning peace, war and treaties.

The chief agents of the Company are: the governor of Bengal who, having supreme authority, takes the title Governor-General; the governor of Madras and the governor of Bombay; the Governor-General having the power, in certain cases, to suspend the others, if and when he deems it necessary to intervene and overrule them in their administration. The number of Europeans living in Hindustan does not exceed, so it is said, forty thousand. One cannot conceive how feeble a number this is when one remembers that the number of natives amounts to more than one hundred million.

But one must not forget that the English government still renders it very difficult for its subjects to set up business in India or to become landowners. The government's experience in North America taught it a lesson: it did not want an Anglo-Indian population springing up on the banks of the Ganges and one day using the word 'liberty' as a signal for independence.

Those posts in the Indian administrative and military services which the Company deems necessary to entrust to Englishmen are tenaciously fought over, for they are generously paid and the source of the rapid acquisition of a fortune. The Governor of Bengal receives six hundred thousand francs per year, the Governor of Madras four hundred thousand and the Governor of Bombay three hundred thousand. Even the most humble employee, who in Europe we would consider to be generously paid at one hundred francs per month, earns no less than five or six thousand annually and thus may indulge in very lucrative speculation.

I was indebted for all this information, which I found most interesting by its very novelty, to my neighbour at table, to Sir Edward Colebrooke[340] whose many years as a high-ranking official in the administrative service in India had made him an irreproachable judge in all these matters. His brother,[341] who is one of the most distinguished scholars in England and to whom the Company's library owes a large number of its most precious documents, was also seated near me; he added his remarks to those of his brother; and thus was my lesson completed and my curiosity fully satisfied.

Mr. Ed***'s family is very large: he has twelve children; this is not a surprising number in England where Heaven blesses marriage *most munificently*. One can say that this is both a clear indication of domestic happiness and the result of a scrupulous adherence to convention, which religion does not a little to perpetuate.

After dinner, there was music, a custom almost universally observed; the prelude to the concert reminded me of those I had attended in Bohemia, in which each member of the family had their part to play, from the youngest to the oldest.

Standing in the middle of the drawing room, Mr. Ed***, armed with a long, glass flute, combined the functions of conductor and choirmaster; around him were grouped a number of his children who, on harp, piano, violin and 'cello, and despite their enthusiastic amateur eagerness, gave me proof that a family concert could not avoid an unfortunate affinity with the performance of outright dilettanti. Much better was the singing: the two eldest girls, accompanying themselves on the harp, sang French and Italian pieces, ending with Moore's delightful tune (*The Last Rose of Summer*).

340 *TN James Edward Colebrooke (1761–1838) In late 1827 Edward Colebrooke was officially Resident and Commissioner at Delhi. He was dismissed, allegedly for acts of corruption, from this post in 1829 by the Court of the East India Company. He had served the Company for 50 years. It is likely that La Garde met him in London at a later date, rather than in Brighton. La Garde is possibly trying to salvage Edward Colebrooke's reputation by his use of the word 'irreproachable'.*

341 *TN Mr. Colebrooke's brother was Henry Thomas Colebrooke (1865–37). Henry had started his career in India as an administrator but had conceived a passion for the history of the country. He wrote extensively on the Sanskrit language and Hindu law, finally becoming Chair of the Bench in Calcutta and honorary professor at Fort William College in the same city.*

Here La Garde gives a French translation of the following song:

'TIS the last rose of summer,
Left blooming alone;
All her lovely companions
Are faded and gone;
No flower of her kindred,
No rose-bud is nigh,
To reflect back her blushes,
Or give sigh for sigh.

I'll not leave thee, thou lone one !
To pine on the stem;
Since the lovely are sleeping,
Go sleep thou with them.
Thus kindly I scatter
Thy leaves o'er the bed,
Where thy mates of the garden
Lie scentless and dead.

So soon may I follow,
When friendships decay,
And from Love's shining circle
The gems drop away.
When true hearts lie wither'd,
And fond ones are flown,
Oh ! who would inhabit
This bleak world alone ?

Then, in the guise of an intermission, one of those Italian men who have so rightly been called martyrs to music, Signor Veluti, provoked in me, despite the wide range of his voice, an uncomfortable feeling as I thought of the extent to which the pleasure he was giving others cost him in happiness.[342] Other distinguished artists, Sola, Begrez and Puzzi, vied in turn to show off their talents and to earn their well-deserved applause.

During the intervals of the concert, all manner of refreshments were handed round, including perfectly preserved crystallised fruits from the Indies, some being very sweet, others so spicy as to burn your mouth. I was delighted by them.

Mrs. Ed*** served us a very particular type of tea.

'It is picked,' she told us, 'in Udsi,[343] in Japan, on the slopes of a mountain which has a better aspect than any others for the cultivation of the tea plant. Its leaves are reserved exclusively for the emperor; however it would appear that much of the crop vanishes illicitly, for it is brought overland by merchant caravan, and I have already taken this very same tea with Madame Divoff in her Moscow residence.'

By eleven o'clock, I was at the York Hotel for the ball given by the baron, still entranced by my memories of such a pleasant morning. Mrs. W***, the baron's friend, was acting as hostess; she performed her duty with all the charm for which she is well known and with no object other than showing kindness to strangers, for otherwise, social conventions are strictly observed, the slighted hint of failure to do so, however brilliant the ball might be, would result in not one person attending.

Amongst the numerous guests, several were noticeable for the variety and opulence of their dress; the most striking were the Neapolitans, the Spanish, the Greeks and the Poles. One particular quadrille was remarkable, the picturesque dress of its dancers recalling so vividly the court of Elizabeth.[344] Many different dances, of many different styles, were performed, amongst them the Mazurka, a Polish dance which the Duke of Devonshire had recently imported following his time as Ambassador in Russia; it is without a doubt one of the most elegant and unusual in Europe; it demands that the dancer be nimble as well as light-footed if it is to be danced to perfection. On seeing it again, my memories carried me back to the happy time in my life which I had passed in that nation, a nation so interesting and yet so wretched.

342 *TN Signor Veluti was a castrato. The castrato voice was already attracting criticism by the 1820s as evinced by the title of an 1825 etching, now in the Victoria and Albert Museum:* 'An Italian singer, cut out for English amusement, or, Signor Veluti, displaying his great parts.'

343 *TN Now known as Uji in English.*

344 *TN Given the exotic description of the dances, La Garde is most likely referring to Tsar Elizabeth of Russia (reigned 1741 to 1761) than to Queen Elizabeth I of England.*

A lavish supper was served; it was perhaps a little bold of a foreigner to want to vie in luxury with the inhabitants of a country where luxury seems indigenous. But when at a ball all the women are pretty or sparkle with jewels, when the dancers are indefatigable, the rooms lit with a thousand candles, the orchestra excellent, the refreshments copious and refined, the service prompt, the glass and silverware abundant and the flowers ubiquitous, what can one ask more? In short, given the *comfort* that was evident that evening, it would have been difficult to convince oneself that it was a ball given by a foreigner in a furnished hotel and, without any doubt, the baron's farewell was quite worthy of the greeting he had received in the town.

Chapter XII

Preparations for leaving – Public conveyances – The Master of Ceremonies – Mr. Henry Colburn – Conversation – Literary reputations – Luncheon at the inn – Atop the stage coach – Meeting with a publisher – Bears and horses – Roads – Appearance of the countryside – Outskirts of the capital – The Elephant and Castle – Arrival in London.

For more than a month, I had been breathing the invigorating Brighton air, giving myself up completely to that indolent insouciance which varies only according to ones pleasures, and which becomes contagious in such watering places. I let my days slip by in the peace of mind and tranquillity which lend so much charm to time, the warp and weft of our lives.

Conscious of all the activity and bustle which prevail in England, and which are conceivable only if you have witnessed them, I did not indeed expect to find anywhere *la dolce farniente*. This town, in company with a very few other privileged watering places, is a happy exception to the rule, for here is to be truly found the *otium dulce*;[345] it is to Brighton that come both the merchant, to escape his troubles for twenty-four hours on a Sunday, and the peer of the realm, to rest for a few weeks from the fatigues of the parliamentary session. In Brighton, *ennui*, that English disease which starts with melancholy and ends in suicide, is forever banished.

Letters which I received from London plucked me from my intoxicating lethargy; and thus I was forced to prepare my immediate departure. As I was sending for a post-chaise, Mr. Mackinnon entered the parlour of the hotel.

345 *TN The expressions 'dolce farniente' (Italian) and 'otium dulce' (Latin) both refer to the pleasure of doing nothing.*

'You would do better,' he told me, 'to take a seat in one of the public conveyances which leave for London at every hour of the day; in the first place, you will avoid solitude at the staging posts, and then, as an observer of our society, you will have the opportunity of meeting as many curious characters as one might find in any stagecoach in any land: I also suggest it for reasons of economy, a principle which we must always recommend to a foreigner in our country. Life lived simply is no more expensive here than anywhere else; on the other hand, a life of luxury costs ten times the price. Believe me, *live within your means*; four simple words, but they form a maxim you should adopt, as it is the source of all independence.'

I acquiesced to this rational argument and sent out to procure a seat inside the *stage coach* which, travelling as rapidly as its name implies (*The Dart*), leaves Brighton at midday and by five o'clock reaches London, having covered in that short space of time, the fifty-two miles which separate this settlement, or should I say this outpost, from the metropolis.

The 'Age' 1828 starting from Castle Square, Brighton, from an engraving by C. Cooper Henderson

---

In the French text, La Garde uses the name l'Hirondelle *meaning 'The Swallow' or 'The Swift' for the stage coach which is to take him to London. Although L'Hirondelle was a popular name given by stagecoach owners to their coaches, there is no record for 1827 of one bearing any of those names plying the London-Brighton route. There was, however, 'The New Dart.'*

La Garde may be assuming 'Dart' was the name of a fast-flying bird. In November 1828, Viator Junior (see Introduction) lists the 'New Dart' as leaving the 135 North Street and [sic] *18 Castle Square at noon each day. There were various coachmen (or dragsmen), teamed with a regular guard but in the view of Viator, it was George Deere and his guard Ned Pattenden who were the most skilled:*

> 'I cannot conclude this article (and my paper reminds me speedily to do so) without once more adverting [*sic*] to the merits of a coach I have already named, the 'New Dart'. Believe me, gentle reader, it is one of the very best on the road; and let me counsel you by no means to omit travelling this autumn with both George Deere and Ned Pattenden; for it would, I assure you, be a service of considerable difficulty to find two better dragsmen or more obliging fellows out of any yard, not in Brighton alone, but the whole of London. I hope the proprietors intend to keep both sides on during the winter, as it will be a thousand pities to throw such artists out of regular employment.'
>
> quoted in *The Brighton Road,* Charles C. Harper 1906 edition

---

I had three hours before the advertised departure time. This I used to advantage to take leave of my acquaintances. Everywhere I received pressing invitations to meet them again in London when they returned for the season.

I concluded my leave-taking at Sir Robert's; it was with sincere regret that I parted from a man of such an excellent heart, and whose spirit is on a par with that heart, but, in the hope that I would soon meet him again, I curtailed those painful moments when one is anxious not to succumb to one's feelings.

On returning to the Glocester Hotel, I had to wait but a few moments for the arrival of the coach. I was immediately and easily able to convince myself that travelling post-chaise would have been to no purpose other than that of vanity, for the elegance and lightness of this present vehicle, with its four horses and their harness, would have made a Prussian margrave be wild to use it in lieu of his state coach.

To complete the illusion, the very capable guard, sitting high on the back seat, was blowing a fanfare on his horn. This sound, more harmonious than the modest cornets used by German postilions, bade a melodious farewell to the wide roads through which we made our way. Soon we were racing out the gates of the *villa Reale.*[346]

346 TN *The 'Royal Town'.*

of the works most recently published in England to recognise immediately Mr. Henry Colburn.[357]

We drew up at the door of a smart inn towards mid-journey and we climbed out in order to take *luncheon,* a sort of dinner provided for travellers. Some passengers sat at table. It was laden, as custom dictates for this meal, with cold meats, puddings, cheese, celery, fruit and all kinds of beer, ranging from *ale* to *porter* to small beer, the latter being much like our own.

The majority of passengers took no more than a large glass of hot water, brandy, lemon and cinnamon, all of which made up a heady punch. We had to be quick: hardly had we sat down than the coachman called on us to return to our seats. In truth, I do not think that a Westphalian postilion would have taken longer to get down from his mount, drink his glass of schnapps, light his pipe and resume his saddle than we took to peck at this unnecessarily copious meal, pay our share and take our leave of *mine host* and his serving lads.

'The reason for this somewhat tyrannical haste,' Mr. Colburn told me, 'is less that of the coachman's pride than the need to save time, which in England we consider to be an invaluable commodity and most lucrative. All the coachmen are much like human chronometers, indeed some of them own excellent watches worth up to eighty pounds, and for the simple reason that they are not allowed to exceed, even by one minute, the advertised timetable. When the coaches arrive, family, friends and servants are at the designated alighting point to greet the travellers and their packages. All this is a consequence of the principle, without which all is chaos and ruin, and which states: be accurate in your reports and punctual in your movements.'

Mr. Colburn and I had soon settled back into our mobile chamber: the manoeuvre was somewhat more complicated for our travelling companions, amongst whom there were some women. A long ladder is placed against the coach to facilitate the climb to the top. That is not all; once the passenger is seated, he does, indeed, need a certain familiarity with such a perch, and not be subject to vertigo, if he is to maintain, even whilst asleep, the requisite balance.

It is, in the main, the two passengers seated on the outer ends of the bench seat who must keep most alert: these two extremities extend considerably beyond the width of the box and are protected by a little iron armrest no more than a few inches in height. Often, it is only half the passenger's body which is supported on the seat, the other half being suspended over the void: and when the coach is

357 *TN Henry Colburn (1784–1855) Colburn was in serious financial difficulties by 1830.*

The Stage Coach, 'Comet', on the Cuckfield to Reigate run
This early nineteenth-century painting of a Sussex stagecoach does indeed make the outside passengers look as if they are taking their lives in their hands.
Image reproduced by courtesy of Cuckfield Museum

being pulled along with the speed of the wind, the inexperience traveller makes every effort to cling on, often in terror, whilst at the other extremity of the seat, the regulars sway and cavort with the ease of sailors at the tip of the yardarm.

We had taken aboard no other inside passenger: I congratulated myself on this fact, for I wished to continue my conversation with my amiable travelling companion.

In the space of no more than a few minutes he had given me a course on practical literature; we rapidly reviewed all the new publications which revealed the taste of the period, and I learned enough about them to appear none too ignorant in a meeting of *blue stockings*[358] and who are most adept at holding forth on literary merit.

It was a splendid day; the countryside was still beautiful and took on the most brilliant hues in the sunshine.

358 AN The name given in London to scholarly women, somewhat akin to our own ladies of learning.

We were driving on a road as smooth and as well-drained as a garden path; wherever you looked, your delighted gaze came to rest on enchanting sights. Here, extensive parks spread before us their abundant foliage and all those luxuriant vistas which the English owe to the descendants of Brown[359] and Kent,[360] the landscape gardeners. The talents of these skilful imitators of nature often enabled them to combine, within a very limited area, the different aspects of that beauty which is everywhere to be found in the natural world; thus they were able to combine darkling forests, rolling prospects, leaping fountains, rocks, and running water, sometimes in the form of azure lakes, sometimes as silver ribbons snaking through green meadows dotted with flocks of sheep and fine cows from many climes, the whole being scattered with innumerable herds of roe deer and stags; here, everything seems to indicate that the beautiful is united to the useful.

Further on, we saw a multitude of summer cottages, each built to a different plan, nestling amongst thickets of Portuguese laurel, azaleas, rhododendron and other exotic plants, all of which keep their leaves throughout the seasons to cheer barren winter; it is with the most exquisite taste that farm houses and labourers' cottages have fanned out across the landscape in the most romantic and the most picturesque situations. These cottages with, before them, no more than a simple lawn surrounding a well-filled bed of flowers, have around their doors and windows garlands of jasmine and roses, creating the illusion of fragrant, vaulted arbours.

Further north, the sinuous, rampant shoots[361] of the hop fields reminded me of the green vines which furrow the Lombardy countryside. Indeed, the very hamlets through which the road passes have their own charming buildings which evoke the follies built to enliven secluded corners of parkland and which, from their exquisite cleanliness, much resemble Dutch villages without their dreary uniformity; everything seems to exude ease and happiness. The barren

---

359 *TN Lancelot (Capability) Brown (1716–83). Brown landscaped the grand parks at Warwick Castle, Blenheim Place, Woburn Abbey and Althorpe, amongst many, many others. Brown had worked as a landscape gardener under William Kent (see below) at Stow in the 1740s.*

360 *TN William Kent (1685–1748) Kent was a pioneer of the naturalistic design of landscaped gardens.*

361 *TN La Garde lets his imagination run away with him somewhat. He left Brighton in late November. The chance of seeing jasmine and roses was remote. It is also most unlikely that he would have seen 'rampant hop shoots' in November. On 29 November the* Brighton Gazette *reported:*

The weather has been exceedingly and unusually variable this week. Snow and frost of [*sic*] Thursday, til the end of the week, succeeded on Sunday by a heavy rain and thaw, since which time the temperature has been again as mild and warm as it was before.

surroundings of Brighton had not in the least prepared me for these enchanting sights; my travelling companion took great delight in my enthusiasm which, over the last several miles, had been continually stirred and he did the honours of this gallery of landscapes as best he could.

At the top of a hill, he pointed out the distant Thames, the queen of rivers, as she wound her way majestically through an ocean of greenery, with her forest of masts aiming their arrows towards the sky like so many giant crossbows, and a thousand sails spread across her waters.

'There is our River Pactolus,'[362] Mr. Colburn told me.

'Yes, your Pactolus, which, from each hemisphere, constantly brings you the raw and rough-hewn treasures of other peoples, and which you return to them, transformed and enriched by your industry; all this wealth is due to your position in the very midst of a sea which festoons your shores and makes easy all your contacts with the furthest flung points of the earth, from which, at first sight, it would appear to separate you: it is a happy accident of nature which gives you this power of which other nations might certainly be jealous, even though you do not abuse that power.'

'And what of our roads, sir,' continued Mr. Colburn, 'these routes throughout Great Britain are a true miracle; indeed it is for that reason we may claim in, as you say, a play on words, that the *ways* of this country have always been the main source of its *means*. Such is the ease with which distant friends can meet, that England is but forty-eight hours in length and thirty-six hours in width. Praise be to Mr. MacAdam![363] We owe him the advantages which come from speed; nowadays, one is able deal with one's own affairs, thus adding security and the pleasure of personal, friendly relations to mere mercantile transactions. The resultant savings are immense; in the past, if a man had to make a short journey across our island, he had to devote one twelfth of the year and a considerable part of his business life to it; today, he spends no more than four days

362 *TN The River Pactolus (in modern day Turkey) has a very high content of the gold and silver alloy knows as electrum. Greek mythology explained the presence of this metal by saying that King Midas had rid himself of his unwanted power of turning everything he touched into gold by washing his hands in the river.*

363 *TN John Loudon McAdam (1756–1836), Scottish engineer and inventor of a process for surfacing roads with a smooth, hard, impervious surface.*

in the month and devotes the remaining twenty-six to other occupations.'[364]

I was listening attentively to this interesting speech when it was interrupted by a violent jolt of the coach and cries of distress from our neighbours on the outside. We soon learned the cause of this disturbance when we saw the head of one of the lead horses appear at our window, for the coachman had not been able to hold him. At the time, the coach was climbing a steep rise and we were open to the double danger of overturning and being trapped or of being thrown out; the second alternative was of little comfort to us and even less to the passengers perched aloft.

It was not without a great deal of effort that the coachman managed to bring his team to order. He declared that such a thing had never happened to him before.

'Seeing such a strange and sudden apparition at our window,' Mr. Colburn informed me, 'might have frightened us into thinking that it was the horse of one of those mounted robbers (*highway men*) about whom we find so many stories in our novels of yore and obsolete newspapers; but these *gentlemen of the road* appear far less frequently nowadays, since the establishment of a mounted police force which has relieved us of these dangerous visitors.'

Nevertheless, at the top of the hill, the horses started to rear again, and we soon found out why: before us, a caravan followed by a menagerie of animals was slowly making its way to Greenwich Fair, and tied beneath the caravan was a very large bear; the horses' sense of smell had warned them of the proximity of this uncouth traveller even before they had caught sight of it: the caravan stopped and we passed by without upset. I put our horses' instinct down to the management and the care given, without exception, to horses in England, for such attention preserves their innate reflexes; in other, less conscientious, countries the horse's nature is almost always corrupted by excessive bad treatment and fatigue.

My comment lead Mr. Colburn to tell me about the Act of Parliament which renders anyone who mistreats an animal liable to a fine: 'It is only humane,' he explained, 'to protect them against the barbarity of their masters and, in cases

---

364 AN Bacon was right when he said, speaking of discoveries, that one did not know all the offspring of the times. Since my conversation with Mr. Colburn, the improvements brought about in the railways is going to make communications vastly more rapid and more safe.
On 15 September 1830, the famous Liverpool to Manchester railway was opened: a distance of thirty-two miles, the equivalent of thirteen leagues in France, can now be travelled in seventy minutes for the modest sum of five shillings per person. Within ten years, England will be criss-crossed by railways in every direction: and France will be only too well aware of their importance not to imitate her neighbour. What an influence these innovations will have on politics, trade and general well-being!

of ill-treatment, there is no indulgence shown to the guilty: the amount of the fine, depending on the seriousness of the case, is decided by the magistrate or the Justice of the Peace.

'It is thanks to a Bill, which bears the name of Mr. Martin, Member for the county of Galloway,[365] that we now have an Act stating that horses and animals deserve first-rate treatment, thus practically turning animals in England into rational beings.'

'But, sir, cock fighting is very much encouraged in England. How do you justify that?'

'With a very simple argument: the two champions can defend themselves as equals, the one against the other, neither plays a passive role and that puts them in the position of each having every chance of winning the fight.'

At last we caught sight of London: we had already made our way though a long series of villages which had every appearance of being the outskirts of a large town and the streets were becoming alive with the large number of people whose comings and goings seemed to indicate the proximity of a city. I have seen the outskirts all the capitals cities of Europe; as far as liveliness and bustle is concerned, there is not one which can hold a candle to London.

A vast variety of vehicles of every sort cut across each other, tangling and untangling themselves with remarkable speed, thus justifying the reputation of English coachmen as the most skilful *whips* in the world; then there is the crowd of men on horseback and pedestrians who rush about and run into each other, often roughly and for no reason; there are the numerous roadside taverns, their galleries and arcades adorned with smokers and drinkers emptying shining pewter pots overflowing with the white froth of *ale* or *porter*; there are groups of sailors, merchants and workmen whose physical appearance and dress are such that, without flattering them, they might prompt the question: '*But, where are the common people?*' as queried the Tsar of Moscow. This crowd swamping the roads and the footpaths laughs and sings, not reticently but with that frank expression of joviality which characterises *Old Merry England.* Indeed, there was nothing of the cantankerous solemnity, and even less of the vulgar rough behaviour that

365 *TN Richard Martin (1756–1834) was MP for Galway in Ireland (and not Galloway in Scotland as La Garde incorrectly states). Martin's fight to improve conditions for animals resulted in the passing of the 'Ill Treatment of Cattle Bill' in 1822. The Society for the Prevention of Cruelty to Animals was set up in 1824, possibly at his instigation and probably with his support. It was not until the 1880s that similar societies were set up to protect children.*

Harmony in Leicester Square, 1848
Leicester Square was popular with French hoteliers and their continental clients. N°s. 24–26, Brunet's Hotel, had been in the hands Louis Brunet since 1800. He passed the hotel to his half-brother, Francis Jaunay in 1815. The three building were demolished in about 1840, but it was not until 1851 that they were superseded by the Royal Panopticon of Science and Art (1853–58) which evolved into the Alhambra Theatre (1859–1933). The Alhambra was demolished to make way for the Odeon Cinema, opened in 1937.

would, so I was told, strike me as I drew nearer to London; far from it. All the scenes I saw made up an overall picture of general ease, health and happiness, the origins of which are to be found where men are subject to laws alone and are neither slaves to favouritism nor martyrs to poverty.

Before arriving in London, we halted at the Elephant and Castle inn.

'It is from this central point,' Mr. Colburn told me, 'that, after a brief halt, countless numbers of coaches set off, daily, to every corner of England. You could call it, in accounting terms, the preamble to the great double-entry ledger into which we are about to plunge: to our right is the City which represents income; to our left is the *Westend*, the aristocratic area, which represents expenses; it is here, in general, that travellers take leave of each other; may I ask you where to intend to go?'

'To Jaunay's Hotel[366] in Leicester Square.'

'In that case, you are well on your way; this coach will put you down at Charing Cross, which is close by. Allow me to give you my address and please consider my home to be your own.'

'I thank you, sir, and I will retain the memory of our meeting which could well serve as an introduction to my book.'

But subsequently, and by chance, it has become the conclusion.[367]

Upon these words we shook hands; he walked off and my coach continued on its way.

After crossing Westminster Bridge, we stopped at Charing Cross, at the far end of Parliament Street, exactly opposite the equestrian statue of the unfortunate Charles I.

I had arrive in London, eager to continue my observations, ready to challenge common prejudices, the motto of which is *nil admirari* [368] and which would have us believe, quite mistakenly, that when we are unable to equal a rival, we must malign him.

END

366 TN *This was the Sablonière Hotel, managed by François Marie Jaunay at this period.*

367 AN This work forms the continuation of a series of 'Travels' in various parts of Europe and the section on England will complete the series. Mr. Colburn published the first two volumes in London under the title *Journal of a Nobleman.* It has appeared in French, published by Treuttel & Würtz under the title *Voyage de Moscou à Vienne, par Kiev, Odessa, Constantinople, Bucharest et Hermansadt.*

368 TN *'Marvel at nothing'.*

Appendix A

The Brighton Pedestrianism Mystery – 1827

In 1809 Captain Robert Allardyce Barclay walked 1000 miles in 1000 consecutive hours on the heath near Newmarket race course. In 1827 Richard Sutton walked 1200 consecutive miles in 1200 consecutive hours in a circuit around the Royal Cricket Ground, Brighton. Or did he?

In the first few years of the nineteenth century, pedestrianism was at its height. The Prince Regent was betting heavily on any and every sport. That included betting on Captain Barclay's walk. Amongst the Fancy, those high-playing, high-paying aristocrats who, at the time, ruled the ring and the turf, enormous sums of money were changing hands.

By late 1827, the King, George IV, had already paid his last visit to Brighton. The Fancy was a shadow of its former self. Sport was becoming more plebeian, and possibly less professional. However, in Brighton, perhaps because the town was beginning to lag a little behind the times, pedestrianism still aroused interest.

> 'A poor woman, aged 61, who calls herself Mary McMullen, undertook on Monday evening, to walk 93 miles in 24 hours. She started, on a level piece of ground, near the Hanover Inn at six o'clock in the evening, proceeding half a mile out and half a mile in, and is said to have accomplished the task within the time limit.'
>
> Sussex Advertiser 10 September 1827

Mary McMullen was 'poor' only in the pecuniary sense. She would rely on donations during her exertions, and did not make a luxurious living. She was, however, physically strong. The distance of 93 or 94 miles was her 'speciality'. A tall, lean woman, she would walk unshod and, according to all accounts, showed little signs of fatigue at the end of her exploits. She was certainly a more accomplished pedestrian than her sons, Peter and Bernard. In September 1827, the distance she chose was the measured half-mile from the northern corner of Union Road (site of the long-vanished Hanover Inn, about a mile inland from the beach at Brighton) ending at the Bear Inn at the bottom of Bear Road. This stretch of the Lewes Road she covered 186 times, successfully completing her task on the Tuesday evening.

Three weeks later, Richard Sutton, performed the 'curtain raiser' to his attempt to walk a record 1200 miles in 1200 successive hours. The nature of this preliminary feat was bizarre, to say the least, if we can take the word of the *Brighton Gazette* on 1 October:

> On Monday morning, Sutton, the Kentish pedestrian, accomplished the arduous undertaking of walking thirty miles backwards in eight successive hours, on the Lewes-road, starting from the Bear public house, half a mile out past the Cavalry barracks and back. The weather was rather unfavourable; he however performed the distance, exhibiting considerable fatigue, with 26 minutes to spare.

Remember that this was not the smooth, if busy, Lewes Road that is known today. No DIY stores, no twentieth century churches or imposing factory buildings lined the route. This was a muddy valley bottom, treeless, rutted, exposed and deep in horse manure. But this event probably won the attention needed before he embarked upon the main attraction.

Information about Richard Sutton is very sparse, but if this type of walk was his trademark, he might well be the same Sutton who as late as 1837 was still entertaining the crowds, this time on Waterloo Bridge where he undertook to:

> walk one mile backwards, one mile forwards, to run a mile, to wheel a barrow a mile, and pick up fifty stones a yard apart, and deliver them into a basket— all to be performed within an hour, and which he accomplished in 59 minutes, or one minute within the time.
>
> The Idler and Breakfast Table Companion 1837

Apparently the walking backwards was 'particularly admired', as was his performance in Lord's Cricket Ground at St. John's Wood. Here he walked

305 miles, 'half of them backwards'. In an attempt to trace the earlier part of his career, we can only speculate whether this was the same Sutton who, in 1812, was described as:

> a painter in the neighbourhood of Eastcheap, [*who*] for a wager of £5 undertook to go on foot from London-bridge to Shooter's-hill, and back again, in two hours, distance Sixteen miles, which he completed three minutes within the time.[369]

So now we have some idea of the type of man Sutton was. What about his wager in the Royal Cricket Ground at Brighton?

Captain Barclay had undergone rigorous, scientifically-based training before his walk. There is no evidence that Richard Sutton did not train extensively.

Captain Barclay had roped off his course and had had oil lamps rigged up for night-time walking. There is no evidence that Richard Sutton did not prepare his course, although it does seem that he had nothing more than a lanthorn to light his night hours.

Captain Barclay had dressed carefully in 'blue-flannel breeches ... lambswool stockings and strong shoes.'[370] There is no evidence that Richard Sutton did not choose suitable clothing.

Captain Barclay had walked for, and won, a purse of 1000 guineas. Richard Sutton stood to gain 100 Sovereigns – and possibly his cut of the admission fee as advertised in the *Brighton Gazette* on 25 October:

> Every Accommodation will be made for Visitors during the Herculean Task – Admission. Three-pence Each.

Captain Barclay had surrounded himself with a team of assistants to feed him, to wash him, to wake him, to keep away any ill-intentioned spectators and to welcome any notable guests at the course-side. There is no evidence that Richard Sutton did not have assistants.

Captain Barclay walked one mile before the hour and one after, thereby giving himself ample time to rest in between walking – day and night. And Richard Sutton? Well the 'press release' published in the *Brighton Gazette* on 25 October was a little ambiguous:

369 *The Sporting Magazine: Or, Monthly Calendar of the Transactions of the Turf, the Chase and every Other Diversion* (1812), page 301.

370 Peter Radford *The Celebrated Captain Barclay – Sport, Money and Fame in Regency Britian*, Headline Books 2001.

> Sutton, who is walking a match of 1200 successive miles in 1200 successive hours, in the Royal Pleasure Grounds, starts every morning at a quarter before 7 and a quarter after, and at similar times before 9, 11, 1, 3, and 7 o'clock. He commenced on Monday morning, and is going on well; if he is successful, he will achieve a greater feat than any yet accomplished. The Barclay match, it will be recollected, was 1000 miles in 1000 successive hours.

Yet he, too, must have walked day and night otherwise the concept of 'successive hours' would be meaningless.

Captain Barclay set off to walk 1000 miles between 1 June and 12 July, 1809. Richard Sutton set off to walk 1200 miles on 29 October 1827. June and July can be very hot. Especially in East Anglia. Captain Barclay did, indeed, suffer from the heat and over the course of his walk, lost some two stones in weight. But what on earth induced Sutton to plan his walk for the months of October to December? The residents of Brighton will be painfully aware of the storms that can beset the town at that time of year. The event had already hit problems as Sutton had had to delay his start from earlier in the week 'Owing to the wetness of the soil, and the falling moisture.'[371] However, start he did, and by 5 November he had attracted

> 'The Earl of Uxbridge, and others of high rank and fashionable distinction [*who had*] visited him during the week past, and were liberal in their donations for the steady resolution he manifested.'[372]

The newspapers then lost interest in Sutton for virtually the whole of November. The weather was bad. Although the Season was not yet ended and the Lady Patronesses were still giving their weekly Almack's balls in the newly refurbished Assembly Rooms in the Old Ship Hotel, Lucombe had already closed his evening entertainments at the end of October and Tuppen closed his Library the following week. The great and the good were drifting away from Brighton and presumably the not-so-great and the not-so-good had followed their masters and mistresses back to Town or to the stately home or quite simply had other work to do.

Interest picked up again as the advertised finishing date of 11 December approached. The pedestrian is reported as being in rather a sorry state:

---

371 *Sussex Advertiser* 20 October 1827.

372 *Sussex Advertiser* 5 November 1827.

> Sutton is continuing his task in the Royal Grounds. He has now completed (ten o'clock last night) 736 miles, and feels confident of performing the remainder with ease. He even goes so far as to say that should he walk the 1200 miles, and his fatigue not be too great, he will continue to 1500 miles, but we doubt at present his ability to accomplish this. He was considerably distressed during the frosty weather, and his legs are swelled very much; they are now better, but not entirely free from swelling. [...] He generally does his mile in from 14 to 16 minutes, and sometimes, if desired, walks the distance backwards. The feat has not attracted any great number of spectators, but there have been frequently people to see him.
>
> Brighton Gazette 29 November 1827

A week later the same newspaper was reporting, perhaps a little more optimistically:

> Sutton, although he is very much distressed, is still confident of accomplishing his task. At ten o'clock last night he had walked 904 miles, but his swelled legs and his thin, pale countenance appear very much against him. A gentleman for a very small wager a few nights since, walked a mile with Sutton, but the pedestrian proved too much for him, beating his opponent in fine style; the gentleman was obliged to run the latter part of the mile, which was walked by Sutton in eight minutes and twelve seconds. On a former occasion some person was sent to Sutton (no doubt a hoax), there being talk that he wanted a man to watch him at night, and offered his services; Sutton directed him to take the lanthorn, and walk the ground with him, but the man found that he could not keep with him; he was obliged to run, and was several times nearly knocked down by Sutton passing him; that mile was accomplished in little better than seven minutes. The man was then told his services were not required. Sutton will finish, if he continues walking, on Tuesday se'night.[373]

By this time, Sutton felt the need to get the public on his side. He needed all the support he could get, so he wrote the following letter which was published in the same edition:

> Sir – Pardon me for taking this liberty of intruding on your goodness, to insert the following account of my performance. This morning at six o'clock having performed 888 out of 1200 miles, I am fully confident

373 *Brighton Gazette*, 6 December 1827.

> of completing that arduous task, although exposed to the inclemency of the weather last week. My legs are swelled, and the arteries of my right leg strained; my attendants complain of great trouble in waking me at night, having more than once been obliged to throw water on me to make me sensible, during the last windy and rainy night. There have been a great many visitors out this week, when the weather would permit. Kind Sir, should you be so kind as to insert a small paragraph in your valuable paper of Thursday next, you will be obliging your humble Servant
>
> Wednesday morning RICHD. SUTTON

By 13 December, the expected finishing date for the walk had come and gone. Almost in desperation, Sutton writes to the same newspaper yet again. There is perhaps just a hint of self-delusion in his words:

> To the editor of the *Brighton Gazette and Lewes observer*
>
> Sir, – You will oblige me by inserting in your valuable paper that I have just completed 1056 miles, and I am going on favourably towards completing the undertaking of walking 1200 miles in as many hours. The weather has been much against me this week, and the state of the ground is very bad, owing to the heavy rains that have fallen of late. My legs are still much swelled, and I find a good deal of trouble, when called, to get myself awake; but still have confidence of completing the arduous undertaking, and if I should, I have been matched to walk 200 miles further on the same task, making the whole 1400 miles; 100 of the last 200 to be walked backwards. – Should the weather be favourable, I think that I should be able to complete the task. I have a great number of night visitors as watchers against me. The rain fell in torrents last night with much wind.
>
> I remain yours, &c. Wednesday morning, Six o'clock R. SUTTON

On Tuesday 18 December 1827 Richard Sutton stopped walking. We know because the *Brighton Gazette* said so. Why, then, does the name of Richard Sutton not appear in any of the record books? Why have virtually no sports historians ever heard of him?

The problems seem to have started towards the end of November. At the 736 mile mark, as we have seen above, despite the frosty weather, Sutton appeared to be in fairly good heart. But all was not well. The same newspaper item

(Gazette 11 December) contained, in its central section, this ominous sentence:

> We understand several large bets are laid; the odds are quite 3 to 2 against him. A rumour has gone abroad that he does not walk in the night; but he says that £10 will be given to anyone who shall detect him not then walking, and he was being watched, (among others by Mr. Pierpoint), unknown to himself.

It is clear from Sutton's comment in his letter quoted above, that he was aware of the suspicions being harboured against him: "I have a great number of watchers against me". But watchers there were, and there is no indication in any of the newspapers that the £10 reward for catching Sutton out was ever won by a person or persons who had observed that Sutton had failed to walk in 'successive hours'.

There was further indication that Sutton's observance of the rules was not as meticulous as it should have been. On 17 December the *Sussex Advertiser* gave a clue as to where a further problem might lie:

> Sutton, the pedestrian, in extraordinary condition, considering the fatigue he has had, being yet able to cross a mile of ground in about 16 minutes, is yet pursuing his labours of walking twelve hundred miles in twelve hundred successive hours, and which task, should he continue it, he will accomplish tomorrow se'night. A regular journal of the exploit, properly attested in the event of success, might do him some service with the public.

Alas, Sutton and his team had not kept a log-book of the walk, and even his good health seemed to have been a black mark against him.

In its Christmas Eve edition, at the conclusion of the walk, the *Sussex Advertiser* merely stated, in its low-key way:

> Sutton, the Kentish pedestrian, is said to have accomplished his task of walking 1200 miles in as many successive hours, on Tuesday last – but no diary of the exploit, suitably attested, has yet appeared.

The *Gazette*, the newspaper to have covered the event in the most detail thus far, seems to have washed its hands of the man and the event. In the *Gazette*, there is no report of the end of the walk. It was left to the *Brighton Herald* to raise the real doubts as to Sutton's probity. This was done in a rather mealy-mouthed line inserted into the newspaper on Saturday 22 December:

> Sutton completed his task of walking 1200 miles in 1200 successive hours on Tuesday last, – at least, so it is said, and, certainly, we are not competent to prove the contrary, nor do we presume to doubt the fact.

Did Richard Sutton walk 1200 miles in 1200 successive hours? He kept no journal. He had no referee. There was no log. He was left with no credibility. If he had not walked the walk according to the rules, he deserves to be forgotten as a charlatan. But suppose he really had tortured himself for 52 weary days and nights? Not only had he lost the purse of 100 sovereigns (approximately £5,000 in the early 21st century) but must have lost many illusions, faith in his fellow human beings and, most importantly, faith in himself. A cautionary tale for all sportsmen and women.

Bibliography

Allan, David, *Making British Culture: English Readers and the Scottish Enlightenment*, Routledge, 2008

Anon., *The Watering Places of Great Britain and Fashionable Directory*, J Robins, London, 1831

Anon., 'Clio Grub at Brighton' (satirical poem), *New Monthly Magazine and Literary Journal* Vol XX N°. LXXXV, 1828

Auguste, Comte de la Garde (translator unknown), *The memoirs of Hortense Beauharnais*, Key and Biddle, Philadelphia, 1833.

Barton, Margaret and Sitwell, Osbert, *Brighton*, Faber and Faber, 1935

Blew, William C., *A History of the London to Brighton Road*, J. C. Nimmo, 1894

Carder, Timothy, *The Encyclopaedia of Brighton*, East Sussex County Libraries, 1990

Collins, Michael, *The Mechanics' Institute – Education for the working man?*, Adult Education Quarterly, Vol 23, Issue 1, September 1972

Cruikshank, Robert, *Brighton: A Comic Sketch*, William Kidd, 1830

Fisher, Michael H., 'Preface' to *The Travels of Dean Mahomed: An Eighteenth-Century Journey Through India*, University of California Press, 1997

Fleury, Comte de, 'Introduction' to *Souvenirs du Congrès de Vienne 1814–1815*, Librairie historique et militaire, 1901

Gilbert, Edmund M., *Brighton: Old Ocean's Bauble*, Flare Books, Hassocks, Sussex, 1975, first published by Methuen & Co. Ltd, 1954

King, Maude Egerton Hine, *Round About a Brighton Coach Office*, J. Lane, London, 1896

Harper, Charles G., *The Brighton Road*, Chapman and Hall, 1906

La Garde, Comte Auguste de, *Souvenirs du Congrès de Vienne 1814–1815*, Publié avec introduction et notes par le Comte Fleury, 1842

Lewer, William, *The Athenaeum, Literary and Critical Journal*, London, 1828

Melville, Lewis, *Brighton: Its History, Its Follies and Its Fashions*, Chapman and Hall Ltd, 1909

Oxford English Dictionary (online)
Parry, J. D., *An Historical and Descriptive Account of the Coast of Sussex*, Wright and Son, Brighton, 1833
Pigot's Directory (Brighton), 1828
Porter, Henry C., *The History of Theatre in Brighton*, King and Thorne,1886
Radford, Peter, *The Celebrated Captain Barclay – Sport, Money and Fame in Regency Britain*, Headline Books, 2001
Reece, R., *The Monthly Gazette of Health*, vol. 10, 1825
Sicklemore (Snr.) R. *The History of Brighton and its Environs*, 5th Edition, C. and R. Sicklemore Jun., 1827
Stone, Michael (editor), *The Diary of John Longe, Vicar of Coddenham (1765–1834)*, Boydell Press 2008
Vandam, Albert Dresden, *Anecdotal recollections of the Congress of Vienna by Auguste de la Garde* (Translation), Chapman and Hall, 1902
Various, *The Story of Queen's Park, Brighton*, Brighton Town Press, 2009

Index